UNSOLVED
VICTORIAN
MURDERS

T0315906

UNSOLVED
VICTORIAN
MURDERS

Jonathan Sutherland

irst published in Great Britain byThe Breedon Books Publishing Company Limited
Breedon House, 44 Friar Gate, Derby, DE1 1DA. 1999

This paperback edition published in Great Britain in 2015 by DB Publishing, an imprint of
JMD Media Ltd

ISBN 978-1-78091-501-2

Printed and bound in the UK by Copytech (UK) Ltd Peterborough

CONTENTS

DEDICATION

For Betty Jayne and Michael

ACKNOWLEDGEMENTS

The author would like to thank Steve and Ray at the Metropolitan Police Museum for their help, hospitality and guidance in collecting information about the 12 cases. Thanks also to Chris Leggett and, as always, my partner Diane.

INTRODUCTION

THE VICTORIANS believed in their Queen, their God, their Empire and their destiny. They believed in their judges, their penal system and their punishments. They believed in the death penalty, the birch and the whip, foolproof methods of dealing with criminals and anarchists who, without punishment, would bring society crashing down around their ears. Above all, they believed in themselves and their mixture of piety, steadfast knowledge of their position and righteous indignation, and fostered a God-fearing desire to inflict retribution on malefactors wherever they were found. They would never have accepted that their systems of justice were flawed, or acknowledged that hearsay evidence was completely inadmissible. Incredibly, a defendant was not allowed to give evidence at his own trial until 1896. Nor would many Victorians have seen and believed that in fact, murder, crime, prostitution and fraud were all around them, and that criminals were not just from the under-classes marginalised by society, but also from the ranks of the respectable middle or upper classes.

By the time that Victoria ascended the throne in 1837, *The Observer* was devoting some 20 columns a week to the coverage of crime. When *The News of the World* made its debut in 1843, crime coverage was the staple of the paper and the readers loved it. Founded in 1855, *The Telegraph*, by the beginning of the 1870s, could claim a circulation of over 200,000 copies a day, due largely to its comprehensive crime coverage.

Victorians were acutely aware of the crime going on around them, and the middle classes, that were exposed to the crime coverage in the daily papers, gradually discovered that murder was a part of their class. The writings of Dickens, Wilkie Collins and William Harrison Ainsworth also brought murder, robbery, arson and other villainies into the homes of Victorian Britain.

Throughout the whole of the period, thanks to elementary mistakes and the relative clumsiness of the police, horrendous murders took place for which no culprits were ever identified. This was a time when forensic science was in its infancy, when the accused could not give evidence in court and juries were led by the nose to absurd and dangerous conclusions. Many convicted individuals did not have the luxury of an appeal, and were abandoned to the ministrations of an executioner on a cold morning only days or weeks after the trial. One of the cases detailed in this book did end with someone hanging at the end of a rope, but it was such a grave miscarriage of justice that it remains, to all intents and purposes, unsolved.

This book features 12 cases, notorious at the time and perplexing to this day. Scholars and lawyers have spent years examining case notes and pulling the investigation processes to pieces. Ultimately, the only truth is that we may never know what really happened. This book seeks to set the facts away from the fiction and focus on how real lives were ended. What were the motives behind the killings? Why did the investigating officers and courts arrive at the decisions they did? What were the ultimate fates of those involved? Was justice done to the victim and the accused?

My Poor Brother looks at the Charles Lyddon case, which occurred in Faversham, Kent, in 1890. It seems to be a straightforward case, but unravelling the detail may well lead us to the same conclusion as the Old Bailey jury, 'not guilty'. Questions, however, still remain. What was really going on in the Lyddon household in 1890? Was Dr William Lyddon a habitual drug user who took his own life by mistake or design? Why was he so neglected by his mother and half-brother? What actually happened on the fateful night of 26 April?

Catch Me When You Can looks again at the 'Jack the Ripper' murders in Whitechapel in 1888. This is a truly perplexing case, much written about, yet still unsolved. Thus it may ever be, since all chance of uncovering the truth now seems long since lost. With over 20 suspects proposed over the years, confusion about the number of murder victims and the proliferation of pet theories of criminologists and writers, the case is as unfathomable today as it was then. Why were the victims mutilated? Was this the work of one man? Did the police bungle the investigation and unwittingly release the murderer to continue his work?

Poor But Honest delves into the murder of Jane Clouson and the eventual trial of Edmund Pook for battering her to death in a dark lane in 1871. Edmund Pook was a seemingly respectable middle-class man, implicated only by rumour and the fact that Jane Clouson had worked for his mother. Pook was acquitted, as the evidence against him was circumstantial. After his acquittal, Pook fought and won a libel case. However, many still believe that Pook was the murderer. Did the police mismanage the case or did Pook manage to get justice?

The Bootlace Murders links two crimes committed on or near Great Yarmouth beach in 1900 and 1912. Herbert John Bennett, the husband of the first victim, had already been hanged for the crime at Norwich in 1901. Why then was there a second, almost identical murder in the same place 11 years later? The murder weapon was a bootlace in both cases. Bennett was convicted on the flimsiest of evidence, so was the jury wrong?

Madeleine's Love Letters investigates the trial of Madeleine Smith in Glasgow in 1857. She was a respectable 21-year-old woman, who allegedly poisoned her French Channel Island lover. The trial took Glasgow and the country by storm. Victorians were shocked by the frankness of her love letters. Was Pierre Emile L'Angelier an arsenic-eater, seducer and blackmailer with suicidal tendencies, or did Madeleine administer the fatal dose of 82 grains of arsenic herself? On 9 July 1857, the Scottish jury returned a 'not proven' verdict and

Madeleine went on to live to the ripe old age of 93. The 'not proven' verdict neither convicts nor acquits the accused; it simply leaves a question mark over the case. The Madeleine Smith trial remains a fascinating insight into Victorian society and morals.

The Blind Killer looks at the seemingly impossible death of Thomas Farrant in Bristol in 1867. Thomas Farrant was either pushed or fell from the top storey of the Colston's Arms. He was living with the wife of a blind man called Giles Clift, his own great uncle. On the fateful day, somehow Farrant managed to squeeze through a two-foot square window to his doom. Was there a fight, or was the victim so desperate to evade his relative that he slipped and fell? Giles Clift was acquitted of the murder, and he was a blind, thin and weak 53-year-old, but could he have put the fear of God into Farrant? Did he actually murder his 25-year-old rival and nephew?

She Should Tell Us How She Did It attempts to unravel the murder drama surrounding the death of Edwin Bartlett in London in 1885. This is a bizarre poisoning case that baffles the experts to this day. Did Adelaide Bartlett administer poison to her amorous husband? The cause of death was ingestion of chloroform, but how was the deadly dose given to the victim? The jury could not find her guilty, but did she hypnotise Edwin or was she the victim of his own odd medical beliefs and paranoia?

What Art Can Turn Him Into Clay? features another poisoning case, the strange and unsettling death of Charles Bravo in Balham, in 1876. Did Florence Bravo connive with her companion Jane Cox and her lover Dr Gully to murder her husband? Why did she call for the assistance of Sir William Gull, the most famous physician in England at the time, to examine her ailing husband? The first inquest returned a verdict of suicide, but the second, after the newspapers had uncovered many unsavoury facts, became almost a trial of the two women. Despite that, was there really insufficient evidence to bring anyone to trial? Whatever the truth, the experience ruined Florence Bravo, who died an alcoholic just 19 months later.

The Ireland's Eye Tragedy may have been a conventional, if rather unusual murder case, or a great miscarriage of justice. The death of Maria Kirwan led to the conviction of her husband William in 1852. Did the professional artist murder his wife, or was she the victim of a tragic swimming accident? When the corpse was exhumed, the cause of death was said to be asphyxia, but had the woman died from the results of a fit? Kirwan spent over 25 years in prison, but to the end he protested his innocence. He was no saint, and had at least seven illegitimate children, but was his love for Teresa Kenny enough to drive him to murder his wife? After his release, he was told to leave Ireland and disappeared into history forever.

The Southern Belle looks at the trial and conviction of Florence Maybrick in Liverpool, in 1889. Although the American Florence Maybrick was charged and found guilty of the murder of her husband James, the case is held to be one of the major miscarriages of justice of the era. Prejudice against unfaithful women and the damning summing up of the judge made her fate inevitable. Nevertheless, she escaped the hangman's noose, instead spending 15 years in prison, but did the evidence really point to her guilt? Many believe that it did not.

Mr Cecil Has Shot Himself covers the bizarre and complex trial of Alfred John Monson in Edinburgh, in 1893, for the murder of Cecil Hamborough. Did Monson's complex financial dealings finally lead to murder? Was the tangled web of insurance policies and frauds the reason for the death of Cecil Hamborough? Or did the young man take his own life? What of the accusations that Monson had tried to drown him the day before his death? The jury returned a 'not proven' verdict, just as they had in the Madeleine Smith trial.

The Unconsummated Marriage goes back to Paisley in 1843 and investigates the capture and trial of Christina Gilmour. The apprehension of the suspect has echoes of the even more famous Crippen case. When Christina married John Gilmour, she quickly realised that she had made a mistake and was determined, by some accounts, to end it as quickly as possible. Her preoccupation with her own unhappiness coincided with the illness and death of her husband. Did she flee the country after the body was exhumed? Was the circumstantial evidence sufficient to convict her of poisoning? The jury thought not and she lived for another 62 years.

I have tried throughout to seek original and contemporary material for each of the cases. This has not always been possible, but it is hoped that while there is little new in terms of evidence in my treatment of the trials and cases, new insights and reordering of evidence may help the reader to draw more informed conclusions.

With the passage of time and the fact that we can no longer question any of the witnesses or protagonists, we are at the mercy of those who investigated or covered the stories as they unfolded at the time, and must always be prepared to filter out comment from fact. Without doubt, many of the cases could now be simply solved given the advances in criminal detection, forensic science, offender profiling and a host of other investigative aids. The trick is to step back, view the evidence without preconceptions and look for motives and opportunities. Most of the cases have both.

Jonathan Sutherland
Suffolk, October 2001

CHAPTER ONE

MY POOR BROTHER

The Death of William Lyddon – Faversham, Kent, 1890

D R WILLIAM REEKS Lyddon practised medicine in Faversham, Kent, from 1878 until his death in 1890. By all accounts he was a successful practitioner and well-liked by the majority of his patients. Despite growing personal problems that began in 1889 he still managed to maintain the practice and retain his patients' loyalty.

By 1890 Dr Lyddon was a 44-year old widower. Lyddon's mother had died and his father, the collector of taxes for Canterbury, had remarried, this union producing a son, Charles, who was 16 years younger than Dr Lyddon. Charles Lyddon also had medical leanings and had managed to pass his first examination with the College of Surgeons. He had also been successful in passing two further examinations with the College of Physicians. Charles had begun assisting his half-brother as a dispenser when the practice was opened. He was entitled to do this despite the fact that he was not a qualified doctor. Charles was paid a salary of £50 a year by Dr Lyddon, but continued to live in Canterbury with his parents, making the daily trip of eight miles to Faversham. It appears that Dr Lyddon often failed to pay him his salary, but Charles received an allowance from his father of up to £300 a year.

The Lyddon's father died in 1886. Charles was left with nothing. At around this time one of his uncles also died, leaving him £270 and most of his effects. Charles continued to receive a small allowance from his mother.

The death of the Lyddon's father brought about what should have been an ideal household arrangement, both in business and financial terms. Charles and Mrs Lyddon, his mother, moved into 12 West Street, Faversham, with the doctor.

For at least two or three years it appears that the household ran fairly smoothly, although

William and Charles did have their differences. It seems that both men drank an excessive amount of whisky. During their binges they quarrelled and often became violent towards one another. The root of most of the arguments was money and invariably Charles would threaten his elder half-brother. When they were sober neighbours and witnesses attested to the fact that they were affectionate to one another and generally co-operative.

Some time in the spring of 1889 Dr Lyddon required an operation on a stomach ulcer. In those days such an operation was not as routine as it is today. It was a wise precaution, therefore, when Charles asked Dr Lyddon for a legal statement which would safeguard his own and his mother's interests should the worst happen and his half-brother die on the operating table. The two brothers consulted John Wiggins, a solicitor from Whitstable, about drawing up the deed, but it was in fact drawn up by Frederick Gibson, another solicitor based in Sittingbourne. It is, perhaps, significant that Gibson did not see Dr Lyddon, despite the fact that he recommended that the doctor use his own solicitor, to ensure that everything was in order.

The Deed of Assignment seems rather far-reaching, and it is very surprising that Dr Lyddon chose to sign it at all. The deed meant that the doctor would have to repay, on demand, Charles's 12 years of outstanding wages, plus numerous loans that Charles had made to his half-brother over that time. Charles would be able to claim the whole debt whenever he saw fit. If the doctor was unable to repay the debt then he would have 'absolutely to sell and assign to Charles Lyddon all his interests and goodwill in the practice, the debts, stock-in-trade, horses, carriages, furniture, plate and effects.' Soon after the deed had been signed and witnessed by Richard Dunn, a neighbour, it was said that Charles had said to George Amos, his coachman, 'I am the master of everything now'.

In the event Dr Lyddon did not die on the operating table but spent two months recovering from the operation in St Thomas's Hospital in London. When he returned to Faversham in August he asked for the document to be destroyed, but Charles refused. From then on Charles, with the document safely in his possession, could dictate terms to his elder half-brother.

Much of what we know about the intimate details of the household and the relationship between the half-brothers is derived from the various servants and employees that saw their less-public faces. There were three employees who worked for the household that lived in their own homes. Henry Lyons assisted George Amos, the coachman, and his replacement Mr Ford. Mrs Hunt was a laundry woman who made three or four visits a week to collect and return the household's laundry. One 15-year-old local boy, Charles Naylor, joined the household in the same month that Dr Lyddon returned from his convalescence in St Thomas's Hospital. Although he was described as a page boy, his duties were, in fact, far more wide-ranging. He helped Mrs Lyddon with the cooking and the general maintenance of the house, answered the door to callers and assisted in the surgery, gradually learning dispensing.

It is not clear whether Dr Lyddon was already addicted to morphine prior to his stomach ulcer operation, but after his convalescence he used increasing amounts of the drug, to which he had ready access. Charles Lyddon used this addiction as another avenue of attack against his half-brother and it seems that during their drinking binges threats were made by Charles to evict the doctor, because his addiction was not only financially ruining the practice but also affecting its reputation. Several of these arguments were witnessed by Charles Naylor, who claimed that the half-brothers were becoming more violent towards one another. George Amos also witnessed incidents, including one in which he claimed to have seen Charles give his brother a black eye by punching him in the face and knocking him to the floor. Amos also claimed to have seen Mrs Lyddon beating the doctor with a stick and bruising his arm.

Around three months after the doctor had returned from hospital, George Amos was called out of the stables by Charles, who said that he should attend the doctor. Charles told him that his half-brother was both drunk and delirious and was thrashing about in the bed. Amos found the doctor in no such state, and later remarked that it was Charles that appeared to be drunk. He also claimed to have seen Charles strike the doctor several times. When Amos stepped in to protect his original employer Charles turned his anger and violence on the coachman. Charles threatened to kill Amos and launched himself at him. It is not clear whether blows were exchanged but the outcome, according to Amos, was that he wrestled Charles to the floor before leaving the room.

Some time later Amos again witnessed the conflict between Charles and William. Responding to noises and shouting Amos entered the doctor's bedroom. He saw William lying on the floor as his half-brother screamed that he had stolen the whisky and hidden it somewhere in the room. Amos claimed that Charles ransacked the room and, when he found some locked drawers, went downstairs to find a chisel. Systematically he forced the locks on the drawers, even disappearing for a short while to collect a larger chisel in order to open a drawer that he had failed to prise open. In this final drawer were various letters and mementoes that William had kept in memory of his late wife. Charles threw them around the room despite William's protestations. Amos claimed that Charles yelled 'Oh bugger your wife!' to his distraught half-brother. On this occasion, uncharacteristically, Amos decided to spend the night in the doctor's bedroom in order to protect his employer. Later that night Charles again entered the room looking for whisky. He searched the room again and threw ornaments and other items onto the floor.

Although it is not clear exactly when this happened, one day Henry Lyons, who worked with Amos, was called into the house by Mrs Lyddon. She instructed Lyons to tie the doctor to a kitchen chair. She claimed that he was delirious, although the doctor exclaimed 'They will not let me have a moment's peace'. Lyons claimed that at this point the doctor tried to get out of the chair, whereupon Charles hit him in the face and Mrs Lyddon punched his arm.

One Saturday evening during September 1890, Charles Naylor rushed to the police station for help in dealing with a potentially dangerous situation in the house. Luckily he met Inspector Fowle on the way, and the two quickly made their way back to West Street. The inspector saw Charles Lyddon sitting near the dining room door with a double-barrel shotgun across his knees. It was William who spoke first, saying to the police officer 'my brother is threatening me with a gun and I cannot go into the surgery to do my business'. Before the inspector could comment, Charles put in 'yes, and if you come near me I will use it'. There then appears to have been a considerable verbal exchange and slanging match between the half-brothers and the inspector. Charles eventually set the shotgun aside, claiming that it was only loaded with blanks. Having seen his brother set aside the weapon, William made to walk into the dining room, but Charles punched him in the stomach. Charles shouted at his half-brother 'Your breath stinks and I don't want it in my mouth'. At this William went into the surgery. The inspector was sure that Charles had been drinking heavily and took him aside into the dining room out of the way of his half-brother. Inspector Fowle lectured Charles about his behaviour and told him of the serious consequences of threatening someone with a gun. No further action was taken against Charles at this time.

Later in September Dr William Hill, an old colleague of Dr Lyddon, visited his friend during a stay in Faversham. He found William suffering from pneumonia and was appalled at the state of his bedroom and the apparent disinterest of the rest of the household. Dr Hill was further concerned with the physical appearance of his friend, whom he believed had not been eating properly for some time. He made several visits to William and brought him food, including Brands Essence and a chicken. When his stay in Faversham came to an end, Dr Hill advised Charles to call in a local doctor as he was concerned for his friend's welfare.

Rather surprisingly, Charles took Dr Hill's advice and another Faversham doctor, Dr Boswell, visited William at 9pm on 30 September 1890. It appears that Dr Hill had already warned Dr Boswell about what to expect. When Dr Boswell rang the doorbell it was eventually opened by Charles Naylor. Charles Naylor told Dr Boswell that William was asleep and would be unable to see him. Dr Boswell was insistent, saying that he had an appointment to see William and that Charles Lyddon was responsible for his half-brother. By this time the doctor was already in the hall and although Charles Naylor protested, he reluctantly led Dr Boswell up the stairs. Boswell found an inert Charles Lyddon lying on the landing. He was clearly very drunk, and the scandalised doctor also noted a young woman lying on the landing floor, also very much the worse for drink. Charles Naylor led the doctor into William's bedroom, where he found his patient to be seriously ill. Not only was William extremely dirty but the room showed signs of long-term neglect. Dr Boswell asked Naylor whether William had been fed that day to which the boy replied that he had been given a cup of tea and a glass of beer. Boswell also asked who was nursing William and Naylor explained that the drunken woman on the landing was the nurse.

Dr Boswell did what little he could for William and then asked Dr Hill to meet him at his surgery in Faversham. They were both under the impression that if William remained in the house in West Street for much longer then he would die. William needed urgent nursing and medical attention.

On 1 October Dr Boswell returned to West Street and found Charles Lyddon slightly less drunk than he had been the previous evening. He told Charles that his half-brother needed to be admitted to the Cottage Hospital. Charles asked Dr Boswell 'Do you think my brother is going to get better?' Dr Boswell caustically replied 'I hope so, but it is no thanks to you that he is not dead now'. Before William was removed from the house and taken to the hospital he gave Charles Naylor £1 5s 6d, explaining to the boy 'Charles takes money out of my pockets' and asking him to look after it until he returned home.

William remained delirious for virtually the whole of the first week of his stay in the Cottage Hospital. Gradually, however, he began to regain his strength and sense of mind. At some point he confided to Dr Boswell that Charles still held the Deed of Assignment. He also told Dr Boswell that he had been receiving threatening letters from his half-brother and, although he was reluctant to leave the hospital, he felt that Charles would make him suffer for it if he did not return home at the earliest possible opportunity. He said, rather conspiratorially, 'Charles will stop at nothing'. Charles discharged his brother from the hospital on 26 October against the advice of Dr Boswell and other medical professionals that had attended William.

The now-normal state of affairs within the West Street household resumed, with the police attending calls made by one or other half-brother as a result of violent disturbances. Charles demanded that the police evict William from the house, claiming that he was the master of the house and that his brother was the cause of all of the problems between them. Charles even visited Mr Gibson, who had drawn up the Deed of Assignment on his behalf many months before. He instructed the solicitor to enact the Deed of Assignment and evict his half-brother. Mr Gibson advised Charles not to proceed with this course of action.

Events began to spiral out of control, and Charles Naylor reported hearing Charles Lyddon talking to his mother about the state of the practice, after, it was claimed, William had refused to treat two patients in the surgery. At around this time Charles Lyddon telephoned the solicitor Mr Wiggins in a further attempt to enact the Deed of Assignment. The solicitor met the half-brothers in the drawing room at West Street. At least twice during the meeting William Lyddon called Charles Naylor and instructed him to telephone a solicitor to represent him. Unbeknown to the doctor, Charles had already told Naylor to ignore any instructions given by William. However, despite William's lack of legal representation at the meeting, Mr Wiggins was no more inclined to accede to Charles Lyddon's demands than Mr Gibson had been. It was finally agreed that Mr Wiggins would consider the situation and attempt to formulate a mutually acceptable solution to the impasse.

As soon as the solicitor left the house, Dr Lyddon, in an attempt to avoid his mother and quarrelsome half-brother, went and sat down in the dining room. According to Charles Naylor, there was another loud argument between the three principal protagonists. Presently Mrs Lyddon went upstairs to dress for a visit out and Dr Lyddon left the dining room and sat in the drawing room. Both brothers had been drinking. Naylor heard Charles shout 'You will either go to Herne Bay or go out of the house!' Soon after this the household's carriage was drawn up outside and Charles drove his half-brother and Mrs Lyddon to the railway station. It appears that by 5pm both Mrs Lyddon and William were in Herne Bay. A local cabinetmaker, Ronald McDonald, saw Dr Lyddon stumbling along the road, holding on to anything for support. McDonald realised that the man was either ill or very drunk, and watched as Dr Lyddon failed to support himself by hanging onto a shop blind and fell to the ground. McDonald described how the doctor knelt with his forehead on the ground and his legs in the air. Unable to decide whether the man was drunk or in distress, McDonald approached the doctor and said 'Allow me to lend you a hand brother'. William replied 'I am alright, I only want another glass'. With the aid of another passer-by, Mr Weatherly, McDonald dragged the inebriate doctor to his feet and they asked him where he lived, to which he replied 'Marine Terrace'. At this point Mrs Lyddon appeared on the scene and McDonald asked 'Do you know him?'. She replied, 'He is my son, one of the leading doctors in Faversham, do help him.'

Weatherly and McDonald, with Mrs Lyddon in tow, man-handled William to 1 Marine Terrace. The building was a boarding house run by Mrs Sarah Stuart. Mrs Stuart welcomed the Lyddons as they had stayed at her boarding house on several occasions. Although she had never seen William that drunk, she was aware of the family's general propensity for whisky. What struck Mrs Stuart at the time was the fact that although William appeared to be drunk, he did not display behaviour that she would normally attribute to drunkenness. She noted that he could talk perfectly normally, but seemed to have no control over his legs. Despite Mrs Lyddon's assurances that her son had been drinking heavily, Mrs Stuart took it upon herself to call a local doctor. When the doctor arrived he found William completely uncooperative; he would neither talk to the newcomer, nor allow him to take his pulse, and refused to show him his tongue. The doctor left, unable to make any clear diagnosis.

Shortly after the doctor had left, Mrs Stuart's son undressed William and helped him into bed. Mrs Stuart stayed at his bedside all night, during which time she witnessed his groaning and restlessness. When he awoke in the morning he was sick.

Later in the day Charles Lyddon arrived in a carriage to take his half-brother back to Faversham. William refused to move and Charles reluctantly agreed that his half-brother could spend the weekend in Herne Bay and return to West Street on Monday. Over the weekend William further recovered, and on Monday morning he ate breakfast at 8am and drank milk at 10am. William appeared to have regained his senses and complained to Mrs Stuart of pains in the sides of his abdomen which he could not explain.

At 11am Charles returned with the carriage and had lunch with Mrs Stuart at Marine Terrace. During the meal he confided to her that his half-brother was a drug addict and that this was the root cause of the condition she had seen him in the previous Friday. What struck Mrs Stuart was that she had searched William's clothing for his tobacco, at his request, and had found nothing which could support what Charles was now telling her. By the time Dr Lyddon returned to West Street around noon, he was obviously in a much better physical and mental state. Charles Naylor gave him raw minced steak and a glass of stout for lunch at around 1.30pm. William even sat with his half-brother while he ate. By 4pm William was sufficiently fit to go out and visit patients, returning to the house around 7pm.

Two patients came to the surgery in the evening, a Mrs Walters and, significantly, a Mr

Frank Sherlock, who worked at the Ship Hotel. He arrived for a consultation at 8.50pm and was shown into the surgery by Charles Naylor. Sherlock was aware that Dr Lyddon had been unwell and asked him how he was feeling. The doctor replied 'Very much better'. Mr Sherlock noted that the doctor seemed healthy and showed no signs of having been drinking. Mr Sherlock asked to pay his medical bill but Dr Lyddon told him that he had not yet prepared it and they both agreed to meet again later in the week. Shortly after Mr Sherlock had left Dr Lyddon asked Charles Naylor to get him some milk, and by the time Naylor returned from the errand, the doctor had begun drinking. Naylor helped him prepare medicines for patients, then set out to deliver them to the appropriate patients. Charles Naylor returned to the house at about 10.15pm, to find Charles Lyddon waiting to tell him that he had had a further violent argument with the doctor. Again the subject was debts and money and both half-brothers had been drinking whisky and wandering around the house, abusing one another. Naylor did not witness this argument, and on his arrival he found William Lyddon asleep on a couch in Mrs Lyddon's room. Naylor had been back in the house for at least 30 minutes when Charles Lyddon told him to go to the police station and get Inspector Fowle to come to the house. Naylor discovered that Inspector Fowle was out on business and that only PC Stone was on duty at the station. Dutifully, Naylor returned to West Street and reported this to Charles Lyddon. Lyddon immediately ordered Naylor back to the police station and told him to bring PC Stone with him. PC Stone refused to leave the police station, so Naylor again returned to West Street. Naylor was sent to the police station on two more occasions that night until he finally encountered Inspector Fowle.

With great reluctance the inspector accompanied Naylor back to West Street and encountered Charles who said to him 'This Deed of Assignment, you know all about it? I want my brother to leave the house'. The inspector asked Charles Lyddon where his brother was and was told that he was upstairs on the couch. Unwilling to cause a scene at this time of night, the inspector told Charles Lyddon 'If he is upstairs and comfortable, the best thing you can do is to go to bed yourself'. Charles was furious and demanded that the inspector throw the doctor out of the house. Fowle refused. Not only did he point out that it was a cold night, but he told Charles Lyddon that the doctor would not have anywhere else to go at this time of the night.

Charles Lyddon was insistent and said 'My brother is in the habit of taking drugs and I might be accused of it'. Before the inspector could respond, Mrs Lyddon appeared and added 'Yours is very kind advice sir and I am ashamed of Mr Lyddon to want to turn the doctor out, as he is laying very ill and not fit to be turned out'. Even this interruption from his mother did not calm Charles down and he said 'Mr Wiggins wants him out'. The inspector patiently replied 'You are not bound to do what Mr Wiggins tells you'. At this point he told them both to retire and beat a hasty retreat.

Calm seems to have prevailed for a little while, and according to Charles Lyddon he sat down to write some letters before retiring. On his way up to bed Charles claimed that he went in to check to see whether his half-brother was still asleep. He found William wide awake and a further argument commenced. It appears that both of the brothers consumed more whisky after the inspector had left.

The next independent account comes from Charles Naylor, who claimed that at around 11.50pm, after having turned off all the lights on the ground floor, he headed for his own bed. He said that he clearly heard Mrs Lyddon shout 'Don't hit him in the face!' Immediately afterwards he heard William scream out 'Oh Jo, Jo, you blackguard'. The shouting was coming from Mrs Lyddon's bedroom and Naylor saw the doctor leave the room and attempt to gain sanctuary in his own bedroom, but his half-brother and mother followed him. Mrs Lyddon was screaming that her son should be horse-whipped because of his drug abuse and Charles Lyddon told Naylor to 'Go and get me the tanning whip'. Naylor was petrified and remained immobile. He then saw Mrs Lyddon punch the doctor three times on the shoulder, before grabbing a wooden bonnet stand and screaming that she was going to 'crack his head open' with it. Charles Lyddon grabbed the object from his mother and set it aside.

Dr Lyddon was still fully clothed and now took off his coat and waistcoat and threw them onto his bed. Charles told his half-brother that he was not prepared to allow him to sleep in his bedroom and that if he wanted to sleep he would have to do so in the lumber room. There was another violent argument between the Lyddons, at the end of which Naylor suggested to the doctor that he should do as they said in order to avoid further argument. Naylor guided the drunken doctor into the small room, noting as he did so that Charles Lyddon was nearly as inebriated as the doctor.

The lumber room was a cold and uninviting place situated above the downstairs kitchen, with one of its walls occupied by a chimney breast connected to all of the downstairs fireplaces. As there was no bed or light in the room, Naylor lit a candle and collected a sheet and blankets for the doctor. Charles Lyddon was still hovering, and eventually, with the aid of Naylor, he convinced William to go into the lumber room. William had taken his coat with him for additional warmth. Charles Lyddon took the candle from him and locked the door once William was inside. Naylor then collected a partially drunk bottle of whisky from Mrs Lyddon's bedroom, gave it to Charles and prepared to retire for the night. Naylor normally shared the attic bedroom with Dr Lyddon but Charles told him that he wished him to sleep in his bed tonight. Following his employer's instructions, Naylor got into bed, noting that when Charles got in beside him he was still wearing his trousers.

Charles Lyddon awoke at about 7.30am the following morning, probably as a result of the postman delivering mail. When Naylor encountered him a few minutes later it was clear that Charles was still wearing the same clothes that he had gone to bed in the night before. He was reading a letter from the solicitor Mr Wiggins that detailed his proposed suggestions about the dispute between the half-brothers. While Naylor dressed, Charles took the bunch of keys and told the boy that he was going to see how William had fared during the night. Naylor then went downstairs to light the kitchen fire. Meanwhile Charles walked through his mother's bedroom and, seeing her still asleep, quietly unlocked the door to the lumber room to reveal his brother, also still asleep, lying on his back and snoring. Charles decided to leave William where he was and later claimed that although William's breathing was heavy, he detected no reason for concern about his brother's condition and accordingly went back to his own bedroom to wash, have a shave and put on some clean clothes. At some point Mrs Lyddon had also woken up and had suggested to Charles that they get William some breakfast ready.

The doctor was left alone for another half an hour and when Mrs Lyddon and Charles looked into the lumber room again the doctor had not moved and was still snoring. They once more agreed to leave him and they went down to the kitchen to have their breakfast, which had been prepared by Naylor. Having eaten, Mrs Lyddon went back upstairs to try and wake the doctor. She could not rouse him, despite the fact that she mopped his face with a wet sponge. Again she left him.

At 9am Charles told his mother that he was going to call Dr Evers and said of his brother 'This will not do, we must put him to bed with clean sheets'. Mrs Lyddon and Naylor re-made the doctor's bed in his own bedroom, checking several times while they were doing so to see if the doctor had woken up. Once the bed was made Naylor, for the first time, went into the lumber room and took off the sheet, blanket and overcoat draped over the doctor. Naylor tried to wake him but got no response. Mrs Lyddon, joined by Charles, watched Naylor's failed attempt to rouse William. The pair then instructed Naylor to pick up the doctor and put him in his own bed, offering him no assistance in this task. Naylor managed to drag the doctor into his bedroom, but could not lift him into the bed. Rather reluctantly Mrs Lyddon tried to help Naylor and drag William into the bed but still Charles stood by. After struggling for a short time they left William propped up against the bed and went downstairs. Naylor was then sent to Dr Evers with the instruction to say to him 'Tell him that my brother is seriously ill'. While Naylor was away on his errand the doctor's condition worsened, and when he returned he could see that the doctor was barely breathing. Again Charles sent him off, this time with the instruction to tell Dr Evers that his half-brother was dying.

During Naylor's second absence Charles went to seek help in the stables and found Francis Ford, the stableman, in the harness room, talking to a neighbour, Mr Woodruffe. He told them both that his half-brother was nearly dead and urged them to bring Dr Boswell to the house as quickly as possible. When Naylor returned after his second visit to Dr Evers he found Charles pacing around the hall, wringing his hands. Mrs Lyddon was stood on the landing, sobbing.

Despite Naylor's attempts to summon Dr Evers, it appears that either Ford or Woodruffe had managed to impress upon Dr Boswell the urgency of the matter in West Street. Charles took Dr Boswell upstairs, where the inert body of Dr Lyddon was lying face-down on the bedroom floor. Dr Boswell knelt by William's side and quickly realised that he was already dead. His immediate assessment was that the doctor had passed away about an hour beforehand. At this point Dr Evers arrived and they both examined Dr Lyddon's body. Charles Lyddon stood by impassively, watching their every move. It was Charles that spoke first, directing his question at Dr Boswell. 'You have been attending my brother and must know what he died of?' The doctor looked at him squarely and replied 'I do not know what he died of and I shall certainly give no certificate'. Charles then replied 'I suppose neither of you will give me a certificate, so I must send for the police'. Neither of the doctors was prepared to suggest how or why Dr Lyddon had died, so Naylor was sent out of the house again, this time with a message for Inspector Fowle.

At 10.50am Naylor returned to West Street, not with Inspector Fowle, but with Sergeant Frederick Sergent. The police officer was shown Dr Lyddon's body by Charles and the experienced officer noted that the corpse's face was blue, that the right cheekbone was discoloured, as if it had suffered a blow, and that there was moisture around the bruising. Having concluded his brief examination of the body, the sergeant then asked Charles 'Where did your brother sleep last night?' Charles admitted that William had not slept in his bed but had spent the night in the lumber room. The police sergeant was perplexed and asked 'Did he always sleep there?' to which Charles replied 'No. He was ill last night and wanted to sleep there'.

The sergeant then walked across the room and into the lumber room. It was still dark in the room because the blind was drawn. He saw chairs, a dressing table, a chest of drawers and some bedding and clothing strewn on the floor. Then he noticed a medicine bottle. The sergeant picked up the bottle and saw that it had a colourless liquid inside and that it was still corked, although most of the contents had already been used. The sergeant showed the bottle to Charles and asked him 'Can you account for this bottle being here?' Although Charles did not open the bottle, he quickly said 'This settles the matter. I want you to take charge of this bottle'. The sergeant replied 'I intend to'. Curiously, Charles added 'I am glad you found this, as people might say I poisoned him'. He then added 'Oh, my poor brother. I only brought him back from Herne Bay yesterday and to think it has come to this.'

The police officer then ushered Charles away from the scene, intent on ensuring that nobody tampered with either of the rooms until Inspector Fowle arrived. While they waited for the inspector, Sergent asked to be shown to the surgery, and particularly where the drugs were housed. He saw a number of bottles lying in a row on a couch in the surgery, and carefully examining them, he identified a bottle that matched the one that he had found upstairs. Still the exact nature of the liquid had not been revealed but it is obvious that Sergent was suspicious, as he asked Charles 'How much of this do you have in at one time?' Charles replied that they usually had three in stock. Sergent held up two full bottles and said 'Can you tell me what has become of the other one?' Charles shrugged and said that he did not know, but that Naylor might. Having summoned Naylor, Sergent asked Charles a last question. 'Can you say how much was in this bottle yesterday?' Charles replied 'I could not say, but I should think enough to kill a dozen men'. When Naylor arrived the sergeant asked him whether he had seen Dr Lyddon with the bottle the night before. Naylor was sure that he had not. The sergeant pressed him and asked 'Did he have a bottle like this when he went into the little room?' Again Naylor told him that it was unlikely as he would have been sure to have seen it. The sergeant was obviously interested in why the doctor had spent the night in the lumber room and asked Naylor whether he helped him into the room the night before. Naylor replied by saying 'Yes. He seemed to be ill. He took his coat off the bed, put it over his arm, but I did not see any bottle'.

It came as no surprise to either the police or the principal witnesses that the cause of Dr Lyddon's death was poisoning from morphia. The post-mortem indicated that the doctor had ingested at least a quarter of a bottle, or two ounces, of the liquid. There were other slightly more surprising aspects to the post-mortem results. Firstly, there was no whisky in the doctor's stomach. Secondly, there was liquid in his stomach, which surprised the coroner given the witnesses' assertions that he had not drunk anything after midnight. Bruises were found on the body, on the shoulders and the abdomen. The coroner was sure that Dr Lyddon's life could have been saved had a doctor been called promptly at 7.30am when Charles had first seen his half-brother in the comatose state. The coroner's inquest was protracted by the circumstances of the case, and was attended by a large number of interested locals at Faversham Guildhall. During the inquest Charles Lyddon described events as he saw them, leading up to the locking of his half-brother into the lumber room. He also minutely described what had happened when he found his brother at 7.30am the following morning. He attested to the fact that he believed that no one else could have entered the lumber room after he had locked William in at midnight. He claimed that he had the only key, although gossip and rumour that may have originated from Mrs Lyddon herself suggested otherwise. Although Mrs Lyddon did not give evidence at the coroner's inquest, Sarah Wise, who lived in Abbey Street, claimed that she had been told by Mrs Lyddon that she had checked on the state of William at least three times between midnight and 7.30am. She claimed that Mrs Lyddon had told her this while she was helping her lay out Dr Lyddon's body. Sarah Wise explained to the inquest that Mrs Lyddon had asked Charles for the key and that her son had actually accompanied her on at least one visit to the lumber room.

It was, perhaps, inevitable that the jury at the coroner's inquest returned a verdict which stated: 'We believe that morphia was feloniously administered to the deceased by Charles Lyddon'. The jury had been instructed by the coroner that they had the choice of three verdicts; murder, suicide or misadventure. It is clear that the jury was sure that Charles had administered the fatal dose. Accordingly, the coroner told Charles Lyddon 'It is my duty to commit you to take your trial at the next assize to be held at Maidstone upon the inquisition now found against you'.

Charles Lyddon did not, in fact, come to trial at Maidstone but was brought before Justice Hawkins at the Old Bailey. The reason for this change of venue is interesting in itself. It is clear that Charles Lyddon's counsel was sure that his client would fare much better if he were not tried in Kent. The experience of the inquest and the feeling of the coroner's jury made it clear that there was a great deal of ill-feeling against Charles Lyddon. In order to facilitate this change of venue and improve his client's chances of acquittal, his counsel argued that the next assize at Maidstone was so far in the future that it would be unfair to keep Charles Lyddon incarcerated on remand for that length of time.

The trial covered much of the same ground as the coroner's inquest, and particularly focussed on the exact movements of the morphia bottle. It was the prosecution's contention that the bottle had been placed in the lumber room by Charles Lyddon, in order to suggest that his half-brother had inadvertently taken an overdose at some point between midnight and 7.30am. The prosecution pointed to the testimony of Charles Naylor, whose statement claimed that he had not seen the bottle until Sergent had shown it to him in the surgery after the doctor was dead. The prosecution was led by a Mr Murphy, who summed up with the following remarks:

> Although the assignment has been described as a family arrangement, which was satisfactory to everyone, it is difficult to know how it could have been satisfactory to the deceased as it placed everything at the disposal of the prisoner.
>
> With regard to the fluid found in the deceased's stomach after death it must be pointed out that no water-bottle was found in the room which the deceased could have drunk from.
>
> According to the prisoner's evidence he saw the deceased next morning breathing heavily and, although he knew that the deceased was in the habit of taking morphia, he left him there and did not call in medical assistance. Why was that? If medical assistance had been called in, the deceased's life would probably have been saved.
>
> The conduct of the prisoner in leaving Naylor to move the deceased from the room without rendering him any assistance can hardly be realised.
>
> Was the bottle, which was found in the room, there at half past seven in the morning when the prisoner went in?
>
> Must not the prisoner have thought his brother was ill from morphia? The fluid found in the stomach of the deceased was quite inconsistent with the normal state of things, even in the case of a morphia taker. There was no trace of milk, stout or whisky in the stomach. The only way the fluid could be accounted for was by the deceased having taken some drink after he went to the room. How did the deceased get it? There was no water bottle in the room. The inference was that someone went into the room. Who was that person? The prisoner alone kept the key and he must have been the person who went into the room if anyone did.

Mr Dickens was the defence counsel. In his speech he emphasised the close and affectionate nature of the two half-brothers. He referred to their arguments when they were drunk, of course, but the focus of his closing remarks was the circumstantial nature of the evidence against his client.

> The deceased was a confirmed drug-taker and knew that the prisoner objected to his taking drugs. On the evening of 24 November the deceased had taken a dose of morphia and then put the bottle in his coat pocket. The craving would come on him again and, unless he took the bottle with him he would not be able to satisfy it.

Mr Justice Hawkins, the presiding judge, clearly came down on the side of the defence on his summing up.

> The prosecution in every case has the duty cast upon it of establishing the case by

evidence which, in the judgement of the jury, is reliable. If the evidence left a reasonable doubt, then it is their duty to the prisoner, to their consciences and to the public to return an adverse verdict, unless the prosecution established the case by evidence which left no reasonable doubt.

Is it shown on the part of the prosecution that the deceased did not take the morphia with him into the bedroom? There is no evidence that it was not in the deceased's pocket. I cannot see why, if the prisoner wished to administer poison to the deceased, he should have put him in that room as it could have been done quite easily in the deceased's own bedroom.

With the judge's final remarks firmly in their minds, the jury were dismissed to consider their verdict. They were back after just two minutes with the inevitable verdict of not guilty.

On the basis of the evidence presented in the court, there can be no doubt that the case against Charles Lyddon was flimsy and circumstantial. But what exactly happened in those fateful early hours of 25 November? Why was the verdict of the murder trial so different from that which had been returned by the jury at the coroner's inquest?

Once again Mrs Lyddon had failed to contribute anything from her perspective on the events which led up to her stepson's death. It is significant that she neither confirmed nor denied what Charles Lyddon had said, nor the more limited observations of Charles Naylor. Why did she not comment on the witnesses that claimed that she had told them that both she and Charles Lyddon had visited William after midnight? Did Mrs Lyddon see Charles administer the fatal dose to William? Was she party to the murder?

A comment made by the judge regarding the fact that Charles had put William in the lumber room and locked him in there, which would seem a strange thing to do if he intended to poison him, is actually easily explained. Firstly, Charles put William in a place where no one could see him give his half-brother the fatal dose. Secondly, he made sure that Charles Naylor was not in the room adjoining the lumber room. Thirdly, Charles Lyddon did not undress before retiring to bed. Fourthly, Charles Lyddon claimed that no one else had access to the keys. Should he not have assumed that if foul play was suspected, he would be the only individual who could have perpetrated the act?

The answers to the questions posed by this sequence are obvious. If Charles did wish to murder his half-brother that night then it was logical to try to remove William to a place where no one could witness the murder. We do not know whether Charles Naylor was aware of Charles Lyddon or Mrs Lyddon's visiting the doctor during the night. However, the fact that Charles Naylor did not testify that Charles got out of bed that night does not mean that Charles did not visit his half-brother.

What is certainly the case is that Charles Lyddon either wanted his half-brother dead, or was completely indifferent to any natural or self-inflicted suffering that he might be enduring. Looking back to the period when William was suffering from pneumonia, is it reasonable to suggest that Charles's indifference to his half-brother at that time was based on the hope that William would pass away from natural causes? It was certainly not Charles's intention to seek medical assistance for his half-brother, despite the fact that his own limited medical training must have led him to believe that his half-brother was seriously ill. It was only the prompt action of Dr Lyddon's colleague, Dr Hill, that prevented William from dying on that occasion.

What, then, did happen on the fateful morning that led to the death of Dr Lyddon? Is it possible that William inadvertently overdosed on morphia? Given his state of mind and supposed drunkenness at the time, it seems entirely possible. Alternatively, had William Lyddon realised that his half-brother had managed to gain such control over his life that living had become intolerable? Dr Lyddon may have deliberately overdosed with the intention of committing suicide. A further thought, obviously uppermost in the minds of the inquest jury, must have been that Dr Lyddon, presumably almost insensible after drinking so much during the day, and still convalescing from his illness of only a few days before, would have been an easy victim.

At the very least Charles Lyddon and his mother were both culpable for the death of William. Why did they not call for urgent medical assistance the moment they saw the state Dr Lyddon was in at 7.30am? Why did they wait an hour and a half before attempting to call for aid? Surely Charles would have realised from his medical training what was wrong with his half-brother? Why did he not act either himself or by summoning help?

Whatever the actual truth of the case, it is certain that Dr Lyddon did not have to die that morning. Whether Charles Lyddon or Mrs Lyddon was guilty of administering the overdose is almost irrelevant. They were certainly guilty of supreme neglect.

CHAPTER TWO

CATCH ME WHEN YOU CAN

The Jack the Ripper Killings – Whitechapel, 1888

THE WHITECHAPEL murders are, perhaps, one of the most enduring unsolved crime stories in history. There is so much that we do not know; no one was ever brought to justice for the killings, nor are we completely sure how many victims there were and over what period of time. Estimates range from a minimum of five victims to almost impossible figures encompassing every unsolved murder across the country and beyond.

All of the victims were female, had been attacked from behind and had their throats cut. They were all prostitutes and, to a greater or lesser extent, their bodies had been dissected and mutilated, either at the scene of the murder, or elsewhere.

It is popularly believed that the first murder was that of 42-year-old Mary Ann 'Polly' Nichols in Buck's Row. She had been married for 24 years, and at the time of her death, on Friday 31 August 1888, she had not seen her husband for three years. Polly had been in and out of workhouses and had been a prostitute since at least 1882. On the night before her body was found she was seen in the Whitechapel Road area, attempting to make some money to pay the lodging house. She was drunk and the last time she was seen alive was at 2.30am on Osborne Street. At 3.40am Polly was discovered, barely alive, and by the time a doctor arrived at 3.50am she had passed away.

> No murder was ever more ferociously and brutally done. The knife, which must have been a large and sharp one, was jabbed into the deceased's lower part of the abdomen, and then drawn upwards, not once but twice. The throat is cut in two gashes, there is

a gash under the left ear reaching nearly to the centre of the throat. Along half of its length, however, it is accompanied by another one which reaches around under the other ear, making it a wide and horrible hole, and nearly severing the head from the body.

The Star

The second victim was Annie Chapman, also known as 'Dark Annie'. She had been born in 1841 and was said to have been an alcoholic suffering from tuberculosis and syphilis. She had three children but had separated from her husband in either 1884 or 1885. She was last seen alive heading towards Spitalfields Market shortly before 5.30am on Saturday 8 September 1888, in the company of a customer. A witness, Elizabeth Long, described the man as having a dark complexion and wearing a brown deer-stalker hat; he was about 40 years old, possibly foreign and taller than Annie. Her body was found in the backyard of 29 Hanbury Street and examined by Dr George Bagster Phillips at around 6.30am. At the inquest he testified:

> The left arm was placed across the left breast. The legs were drawn up, the feet resting on the ground, and the knees turned outwards. The body was terribly mutilated, the stiffness of the limbs was not marked, but was evidently commencing.

The doctor thought that the injuries had been inflicted by a knife that was at

Mary Nichols' body. (*Penny Illustrated Paper*)

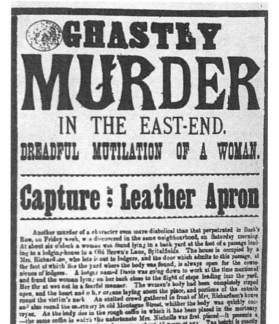

Police notice after the Buck's Row murder.

Buck's Row.

An alternative view of Buck's Row.

least 6 to 8 inches long and that whoever had mutilated the body had some anatomical knowledge. He believed that Annie had entered the yard alive. The post-mortem suggested that the immediate cause of death was suffocation, but the throat had been cut, the abdomen opened up and some internal parts of the body had been removed and taken away. It was the belief of the coroner that the extent of the injuries pointed to the fact that the killer had dissected the body for at least an hour.

The third and fourth victims were both murdered on Sunday 30 September. The first was a 45-year-old Swedish prostitute called Elizabeth Stride, or Long Liz. It appears that she had been registered as a prostitute in Sweden as early as 1865 and had suffered on and off from venereal diseases. By 1866, however, she was in England and had married John Thomas Stride, a carpenter. In 1878 her husband and children died when the *Princess Alice* collided with the *Bywell Castle* on the Thames, although some records, bizarrely, show that her husband did not die until 1884. Liz had been arrested for being drunk and disorderly on a number of occasions. At around 12.35am on the

Hanbury Street, site of the murder of Annie Chapman.

morning of Sunday 30 she was seen by a police constable on Berner Street with a 30-year-old man in a dark coat, wearing a deer-stalker hat. The man was carrying a parcel wrapped in newspaper. At 1am a jewellery salesman was driving his cart into Dutfield's Yard when his pony shied. He went to investigate and discovered the body of Liz Stride with a deep gash on her throat. The body was still warm. The post-mortem at St George's mortuary the following

The yard at Hanbury Street.

day at 3pm revealed a six-inch cut across the neck. It was later believed that whoever had carried out the murder had been disturbed, possibly by the jeweller himself. In any event, there was to be another murder that morning. Catherine Eddowes had been born in Wolverhampton in 1842. She was a fierce-tempered woman with three children; her last son was born in 1875. Since 1881 she had lived with John Kelly, who worked for a fruit salesman. At 8pm on 29 September she had actually been arrested for drunkenness on Aldgate High Street and by 12.55am the police considered her sober enough to be released. Instead of heading to her lodgings in Flower and Dean Street it appears that she was actually making her way back to Aldgate High Street. She passed the entrance to Duke Street and then walked on to Church Passage and into Mitre Square. At around 1.35am she was seen by a commercial traveller at the corner of Duke Street and Church Passage, talking to someone that the witness believed to be a sailor. Her body was found 10 minutes later in Mitre Square and was examined by a police surgeon at about 2am. His report showed that again the victim's throat

had been cut and the face slashed. Again there were signs that the murderer had knowledge of the workings of the human body. The abdomen had been ripped up and some of the intestines left near the neck. The murderer had also cut off part of Catherine's ear.

By now local people were not only terrified by the savagery and frequency of the murders, but were also very angry about the police's lack of progress. The last

Mitre Square, another Ripper murder site.

Front page of *Police News*, reporting the Mitre Square killing.

fully attributed murder occurred on 9 November. The victim was Mary Jane Kelly, who was also known as Marie Jeanette Kelly or Ginger. She was just 25 years old and had been born in Limerick in Ireland, although she moved to Wales as a young child. She had begun her career as a prostitute in Cardiff and had come to London in 1884, where initially she worked in a

Miller's Court, where Mary Kelly was murdered.

brothel in the West End. She moved into a house at 13 Miller's Court, where she lived with Joseph Barnett. Some time in late August or early September 1888 Barnett had lost his job and Mary had returned to her life as a prostitute, which had prompted Barnett to leave her. She had been arrested on 19 September and fined for being drunk and disorderly. Barnett continued to visit Mary, and left her after one such visit at 8pm on 8 November. She was last seen crossing Commercial Street and heading for Miller's Court shortly before 3am. She was accompanied by a man in his mid-thirties who was wearing a dark coat and a soft felt hat and carrying a small package in his left hand.

At 10.45am on Friday 9 November John McCarthy, the owner of Miller's Court, sent Thomas Bowyer to collect the rent; Mary already owed him 30 shillings. He knocked at the door and received no reply so he peered in through the window and saw the mutilated remains of the tenant. He ran straight to the Commercial Road police station and returned to the scene with a police inspector and McCarthy. They smashed the door in and found Mary Jane's remains on the bed. If anything this had been an even more brutal slaying:

> The throat had been cut right across with a knife, nearly severing the head from the body. The abdomen had been partially ripped open, and both of the breasts had been cut from the body, the left arm, like the head, hung to the body by the skin only. The nose had been cut off, the forehead skinned, and the thighs, down to the feet, stripped of the flesh. The abdomen had been slashed with a knife across and downwards, and the liver and entrails wrenched away. The entrails and other portions of the frame were missing, but the liver, etc it is said, were found placed between the feet of this poor victim. The flesh from the thighs and legs, together with the breasts and nose, had been placed by the murderer on the table, and one of the hands of the dead woman had been pushed into her stomach.

Illustrated Police News

There was other evidence; notoriously the words that had been written in chalk on a doorway in Goulston Street along with a piece of Catherine Eddowes's apron, still sodden with blood. It read:

The Juwes are

The men That

Will not

be Blamed

for nothing.

Sir Charles Warren, Chief Commissioner of the Metropolitan Police, ordered that the message be erased before daybreak in order to avoid a backlash against the Jewish community.

So what do we know of the murderer? It seems that he was white, in his twenties or thirties, of around medium height and quite respectably dressed. We also know that he must have had some anatomical knowledge. The police believed that he was a local man. Before we turn to the very contentious topic of potential suspects, of which there must have been hundreds from the outset, can we be sure that these five women were the only victims of Jack the Ripper?

An unknown woman was murdered in an alley off Commercial Road on Boxing Day night, 1887. She had taken the alley as a short-cut home from a pub on Mitre Square. She has been dubbed 'Fairy Fay' and she was murdered by having a stake thrust into her

Sir Charles Warren, Commissioner of the Metropolitan Police.

abdomen. However, the evidence for this case is scanty, and it may be that this potential Ripper victim never actually existed.

Annie Millwood was admitted to the Whitechapel workhouse infirmary on Saturday 25 February 1888. She may have been a prostitute but all we know for sure is that she was a widow of about 38 years old and that she lived in Spitalfields. She was attacked by a man and stabbed in the legs and lower part of her body. Although she recovered from the attack, she collapsed on 31 March and passed away. It was believed that her death in a back yard occurred while she was engaged in business with a client.

On 28 March 1888 Ada Wilson, who lived alone as a seamstress at 19 Maidman Street, Mile End, opened the door to a 30-year-old man of about five feet six inches tall, wearing a dark coat, light trousers and a hat. He forced himself into the house, demanding money, stabbing Ada twice in the throat. It is interesting to note that the term seamstress was often used as a euphemism for prostitute. It is quite possible that this was a Ripper attack as it supports the view that many criminal behaviourists have of serial killers, that they graduate from attacks to mutilations. Ada Wilson survived the attack but at no time did the police link the incident with the Ripper killings.

On 4 April 1888, in the early hours of the morning, Emma Smith was seen talking to a man dressed in dark clothes in Limehouse. When she returned to her lodgings at about 4am she claimed that she had been beaten and raped by three or four men on the corner of Brick Lane and Wentworth Street. Her internal injuries from the attack resulted in her falling into a coma at the London Hospital, where she died four days later. This attack has been connected to the

Ripper on account of the fact that it is still not clear whether the Ripper was actually one man operating alone, or several people.

Martha Tabram's body was found on the morning of Tuesday 7 August 1888, on the first floor landing of George Yard Buildings. She had suffered a frenzied knife attack and it is believed that two weapons were used to inflict the injuries on her. For many analysts of the Ripper case she was the first fully attributable Ripper victim. At the time of her death Martha was 39 years old and was believed to be a prostitute. As far as the coroner, George Collier, was concerned, his description of how the body was found completely matched the other Ripper victims. The lower part of her body was exposed, her legs were open and, unusually, there were definite signs that sexual intercourse had just taken place. Martha had been stabbed 39 times with a bayonet and a penknife.

George Yard buildings, site of Martha Tabram's murder.

On 3 October 1888 the headless and limbless torso of a woman was found in a cellar in Whitehall. Despite press speculation that this was a Ripper victim, the police never believed it to be so. Later the woman's arms were found in the Thames.

On 21 November 1888 Annie Farmer picked up a client and took him back to Satchell's lodging house on George Street, Spitalfields. They arrived together at 7.30am and two hours later the man was seen running along George Street and into Thrawl Street. At the time Annie claimed that she had been attacked by Jack the Ripper. It was true that her throat was cut and bleeding and she claimed that the man had tried to murder her. It was later revealed that she had probably stolen money from the man and put the coins in her mouth; the man had tried to frighten her into giving back the money by running a blunt knife across her throat.

On 20 December 1888 Rose Mylett, also known as Drunken Lizzie Davis, a 26-year-old prostitute and drunk, was discovered at 4.15am in Clarke's Yard, off Poplar High Street, by a police constable. This was just two miles from where the Whitechapel murders had taken place. Unlike the Ripper victims Rose had been strangled and there did not appear to be any other sign of injury to the body. The police never found the string or ligature that had been used to kill her.

Between 31 May and 25 June 1889 various parts of Elizabeth Jackson were discovered in the Thames. She was a Sloane Square prostitute and was heralded by some newspaper reports at the time as being the tenth Ripper victim.

On Wednesday 17 July 1889, at 12.50am, the body of Alice McKenzie, also known as Clay Pipe Alice, was discovered in Castle Alley, off Whitechapel High Street. Her time of death could be accurately established at some time between 12.25 and 12.45am, as it had been raining and the pavement under her body was still dry. The cause of death was the severance of the left carotid artery as a result of two stab wounds on the left side of her neck. There was bruising on the abdomen and chest and a seven-inch wound from the bottom of her left breast to her navel; there were also cuts and scratches around her pubic area. In comparison to the other more established Ripper victims, the mutilations on the body were much more superficial. Only Dr Bagster Phillips suspected that the murder had been carried out by the Whitechapel killer, and even he was unsure. It was generally believed that this was a straightforward murder and not a Ripper killing. A man named William Wallace Brodie later confessed to both this murder and the Whitechapel killings, but it was proved that he was in South Africa between 6 September 1888 and 15 July 1889.

On 10 September 1889, the body of what was believed to be Lydia Hart, a prostitute, was found in Pinchin Street, under a railway arch, by a police constable. The heavily mutilated body had been there for some time and it was possible that the murder had actually taken place on 8 September. It appeared that the body had been dumped after being murdered elsewhere. The stomach had been cut open and the head and the legs had been severed. A newspaper vendor at Charing Cross claimed that he had been told by a soldier in Fleet Street of the murder before it was reported. The man was described as being in his mid-thirties, around five feet six inches tall, with a fair complexion and a moustache. He was carrying a parcel. The state of the body led experts to suggest that the killing was carried out by the same person who had murdered Elizabeth Jackson.

On 13 February 1891, at 2.15am, a police constable walking along Chamber Street, near Leman Street Police Station, heard footsteps heading towards Mansell Street. He shone his light into Swallow Gardens and saw the body of Frances Coles. Her throat had been cut in three places but she had not been mutilated and was still alive. By 2.25am a second officer had called for a local doctor and at some point soon after she died from her injuries. The authorities' investigation immediately focussed on Thomas Sadler, a 53-year-old merchant seaman, who had spent much of the previous day drinking with Frances. Unfortunately for Sadler, in his drunken stupor he had got involved in several brawls and it was believed that Frances had organised for two men she knew to rob him. This did not explain the fact that Frances was out looking for clients in order to pay her landlord. Frances was last seen alive on Commercial Street by another prostitute who remembered the man that Frances was with. It was not Sadler, and the other woman remembered that the man had given her a black eye. Shortly before 2am Sadler had got into a third fight with some dock workers before managing to get back to his lodgings in White's Row. When the police picked him up he was still heavily blood-stained from his fighting. He came to trial at the Thames Magistrates Court on 3 March but the charges against him were immediately dropped. It was believed by many that Sadler had killed Frances but that he was not Jack the Ripper. It is strongly believed that whether Sadler committed the murder or not, the motive was robbery.

Between 23 and 24 April 1891 the only credible Ripper-related victim outside of the British

Isles was killed. Carrie Brown, known as Old Shakespeare, was discovered in a room in the East River Hotel on Manhattan Island, New York. Aside from the strangulation, mutilation and position of the body, the only real connection with Jack the Ripper was the fact that George Chapman, a Ripper suspect, was living in nearby Jersey City. There were numerous cuts and stab wounds all over the body and eventually an Algerian was arrested, convicted and sentenced to life for her murder. He was released 11 years later when it was proven that the bloodstains that had been found in his room had probably been inadvertently or deliberately placed there by the investigating officers. Ameer Ben Ali was released and the murder was never solved. The American press was full of the links between this case and the Whitechapel murders. In the absence of a detailed report from the autopsy, which has never been made available, it is impossible to guess the exact injuries and how they compared to those of the five most well-established Ripper victims. It is always possible that this was a copycat killing.

As if the confusion and argument about the number of Ripper victims were not sufficient, a plethora of potential suspects have been identified, by the police, newspapers and Ripper writers. It is prudent to take them in turn and establish whether there are any connections between the suspects and the murder cases.

Our first interesting suspect is none other than Prince Albert Victor Christian Edward, the grandson of Queen Victoria. He was known as 'Eddy' and it is possible that he had a limited mental capacity and was partially deaf. He was not linked to the Ripper murders until the 1960s, when the train of thought suggested that Eddy had contracted syphilis and that this

condition had driven him mad and made him commit the murders. Sir William Gull was Eddy's doctor and the theory goes on to propose that Eddy, who was incarcerated in a private mental hospital shortly after the double murder on 30 September 1888, escaped from the hospital to carry out the murder of Mary Kelly. After this he was sent to another hospital in Sandringham, Norfolk, where he died in 1892. Unfortunately the story has many holes, not the least of which is the fact that there are no existing records to substantiate the claims that Eddy had syphilis. There have been continual attempts to acquire archive evidence of Eddy's movements during 1888 in order to establish whether he was ever in a position to carry out the murders. So far Buckingham Palace has refused to open the Royal Archives.

Joseph Barnett was a porter who worked at Billingsgate Market. As we have already

Prince Albert Victor, Duke of Clarence.

established, he had a relationship with Mary Jane Kelly and lived for a while with her in 13 Miller's Court. They had quarrelled, presumably on account of Mary's return to her life of prostitution, on 30 October, and his physical description matches the archetypal Ripper described by witnesses: a 30-year-old, medium-built, fair-complexioned man with a moustache who was around five feet six or seven inches tall. Barnett did not emerge as a Ripper suspect until the 1970s, when it was claimed that he carried out the killings

The Duke of Clarence

in order to scare Mary into giving up prostitution. Bearing in mind that he lost his job in June 1888, by the time the Ripper killings officially began Mary was already working on the streets to provide for them both. It was claimed that it was love that had driven him to carry out the murders on local prostitutes. What is fascinating is that Barnett almost exactly matches an FBI psychological profile of Jack the Ripper. The FBI profile was done by William Eckert of the Milton Helpern Institute of Forensic Sciences in 1988, as part of ongoing investigations into the Ripper killings. The profile described the murderer as being white, aged 28 to 36, and living in the Whitechapel area. Barnett was 30 and had lived in Whitechapel all his life. His father had died when he was just six years old; the profile identified that the absence of a father figure was significant. The FBI suggested that the killer was probably engaged in work where he could practice destructive acts; Barnett boned and gutted fish. The FBI also believed that the killings had ceased as a result of the murderer either having been suspected of carrying out the crimes, or as the result of an arrest for a different criminal act. Directly after Mary Kelly's murder Barnett was interviewed for over four hours by the police. Finally, Barnett suffered from a speech impediment and the FBI pointed to the fact that it was likely that the murderer suffered from some physical defect which was at the root of his anger and violence. What may also be significant is the fact that Mary Kelly was found in a locked room; we do not know how many keys there were to the door, but it is reasonable to assume that Barnett still had a copy.

William Henry Bury was hanged in April 1889 for the murder of his wife, Ellen, in Dundee. He was first suspected in 1889 when the *New York Times* noted similarities between the stab wounds on Polly Nichols' body and that of his wife. Admittedly Bury's wife was a former prostitute and many of his known characteristics matched the FBI psychological profile. At the time the police did not take the link between the Ripper and Bury very seriously, but they did send Inspector Abberline to investigate. In the event the connection was discounted.

Stunningly Charles Lutwidge Dodgson, much better known as Lewis Carroll, was also a suspect that emerged in the late 20th century. He suffered from a stammer, later referred to sexual abuse as a child, and died of pneumonia on 14 January 1898. Over 100 years after his death the writer Richard Wallace claimed to have uncovered hidden confessions in Lewis Carroll's writings. Supposedly, Carroll's family had also destroyed parts of his diaries relating to his sexuality. Although Lewis Carroll had many relationships with women, he was suspected by some of being a homosexual, since he was besotted with artists and had a fixation about taking photographs of naked men and women.

Another surprising suspect is Dr Thomas Neill Cream. He was born in May 1850 in Scotland and moved with his family to Canada where he graduated as a medical student in Montreal on 31 March 1876. Cream married Flora Elizabeth Brooks on 11 September 1876, before which he had carried out an abortion on her. The day after the marriage he came to England and became a student at St Thomas's Hospital, where he obtained qualifications from the Royal College of Physicians and Surgeons. He was, however, to return to Canada and set up a successful business as an abortionist. The body of Kate Gardener was discovered in Cream's office, obviously the result of a bungled abortion. He was never charged but he then moved to Chicago and in August 1880 Julia Faulkner died, implicating Cream once more. This time he was charged but not convicted. Cream also dabbled in 'quack' medicines and believed that he had created a liquid which would combat epilepsy. One of his patients, Daniel Stott, sent his wife to collect medicine from Cream's offices. Almost immediately Cream and Julia Stott started an affair. Cream put strychnine into Julia's husband's medicine and killed him on 14 June 1881. When Stott's body was later exhumed, strychnine was found in the body. Cream was convicted of the murder and sent to prison. By 31 July 1891 he had been released for good behaviour and, after collecting a $16,000 inheritance in Canada, he left for England. Within just two days of his arrival he murdered two women, Matilda Clover and Ellen Donworth, by poisoning. Shortly after this he murdered two more, Alice Marsh and Emma Shrivell. It is probable that he would have never been brought to trial had he not accused his neighbour of murder and then tried to blackmail him. Eventually the police became aware of Cream's knowledge of the murders and he was charged and found guilty of murdering Matilda Clover. The fact that he was in prison during the Whitechapel murders did not stop him from confessing that he was Jack the Ripper on 15 November 1892, as he was about to be executed. Neither has this fact prevented various writers from claiming that he is a credible suspect. How can this be? Many point to his defence counsel, Marshall Hall, who claimed that Cream had a double. He and this mysterious man went under the same name of Neill Cream and would use one another's prison sentences as alibis for further crimes. It is interesting that at one stage Cream was charged with bigamy. He was advised by his counsel to plead guilty, but he confidently claimed that he was in prison at the time and could not have married the second woman. When the prison concerned was asked whether Cream was in their prison at the time they confirmed that he had been, and the bigamy charges were dropped.

Frederick Bailey Deeming was born in 1842 and remained devoted to his mother until her death in 1873. It was believed that he had 'an unnatural' relationship with his mother and that at some point after her death he contracted syphilis. En route to Australia he met and married a woman with whom he had four children. By 1887 he was well known to the Australian police for fraud, which prompted him and his family to move to Cape Town in 1888. His reputation as a fraudster necessitated a further move to Liverpool where they lived for a period together until, as he claimed, his wife and children had gone away. Deeming returned to Australia and remarried; again his wife disappeared. At Christmas 1891 he left the house in Australia for good and several months later the owner of the house tried to re-rent and discovered a strong smell in the dining room. After talking to the police and neighbours it was decided that the floorboards should be lifted, and the decomposed body of Deeming's second wife was discovered. Her throat had been cut. Meanwhile, the Liverpool police had been warned to keep a look out for Deeming and when they checked his house there they discovered the bodies of his wife and four children, again with their throats cut, hidden under the floorboards. He was arrested in Western Australia in March 1892 and hanged on Monday 23 May. He claimed in court that he was an epileptic and that he had a brain disease that forced him to do the killings. It was claimed in the newspapers at the time that Deeming had been seen in Whitechapel in 1888 and that he had bought knives there. While in prison awaiting trial in Australia he confided to other prisoners that he was Jack the Ripper. Obviously Deeming was actually believed to have been in South Africa during the murders in Whitechapel, but the cutting of his family's throats has linked Deeming as a potential suspect.

Montague John Druitt's body was found in the Thames on 31 December 1888. He was born in Wimborne, Dorset on 15 August 1857 and was an Oxford graduate and sportsman. Law became his chosen career. On 29 April 1885 he was called to the bar and in the same year his father died. Three years later his mother was confined to a mental institution in Clapton. It was believed, therefore, that he committed suicide because he believed that he would end his life like

his mother. There is considerable argument about exactly when Druitt committed suicide, but it was probably on 4 December. He had just been dismissed from his second job as a teacher at Blackheath School. As far as Druitt being a Ripper suspect is concerned, he does not necessarily fit the physical description. He was living in Blackheath at the time of the murders but he could have easily caught trains from Whitechapel to Blackheath and vice versa. Equally, Druitt's chambers were at 9 King's Bench Walk, within walking distance of Whitechapel. What is most interesting is that there is evidence that he was playing cricket in Bournemouth the weekend before and the weekend after the murder of Martha Tabram. He was also playing cricket in Dorset the day after Polly

Montague Druitt

Nichols was murdered and was in Blackheath on the day of Annie Chapman's murder. Why then is he considered to be one of the more credible Ripper suspects? Sir Melville Macnaghten, the Chief Commissioner of Police, strongly believed that Druitt was the murderer. It appears that he had been informed by a family member that Druitt was insane and perfectly capable of having carried out the killings. Macnaghten points to the fact that a killer of Jack the Ripper's ferocity would not have been in sufficient control of himself to abruptly stop the killings. Something must have happened after the Kelly killing to have placed a full stop in the killer's mind. Macnaghten believed that this must have been death, emigration, imprisonment or a serious illness. Although Macnaghten wrongly believed that Druitt had died around 10 November, and that several other facts proved incorrect, tantalisingly and without revealing his evidence, he was certain that it was Druitt. In March 1889 Albert Backert, a member of the Whitechapel Vigilance Committee, made a very forceful criticism of the police, who believed that because there had been such a long gap since the last murder, there was much less need for concern. He was told by senior Scotland Yard officers that provided he promised not to divulge what they were about to tell him, they would give their reasons why they believed there was no longer any danger. Backert is quoted in the *Woodford Times* as saying:

> Foolishly, I agreed. It was suggested to me that the Vigilance Committee and its patrols might be disbanded as the police were quite certain that the Ripper was dead. I protested, that as I had been sworn to secrecy, I really ought to be given more information than this. 'It is not necessary for you to know any more' I was told. 'The man in question is dead. He was fished out of the Thames two months ago and it would only cause pain to relatives if we said any more than that'.

Although the police interviewed and discounted George Hutchinson as a potential Ripper candidate, various writers have suggested that the man still is a credible suspect. There are only two real suspicions surrounding Hutchinson, firstly that he gave a rather elaborate description of the man that he had seen outside Mary Kelly's room on the night of her murder, and secondly that he did not give this evidence until after the inquest into Mary Kelly's death was finished. It may well be that Hutchinson did see something that night but chose to embellish it in order to ensure that his name appeared in the newspapers and he was suitably rewarded for his information.

Inspector Abberline, the chief investigating officer, actually toyed with the idea that the murderer was not a man but was a woman. The female suspect, although never named, has often been referred to as 'the mad midwife'. It seems that Abberline's suspicions were first aroused by the circumstances surrounding Mary Kelly's death. The time of death was probably between 3.30 and 4am on 9 November, but a Mrs Caroline Maxwell claimed to have seen Mary Kelly twice after the doctors believed she was already dead. She said that she saw Mary looking ill outside Miller's Court sometime between 8 and 8.30am. She saw her for a second time talking to a male outside the Britannia Pub at around 9.30am. She was positive that she had seen Mary Kelly and it is interesting to point out that Mary Kelly's body was found naked and that her clothes had been neatly placed on a chair beside the bed. Is it really possible that someone, presumably a woman, murdered Mary Kelly, then went out disguised in her victim's clothes, before returning and leaving the clothes on the chair? Equally, given the public hysteria in the area and the fact that any man resembling the various descriptions of the Ripper was hounded or apprehended, it would be easy for a female murderer to avoid detection. The second major issue that gives credence to this idea is the belief that the woman may have been a midwife, which would have meant that she could have moved around the area with complete freedom at all times of the day and night, that she would know about human bodies and that any blood seen on her clothing could be easily explained. The fact that Mary Kelly's body was naked when found

Inspector Abberline.

may also point to the fact that she had taken off her clothes for an abortion, little suspecting that the midwife would murder her or borrow her clothes.

Linked to the 'Jill the Ripper' concept is the case of Mary Pearcey. She stabbed her lover's wife and child to death, cut their throats and dumped their bodies in a secluded street. The crime was committed in October 1890 and she was executed on 23 December. She has become a potential suspect simply because her victim's throats were cut, the act was carried out in a private place and subsequently the bodies were left where they could be found.

James Kelly, who died in 1929, first came to the attention of criminologists in the 1980s. By all accounts he was insane and had been in Broadmoor lunatic asylum for nearly 30 years. He knew the East End very well and the only other link is that he murdered his wife by stabbing her in the throat.

A far more interesting suspect is George Chapman, who was born in Poland on 14 December 1865 as Severin Antoniovich Klosowski. He completed his medical studies in Warsaw and probably arrived in England either in 1887 or 1888. He became an assistant to a hairdresser on West India Dock Road but soon was running his own shop in Cable Street. By 1890 he was still working in the East End for a barber on the corner of Whitechapel High Street and George Yard. To begin with some of the evidence is circumstantial. Martha Tabram, if she was a Ripper victim, was murdered in George Yard. There is some confusion about the name that Klosowski was using at the time, which may have been Ludwig Schloski. We know that by October 1889 he had married Lucy Baderski, whom he had met only five weeks before. Unfortunately for Lucy her new husband was already married and had left a wife in Poland. His first wife came to London and it seems that they both lived with him until Lucy produced a son in September 1890. Lucy and Klosowski emigrated to America soon after April 1891; their child having died of pneumonia on 3 March. Klosowski worked in a barber shop in

Jersey City but he attacked Lucy with a knife, prompting her to return to London and live with her sister in Whitechapel. Lucy was pregnant again and gave birth to Cecilia on 15 May 1892. Around June her husband joined her and they seem to have made a reconciliation. However, by late 1893 he had met a woman called Annie Chapman and he lived with her in south Tottenham for nearly a year. She fell pregnant but by now Klosowski was showing interest in other women so she left him. Certainly by 1895 Klosowski was using the name Chapman and for a time lived in Leytonstone with an alcoholic called Mary Spink. He brutally beat her on a number of occasions.

On 3 April 1897 Chapman bought an ounce of tartar emetic and, after dosing Mary with it over a period of time, she finally died on Christmas Day. By this time Chapman was running the Prince of Wales pub in Bartholomew Square off the City Road and it was there that he soon replaced Mary with Bessie Taylor. She, too, after having been threatened by Chapman with a pistol, was given tartar emetic. They moved to run the Grapes in Bishop's Stortford, then took the lease of the Monument Tavern in Borough. Bessie died on Valentine's Day 1901. By August Chapman had found another woman, Maud Marsh; she too was beaten regularly and suffered the same cause of death on 22 October 1902. This time the doctor refused to sign a death certificate and arsenic and antimony were found in Maud's body. Chapman was arrested on 25 October and during November and December 1902 both of his previous victims were exhumed and found to exhibit the same causes of death. He was convicted of their murders on 20 March 1903 and hanged at Wandsworth on 7 April. The most significant aspect of all of this, even given the fact that the methods of killing were poisons rather than stabbings, is that when Inspector Godley arrested him, he immediately contacted Abberline, who reportedly said to Godley 'You've got Jack the Ripper at last'. Abberline had long believed that Chapman or Klosowski was a viable Ripper suspect for a number of reasons. Firstly, his arrival in England coincided with the beginning of the murders, and secondly, there were similar murders in America while he was in New Jersey. Thirdly, all the murders occurred at weekends, when Lucy said that her husband often stayed out until the early hours of the morning. Fourthly, Chapman was a misogynist, despite his intense sexual drive. He had beaten all four women that he had lived with and killed three of them. Only one thing preyed on Abberline's mind; Chapman did not look very much like witnesses descriptions of the Ripper. As for the murder of the prostitute Carrie Brown in Jersey City in 1891, on the face of it, Chapman does match the description given by the only real witness Mary Miniter, who thought that the man she had seen was a German. Could Chapman have left England after the census on 5 April 1891 and been in Jersey City by 24 April to murder Carrie? It seems possible, but what is not credible is the fact that an accomplished mutilator of women would suddenly change his *modus operandi* and become a poisoner, unless, of course, he did not wish anyone to link the two series of killings.

Aaron Kosminski was first mentioned as a suspect by Macnaghten in 1894. He had apparently been identified as the Ripper by a Jewish witness. According to Macnaghten charges were never preferred against Kosminski because he, too, was Jewish and the witness would not testify against him. We know very little of the man but he was probably born in 1864 and died in 1919. It is believed that he was mentally ill but there is no evidence to support the fact that he was a violent man.

Back in January 1911 Marie Belloc Lowndes wrote a story called *The Lodger* which told of a retired couple who had been servants and who had taken in a man to rent one of the rooms in their house. The lodger is a strange man who spends his days reading the Bible and his nights wandering around the area, not returning until the early hours of the morning. At the same time the couple read the story of a man who calls himself the Avenger, murdering prostitutes. It becomes the suspicion of the couple that their lodger is the Avenger. While this is a particularly obvious form of fiction, it appears that the writer got her idea from a conversation over a dinner table. One of the guests told her that his mother's butler and cook were certain that they had rented rooms to Jack the Ripper. There may be a link with a house in Finsbury Street here, where in April 1888 a man going by the name of G. Wentworth Bell Smith had rented a room from a Mr Callaghan. It seems that this gentleman was a Canadian but very odd. He had three loaded revolvers, would change his clothes several times a day, had three pairs of rubber-soled boots, would often shout at prostitutes and the landlord had once seen 60 sheets of paper covered in writing expressing his disgust of whores. On 7 August 1888 he did not return home until 4am. This was the night that Martha Tabram was murdered. Apparently the maid of the house found bloodstains on his bed the following day. The same man had apparently accosted a prostitute in Worship Street and offered her a pound to have sex with him. Fortunately for her, perhaps, she refused. Maybe the most unfortunate aspect of this particular story is that it was only made public a considerable amount of time after the murders.

The lodger may not have been a Mr Smith; he may, indeed have been Francis Tumblety. He was, apparently, arrested during the murders but released on bail. Tumblety was a herbalist and 'quack' doctor from America and while on bail he fled the country via Liverpool. Despite Scotland Yard detectives being sent to New York, Tumblety again gave them the slip. He was probably born in 1833 and he initially sold pornography in Rochester, before working in a drug store. In around 1854 he set up a practice as an Indian herb doctor. He then appears in Montreal in late 1857 where he was arrested as an abortionist; he was released on 1 October. He fell foul of the law again in 1860 when one of his patients died, so he then pitched up in Boston, moving later to St Louis. He arrived in Liverpool in 1874, via Berlin. It seems more than possible that Tumblety was bisexual, as it is believed that he had an affair, certainly until 1876, with Sir Henry Hall Caine. In 1876 Tumblety returned to New York where he was known as a homosexual. He then returned to Liverpool in June 1888, where he was arrested for gross indecency and assault on four men on 7 November. Tumblety was out on bail from these charges when the Whitechapel murders were committed. Although Scotland Yard could not find him in New York when he fled, the New York police tracked him down to 79 East 10th Street. Tumblety evaded them again and disappeared, re-emerging in Rochester in 1893. He died in St Louis in 1903. The connection between Tumblety and Jack the Ripper seems to be based on a letter written by Chief Inspector John Littlechild in 1913. He cited Tumblety as a very likely suspect who fitted many of the characteristics associated with the murderer. It is clear that he hated women and particularly prostitutes, he had the strange hobby of collecting women's reproductive organs, he had a good knowledge of the East End and he had actually been arrested in the autumn of 1888 as a Ripper suspect.

As related in the chapter on the Maybrick case, the 1990s saw the publication of a diary purportedly written by James Maybrick. It remains at the centre of controversy regarding both its authenticity and attention to detail. In all probability the diary, and hence the link between James Maybrick and the Ripper, is a hoax, but many still believe that the diary is authentic and that it provides irrefutable evidence of James Maybrick's guilt.

Michael Ostrog was born in 1833 but over the course of his complex and criminal life was also known as Max Grief Gosslar, who was sentenced to 10 months imprisonment for theft in Oxford in 1863. In 1864, working under the name Count Sobieski, he was sentenced to eight months by a court in Tunbridge Wells. In 1866 he was given seven years for theft and was released in 1873, whereupon he promptly committed several other thefts in Burton upon Trent. This time, to avoid capture, he shot at the police. However, he was caught and convicted in January 1874, and sentenced to 10 years. By 1883 he was out again and seems to have gone to ground for a little while, but in 1887 he was given six months for theft. Released in March 1888 he was given two years in November in Paris on charges of theft. By 1891 he had been committed to the Surrey County Lunatic Asylum but in 1894, 1898 and 1900 he committed more thefts. He was finally released in 1904 and disappeared. Macnaghten first suspected him in 1894 and described him as being a mad Russian doctor who was cruel to women, carried surgical knives and was in the Whitechapel area during the murders. Could Macnaghten have been wrong in linking Ostrog? After all, he was a petty criminal and probable madman rather than a serial killer.

William le Queux, a writer, first suggested Dr Alexander Pedachenko or Count Luiskovo as a potential suspect back in 1928. The bizarre reasoning behind this suggestion of a man said to have been born in 1857 was that he had been sent by the Russian secret police to London to commit the murders with the sole intention of discrediting Scotland Yard. The only other aspect we know with some certainty is that the doctor ended up in a lunatic asylum.

The 'Royal Conspiracy' was put forward in a book written by Stephen Knight in 1976. It purported to be the final solution to the Ripper mystery. It was, indeed, a bizarre story. Knight had tracked down a man called Joseph Sickert, whose father had been the painter, Walter Sickert. Walter had lived in the East End at the time when the murders took place, and according to Joseph his father had told him that Queen Victoria's grandson, Eddy, had initiated a relationship with a girl called Annie Elizabeth Crook. Eddy had got the girl pregnant and not only that, she was a Catholic. Queen Victoria was livid and told Salisbury, the Prime Minister, to sort the problem out. A raid on the house that Annie lived in at Cleveland Street resulted in Eddy and Annie being taken away. The daughter, Alice Margaret, was nowhere to be seen. Now we begin to move into the realms of even greater fantasy.

With the aid of Sir William Gull, Queen Victoria's physician, Annie was put away into a mental asylum where experiments were performed on her to make her lose her memory. But here we now find the link between the Ripper victims and this outrageous story. It seems that Mary Kelly had been Alice's nanny, and it was Mary who had taken the child away when Annie and Eddy had been detained after the raid. She had given the child to nuns and then had returned to the East End to resume her life of prostitution and drinking. Unfortunately she had told some of her friends about what she knew. These were Polly Nichols, Liz Stride and Annie Chapman. They suggested that Mary blackmail the government to keep the story quiet. Salisbury soon learned that this was a threat and engaged the aid of Sir William Gull to deal with the problem. He and John Netley, one of

Sir William Gull.

Eddy's coachmen who knew the East End well, hatched a plan to deal with the women. The two conspirators, with the aid of Sir Robert Anderson, hunted the East End and dealt with the women in the most brutal fashion. It was claimed that the Eddowes killing had been a mistake on account of the fact that she was often known as Mary Kelly. The story goes on to suggest that they then chose a scapegoat in the guise of Montague Druitt. First they set up circumstantial evidence that he could have carried out the killings and then they dumped him in the Thames. The oddest coincidence was that Eddy and Annie's daughter, Alice Margaret, eventually married Walter Sickert and Joseph was their son.

James Kenneth Stephen was born on 25 February 1859 and schooled at Tunbridge Wells and Eton until 1878. James then went to Cambridge and became a Fellow of King's College in 1885. In 1888 he established a weekly newspaper which was an abject failure and by the summer his father had appointed him the Clerk of Assize for the South Wales circuit. He stayed in the job for two years and returned to Cambridge in 1891. He wrote several books during the next few years and died after being taken seriously ill on 3 February 1892. The only real link with Stephen and the Ripper is that he was suggested as a suspect by Michael Harrison in 1972 in his biography of Prince Albert Victor. It seems that Stephen was mentally unstable and a misogynist and it is really through his association with Prince Albert Victor that he has become a suspect. In his defence it is not believed that he knew the Whitechapel area, nor did he show any signs of being violent.

Robert Donston Stephenson, also known as Dr Roslyn D'Onston, was born in 1841 and initially became a Ripper suspect in 1888. The idea was resurrected in a book called ***The True Face of Jack the Ripper*** written by Melvin Harris in 1987. It is believed that the suspect had a great interest in the murders and had access to a great deal of information that would not have otherwise been known. He probably murdered his wife and, judging from his military background, he knew how to kill. He purported to have medical knowledge and he lived in

Dr D'Onston, Ripper suspect.

the East End at the time. Whether D'Onston is as credible a suspect as Harris claims takes a certain leap of faith, but Harris tries hard to build a serious case against him.

The poet Francis Thompson is yet another Ripper suspect. He was born on 18 December 1859 and died in 1907. The evidence which links Thompson to the murders is perhaps as bizarre as anything that we have encountered to date. The Nichols killing took place on 31 August, the feast day of St Raymond, the patron saint of innocence, midwives, childbirth and pregnant women. The Chapman murder on 8 September fell on the feast day of St Adrian, who was martyred when his body was thrown into a furnace. Significantly, his wife kept his hand. Elizabeth Stride and Catherine Eddowes were murdered on 30 September, the feast day of St Jerome, whom Thompson had written essays about. Mary Kelly's death fell on the feast day of St Theodore, who was tortured and mutilated after setting fire to a temple.

The theory that Thompson was the Ripper is based on the significance of the days that the murders took place and the fact that he may have thought himself to be a Messiah who was purging society of its ills by killing the prostitutes. We know that by 1882 Thompson had an opium addiction and between 1885 and 1888 he was living as a vagrant near Whitechapel. He had variously worked as a surgeon, a priest, a soldier and a factory worker. It is also claimed that Thompson fell in love with a prostitute and that he hunted the area to find her. It was during his opium addiction period that he wrote ***The Ballad of the Witch Babies***, which tells of a knight stalking about in the darkness and disembowelling women. Equally circumstantial is the fact that Thompson was left-handed and although it was believed that most of the murders had been carried out from behind the victims, therefore suggesting the left-to-right cut on the throats, a left-handed man could have delivered this cut from the front. Thompson also wore a neck-tie which many believe was the weapon used to strangle the victims. Although he was emaciated when he died, Thompson was of medium height; he had dark brown to black hair and in many other respects resembled witness descriptions of the Ripper. Could this man, who died a lonely and

A Special Constable, 1888.

METROPOLITAN POLICE.

Fac-simile of Letter and Post Card received by Central News Agency.

Any person recognising the handwriting is requested to communicate with the nearest Police Station.

Ripper letters and envelopes.

tragic death as a result of his addictions, be the maddened and vicious Whitechapel killer?

Choosing a credible Ripper suspect, where there is no incontrovertible proof that the crimes were either carried out by one individual, and when we are not even sure how many victims were involved, would be difficult enough if the Whitechapel case were still active today. We do not know whether the suspect had any connections with the East End, nor whether the suspect had any connection with any of the victims. The Ripper letters and the message left on the wall only serve to muddy the waters. Assuming the Ripper was a man, was he a doctor, did he have medical skills, or was he a butcher? Certainly the police focussed on Donston, Chapman, Druitt, Ostrog, Kosminski and Tumblety, although others were the pet suspects of contemporary investigators. Known murderers such as Chapman, Cream, Deeming, James and Kelly were

Inspector Donald Swanson, officer in charge of the Ripper enquiry.

Punch cartoon, 1888.

all potential suspects but their murders did not match the Ripper's methods. We can never be certain whether any of the main suspects were actually involved in the murders. Perhaps the police knew who the murderer was, but it seems most likely that no one has ever identified the correct suspect, and thus that everything that has been written or assumed has been merely conjecture.

CHAPTER THREE

POOR BUT HONEST

The Strange Case of Edmund Pook – Greenwich, 1871

EDMUND POOK was the epileptic son of Ebenezer Pook, a former employee of *The Times*. In 1871 Ebenezer ran a print company in Greenwich and lived with his wife and their two sons, Edmund and Thomas, at 3 London Street, Greenwich. Thomas was the elder son, but had fallen out with his father when he married a woman that his father considered beneath him. Both the brothers were interested in amateur dramatics or, as they were called then, penny readings. Despite 20-year-old Edmund's epilepsy, he was something of a ladies' man and had been involved with a string of local girls, including Miss Durnford, Miss Langley, Miss Wicks and Miss Love. He did not seem particularly interested in marriage.

Edmund's father, something of a social climber, was not impressed by his younger son's liaisons and flirtations. He was absolutely determined that his younger son would not make the same mistake of becoming involved inappropriately and hoped that Edmund would pursue a more virtuous middle-class girl. We also know that Edmund carried a whistle with him which he apparently used to attract women's attention.

In early 1871 it seems that Edmund became involved with the household's domestic servant, Jane Clouson. She was about 16 or 17 years old at the time and, unlike many of the girls that Edmund had paid attention to in the past, she was much more willing to comply with his wishes. At some point they slept together and soon after not only did Jane fall in love with Edmund, but she also fell pregnant with his child. Three months before Jane's death she had told a friend, Mrs Jane Prosser, that she was already pregnant with Edmund's child but, as we will see later, she was only two months pregnant when she died. What is interesting is the fact that there was gossip that Mrs Prosser either carried out abortions or could organise them for people. There is no evidence to suggest that Jane did have an abortion, but the apparent contradiction about the term of the pregnancy remains unclear.

On 13 April Mrs Pook decided to sack Jane on the grounds that her work and, presumably, the standards of the mistress of the house, had not been met. Mrs Pook accused Jane of being dirty and slovenly, but it was later widely believed that somehow Mrs Pook had realised that Jane was pregnant. Jane told her friends that she had been sacked because she had been made pregnant by Edmund and that the Pooks had sacked her simply because they wished to rid the household of a lower-class girl, regardless of the fact that she was carrying their son's baby. It is not known whether Mrs Pook actually knew about the pregnancy, but what seems unlikely is that Jane suddenly became an unacceptable employee after two years of faithful service.

Jane was now homeless and after visiting a former employee of Ebenezer Pook, a Mrs Emily Wolledge, it was arranged that she would lodge at 12 Ashburnham Street with a Mrs Fanny Hamilton. It appears that throughout this period Jane still saw Edmund, who was, by this stage, desperate that the young woman should not tell his father. It would soon become obvious that Jane was pregnant and unless Edmund did something for her, it was inevitable that his father would hear of his transgression. During this period Jane also talked of her affair with Edmund with William and Elizabeth Trott, her uncle and aunt, as well as her cousin, Charlotte.

Eleven days after she had been sacked by the Pooks, on Sunday 24 April, Jane visited the Trotts at their home in Deptford. Elizabeth and Charlotte later attested to Jane's cheerful nature on what was to be the last Sunday of her life. She apparently told Charlotte:

You must not be surprised if I am missing for some weeks, for Edmund says I must meet him either tomorrow night or on Tuesday to arrange to go with him into the country. He says he will have such a deal to tell me, and that we shall have to make all the arrangements. He says he is going to take me to a christening at St Ives. Then we shall go somewhere else to such a nice place where I shall be so happy. But I am not to tell anyone where I am going, or write to anyone for some time, as he does not want anyone to know where I am. You must not be surprised if you miss me for some weeks, but you shall have the first letter I shall write to anyone. Edmund says I shall not want for money, and if it is five pounds I shall have it and I shall be happy.

Later that night, as Jane and Charlotte walked across Blackheath, Jane told her cousin that she and Edmund planned to marry. Jane fervently hoped that Mrs Pook would accept her into the family as she had reluctantly done with Thomas's wife. She also told Charlotte that she had arranged to meet Edmund on either Monday or Tuesday evening at the top of Crooms Hill.

On Monday 25 April Jane received a letter from Edmund. Although Fanny Hamilton, her landlady, and her friend, Emily Wolledge, saw the letter they did not see its contents. The letter presumably carried an instruction from Edmund for Jane to destroy it as soon as she had read it. She accordingly burnt the letter. The two women also claimed that Jane wrote back to Edmund. Jane also told Mrs Hamilton that her plans to seek work locally would now not be necessary as she was sure that Edmund would look after her future needs.

On Tuesday 26 April Jane walked with Fanny Hamilton into Deptford and parted company with her on Douglas Street at 6.40pm. This would give Jane enough time to walk to the west side of Greenwich Park and climb Crooms Hill to meet Edmund at 7pm. Fanny Hamilton, Emily Wolledge and Jane Prosser, as well as Charlotte Trott, were all aware that Jane was meeting Edmund in order to discuss their future together.

What happened between 6.40pm and the discovery of a dying Jane at 4am the following morning is confused, as no one came forward that could positively claim to have seen her during those fateful nine hours.

Tracing Jane's exact steps before her eventual discovery in Kidbrooke Lane is further complicated by the fact that Kidbrooke Lane is not where it used to be in 1871. The old Kidbrooke Lane was actually opposite St James's Church, SE3, and is not the present Kidbrooke Lane in SE9. Jane's rendezvous with Edmund on Crooms Hill, according to his testimony, never occurred. However, Crooms Hill is near Blackheath, and at the time there was only countryside between it and Kidbrooke Lane, which in 1871 was a well-known lovers' lane that was dark and secluded and not overlooked by any nearby buildings. What actually happened can only be assembled from the various statements made by people who were in the area that Tuesday night. One of the witnesses, a Thomas Lazell, claimed to have seen Edmund Pook wearing a hat and dark-frocked coat in a cornfield with a woman at some point after 7pm that evening. Another witness, William Norton, who was with his girlfriend, Louisa Putnam, claimed that they both heard a woman screaming at some point between 8.30 and 9pm. They also said that they saw a man running past them shortly afterwards, panting for breath. He was running in the direction of nearby Mordern College. Unfortunately they could not give a description of the man because of the dark. At some other point in the evening another witness, named Cronk, claimed that he had heard a woman screaming 'Let me go' several times. He was able to partially describe the woman, who was struggling with a man, and said that she wore a dark dress and jacket and a dark hat. He was later able to identify Edmund Pook as the man he had seen fighting with the woman.

What is particularly unusual about the timing of these witness statements is the fact that nothing was discovered until 4am. On two occasions, at 10pm and 1.45am the following morning, police constable Donald Gunn patrolled Kidbrooke Lane. This was part of his regular beat and on neither occasion did he see or hear anything relating to the evidence from the other witnesses. However, it was PC Gunn that first encountered the viciously battered Jane Clouson at 4am.

At first PC Gunn thought that he had encountered a drunken woman crawling along the lane on her hands and knees. Bearing in mind that it was dark, the constable can be forgiven for not noticing Jane's severe injuries. As he approached her he heard her groan 'Oh my head, my head'. By now Jane was within range of the beam of his torch and he could see how badly injured she was. Her right eye was missing, her face was lacerated and bleeding and, most seriously, there was a hole in her skull through which the constable could see her brain. As the police constable knelt down to tend her she fell onto the ground, moaning 'Let me die, let me die'. By this stage Jane's injuries had shocked her system so severely that she was unable to talk, and despite Gunn's attempts he could not even get Jane to tell him her name. Gunn flashed his torch around the surrounding area, quickly noting that the woman's hat and gloves were on the ground a few feet behind her. Unable to deal with the injuries himself, Gunn ran all the way into Eltham and quickly returned in a cab with Sergeant George Haynes. Carefully they lifted Jane into the cab and took her off at speed to Eltham. Throughout the jolting journey Jane continued to moan and the only sense they could make out was her whispering 'Oh save me, save me'.

Jane was tended by Dr King in Eltham, who quickly realised that her injuries were far beyond his own medical abilities, so again Jane was packed off in a cab to Guy's Hospital. Surgeons there also were of the opinion that the woman was too far gone for them to be able to save her. Various witnesses claimed that Jane, after being asked her name, uttered 'Mary Shru'. It was later claimed that this actually sounded like Edmund Pook and that Jane had not been attempting to say her own name. She remained conscious for only a short while before passing away, giving no more clues about either her name or her assailant.

The body was closely examined prior to the post-mortem and it was discovered that at least 12 deep wounds had been inflicted on her face. The doctors believed that these had been inflicted while she was lying on the ground. The most significant injuries were two on the left of her face, at least one of which had lacerated the brain and damaged the temporal bone above the ear. The third major wound had not only destroyed her right eye but had also fractured bones around the eye socket. It appeared to the doctors, and was later confirmed by the post-mortem report, that the assailant had slashed the face of the woman to disfigure her so completely that identification would be as difficult as possible. The post-mortem also confirmed that Jane was two months pregnant.

On the morning of Wednesday 27 April the police began a painstaking search of the area where PC Gunn had found Jane. Not only did they find footprints moving away from where PC Gunn had found her, on account of the soft ground in the area, but there was also blood in the nearby stream. The stream was known as Kid Brook and the police believed that the murderer, thoroughly splattered in blood after the assault, had attempted to wash the evidence from his body and clothes before leaving the scene of the crime. Soon after the police discovered what was to be confirmed as the murder weapon. It was a strange hammer-like object known as a lathing hammer. It had a long handle surmounted with a hammerhead on one side and an axe-like chopper on the other. The weapon still had Jane's blood and hair caked on it.

Despite the investigations and the conclusions of the post-mortem, which clearly pointed towards a murder, the police still had no idea who the murder victim was. It was not until Sunday 30 April that William, Elizabeth and Charlotte Trott began to feel uneasy about Jane's disappearance, coupled with the fact that the newspapers were running lurid stories about the murder in Kidbrooke Lane. With great trepidation they decided to go to Blackheath Road Police Station, where they were interviewed by Superintendent Griffin. He showed them the murder victim's clothes and even at that point they were reasonably convinced that they were Jane's clothes and that she was the unfortunate victim. They were taken to the mortuary at Guy's Hospital where they were shown the horrific sight of Jane's mutilated body, although they were initially unable to give the police a positive identification due to the excessive facial injuries. However, Elizabeth Trott was able to recognise a mole on Jane's left breast, which left her in no doubt that the body was that of Jane Clouson.

The distraught Trotts told Superintendent Griffin of their conversation with Jane the previous Sunday and what she had confided in them about her assignation with Edmund Pook. To confirm the details of the story Superintendent Griffin was accompanied by Inspector Mulvany to 12 Ashburnham Street, where they interviewed Fanny Hamilton and Jane's friend, Emily Wolledge. Having confirmed the details of Jane's last known movements, they were sure that the man that could answer their questions about the demise of the young woman was Edmund Pook.

From the outset Pook was confident and spoke very badly of Jane. He maintained that the last time that he had seen Jane was when his mother had sacked her on 13 April, because 'She was a dirty young woman and left in consequence'. It was Inspector Mulvany's line of questioning that convinced the two police officers that they were standing in the presence of the man who had murdered Jane Clouson. Mulvany asked Pook 'Have you written her a letter?' Edmund Pook replied 'Certainly not', to which Mulvany responded 'People say you have'. Mulvany certainly considered Edmund's further reply damning. 'Do they?' Pook enquired. 'Have you the letter? If it is in my handwriting that will prove it'. Mulvany was acutely aware of the fact that Edmund Pook was no fool and that there was evidence to suggest that he had instructed Jane to burn the letter he had written to her arranging the meeting on Crooms Hill. Mulvany changed tack to establish whether Edmund Pook had an alibi for the night of the murder. Pook claimed that he had returned to London Street at around 9.15pm, after having made a visit to a young lady in Lewisham. When Mulvany asked him whether she could support his assertion that he was in Lewisham, Pook told him that the lady had failed to honour their arrangement to meet. As far as Mulvany and Griffin were concerned, Edmund Pook's clothes finally confirmed that they had found their murderer. Just as Thomas Lazell had described, Pook agreed that he was wearing a billycock hat and a dark-frocked coat on the night of Tuesday 26 April. Mulvany asked to see the clothes in question and could immediately pick out what he believed to be bloodstains on the coat. Now certain that they had found the murderer of Jane Clouson, they arrested Edmund Pook.

The evidence appeared damning but ultimately the whole case was hopelessly mishandled by the police, who later received severe criticism from the Lord Chief Justice. Questions were even asked in the Houses of Parliament about the handling of the trial and the outcome. The evidence against Edmund seemed unequivocal. Blood was found on both his hat and on the clothes that he had admitted wearing on 26 April. A witness who ran a shop claimed that Edmund had asked her to clean the mud off his clothes. It was beyond doubt that Kidbrooke Lane was muddy and further that Edmund's clothes would be dirty after floundering around in Kid Brook in his attempts to wash the blood away. In addition to this, another shopkeeper positively identified Edmund Pook as the purchaser of the lathing hammer used as the murder weapon. If this were not enough, the police had also found what they believed to be Edmund Pook's whistle near the murder scene. Edmund was inextricably linked to Jane Clouson, on account of the fact that she had worked for the family, and, more damningly, by the evidence given by the Trotts, Fanny Hamilton and Emily Wolledge that Jane was not only carrying his child, but that he had proposed to meet her on that fateful night. It seemed clear from Jane's confidences to Charlotte that Edmund intended to get Jane out of the way by some means. Thus Jane went willingly to her death, never suspecting what Edmund Pook intended for her.

Jane Clouson was buried on 8 May 1871 and soon afterwards there were demonstrations outside the Pook's home in London Street. The local population had been whipped up by numerous newspaper reports which sought to incriminate Edmund. When Edmund Pook finally came to trial the prosecution was not only poorly prepared, but had foolishly believed many of the supposed witnesses that had flocked to the police claiming that they had vital evidence to incriminate the defendant. Without having to show a great deal of skill or resolve, Edmund's defence counsel demolished the testimony of many of these 'late-comers', which seriously undermined the whole case against Edmund Pook.

Ebenezer Pook, meanwhile, had mobilised the assistance of the editor of **The Times,** who ran a series of articles rubbishing the prosecution's claims of Edmund's guilt. Throughout the case the Pook family stood solidly behind their wayward son, determined that the family name should not be associated with such a heinous and notorious crime. Systematically the defence was able to unravel much of the evidence against their client. Bearing in mind that blood could not be tested in the same forensic manner as it can be today, the blood on the clothing was explained away by the fact that Edmund Pook was an epileptic and suffered from heavy nosebleeds. As for the mud story, the defence claimed that Edmund had fallen over in the mud in Lewisham where he had been spying on a man whom he believed to have been showing an unreasonable interest in one of his girlfriends. Mrs Pook in the witness box steadfastly renounced the possibility that her son ever had an affair with the dead woman, or got her pregnant. Even the evidence related to Edmund Pook purchasing the lathing hammer was undermined by a clever defence counsel who tempted the witnesses into confusion and contradiction.

Lord Chief Justice Bovill refused to allow either the Trotts, Fanny Hamilton or Emily Wolledge to testify about what Jane had told them about her relationship with Edmund and their future plans. As far as Bovill was concerned, it was hearsay and not admissible in court. The jury never knew of their evidence and were unable to incorporate it into their deliberations. The only thing that Elizabeth Trott was allowed to testify to related to the identification of Jane's body by the mole on her left breast. Without the damning evidence which incontrovertibly linked Edmund Pook to Jane Clouson, the jury could only take Mrs Pook's word for the fact that her son had no association whatsoever with the former servant girl.

The other aspect that we must be constantly aware of is the fact that defendants could not give evidence in court on their own behalf. This law was not amended until 1896, so the prosecution did not have the opportunity to try to unravel or question Edmund Pook's version of the events leading up to 26 April. It also appears that Lord Chief Justice Bovill was not exactly on speaking terms with the Solicitor General Sir John Coleridge, who was the prosecution counsel. It was believed that Bovill was quite happy to undermine Coleridge's case against

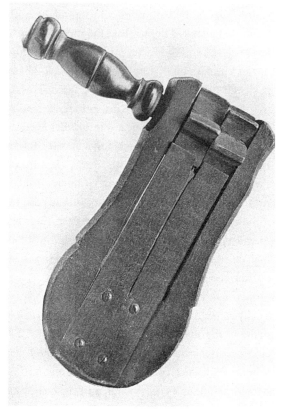

Police rattle.

Edmund Pook. It is not, therefore, surprising that in his summing up the judge was not impartial and drew the jury's attention primarily to the holes in the prosecution's case. He was negative about much of the testimony given by the prosecution witnesses.

Consequently, after just 20 minutes, the jury returned to the court and pronounced Edmund Pook not guilty of the murder of Jane Clouson.

If the Pooks had thought that the nightmare was over, they were wrong. In fact, it was only just beginning. The newspapers still believed Edmund guilty of the crime, as did most of the local population. There were many demonstrations outside their house in London Street.

The Monday after Edmund's acquittal crude effigies were made of Edmund Pook and Jane Clouson. The dolls depicted a crazed Edmund smashing in Jane's skull with a lathing hammer. This was paraded past the Pook's house, followed by a crowd of around 4,000 people.

Newton Crossland, a wealthy London businessman, wrote a pamphlet called *The Eltham Tragedy Reviewed,* which clearly outlined the supposed guilt of Edmund Pook. It sold extremely well in the Greenwich area at 2d per copy. It was very critical of the judge, the trial and the rules against hearsay evidence, and was clearly meant to elicit a response from the family. Part of the pamphlet read:

Now I will tell you how I shall conduct myself when I commit a murder, and I wish to let the judge, jury, police, counsel and the public know beforehand how I intend to act under the circumstances. I shall prepare myself for my diabolical task and cultivate my natural callousness and villainy by a devoted study of the most popular and sensational novels of the day. The girl I once loved and who is desperately in my way shall be my victim. An evening walk down a dark unfrequented lane and a small axe will supply me with all the conditions I shall require for accomplishing my design. Fifteen blows in fifteen seconds will be enough. When the deed is done, I shall not be miserable; I shall feel the same relief that a surgeon would feel after lopping off a mortified limb. But if my nerves should be a little agitated, a quick run home through the evening air will restore my equanimity.

Knowing that the police can discover nothing special against me, I shall give them every facility and treat them with the greatest apparent frankness. If they ask for any explanations why spots of blood are on my clothes, I shall promptly reply that my nose bled and this answer shall be considered conclusive and satisfactory forever after. I shall be very unlucky if the witnesses against me are not stupid and sadly out of their reckoning of time. All hear-say evidence against me will of course be illegal, and I shall be acquitted amid the applause of an excited and bamboozled multitude.

In anticipation of the inevitable libel case that would follow such a derogatory version of Edmund Pook's case, Newton Crossland had already engaged counsel to fight the case in the law courts. Unluckily for Edmund, his father, Ebenezer, saw an ideal opportunity to extract a punitive level of damages from Newton Crossland while appearing to be simply defending the honour of the family. Edmund would have to go into the witness box and be cross-examined to ensure that the libel case could be won. Neither of these things had occurred during the murder trial. Newton Crossland was represented by one of the foremost counsels of the day, Serjeant Parry. During his cross-examination of Edmund he clearly accused Pook of actually murdering Jane Clouson and what is more that he had duped the Old Bailey jury into believing this was not the case. Part of his summing up made clear accusations:

It is obvious that there are many circumstances which point to the young man being the murderer, and he cannot get over them. If the girl's lips had not been sealed by death, and she had repeated those statements on oath, where would the plaintiff be now? Why, undergoing penal servitude for life.

This was a clear reference to the fact that the damning hearsay evidence that could have been given to the court by the Trotts, Fanny Hamilton and Emily Wolledge would have convicted Edmund Pook. In the event, the jury had no choice but to find in favour of the plaintiff. In their view Newton Crossland had libelled him because Edmund had been found not guilty at the Old Bailey trial. It was not for the Civil Court to say whether the murder trial verdict was right or wrong. It is perhaps telling that the jury only awarded the Pooks £50 in damages. We can draw our own conclusions from this paltry sum, but it seems likely that they too believed that Edmund Pook was guilty of the murder of Jane Clouson and that he had, through a legal technicality, got away with it.

Two further versions of the events only serve to muddy the waters even further. The first was that Jane Clouson had attempted to say Edmund Pook's name in Guy's Hospital in order to conceal the true identity of the father of her unborn child. The story contended that she had met this mystery man and had spent the evening with him in Greenwich, after which she had walked with him to Kidbrooke Lane sometime after 11pm. It was here that this strange unknown assailant attacked her and left her for dead until PC Gunn found her at 4am.

Strangely the other story seems to have originated from the Pook family. They claimed that Jane had been intimate with a seaman to whom she had confessed her association with Edmund. It was this man that had murdered Jane for her indiscretions and, directly after carrying out the murder, he went back to sea. The most obvious hole in this story is that if the man had any affection for Jane then surely it would have been Edmund that he attacked and not his pregnant girlfriend.

Unravelling the various newspaper reports and speculation of the time does little to throw any real light on the true facts of the case. What appears to be beyond doubt is that Jane Clouson willingly met or accompanied her murderer to Kidbrooke Lane on 26 April. Whether her murderer was Edmund Pook or an unknown man remains unclear to this day.

CHAPTER FOUR

THE BOOTLACE MURDERS

The Hanging of the Innocent Herbert Bennett – Great Yarmouth, 1900

HERBERT JOHN BENNETT was born in Gravesend, Kent, in 1880. His contemporaries described him as being intelligent, despite the fact that he had little formal schooling. His father was a foreman at a cement works, but Bennett spurned this occupation, becoming first a newspaper seller and later an assistant in a grocers shop. In 1896, he met the 19-year-old Mary Jane Clark, which meeting directed his life towards a fateful end some five years later at the end of a rope in Norwich.

Throughout his life, Bennett was not averse to perverting the truth for his own purposes. Indeed, this less than saintly figure had a colourful history. All his schemes were designed to provide him with untold riches. It seems clear that Mary Jane Clark was a willing accomplice to many of Bennett's illegal dealings.

When Bennett met Clark she was living with her grandmother in Northfleet. He would walk from his home in Swanscombe in order to meet her when she left chapel on a Sunday. The pair had first met when Bennett replied to an advertisement Clark had placed offering lessons on the

Close up drawing of Bennett.

violin and piano. She was a little over 5 feet tall, with titian, shoulder-length hair; she wore glasses and was slightly deaf and Bennett was her first pupil.

Despite the fact that Clark's parents were in opposition to her marrying a shop assistant with the Northfleet Co-operative Stores, earning just 15s per week, the inevitable happened and their daughter fell pregnant. Despite the impending birth, Bennett's parents were also set against their son marrying the girl and the proposed ceremony in Northfleet church was scuppered by Bennett's own father telling the vicar that his son had made a false declaration about his age. Bennett and Clark were not to be swayed from their decision and they were married on 22 July 1897 at Leyton Registry Office near Mary's grandparents' home.

Soon after the wedding Bennett lost his job with the Co-op and seemed to be content with wandering around the local marshland with his shotgun. It is unclear whether their child was stillborn or died a few days after the birth, but it did not survive. Whatever the circumstances, this event seems to have dissipated some of the tension between the young couple and Mary's parents, with whom they had been living since the wedding. They then moved to West Ham to live with Mary's grandmother. The old lady died in April 1898 leaving Mary her much-treasured gold necklace, which plays an important role later in this saga. Mary wore the necklace alongside a silver watch which had been given to her by her father for her twelfth birthday. Soon after the old lady died, Bennett and Mary's father began arguing about the dead woman's possessions. It was said that Bennett actually threatened his father-in-law with a shotgun. This appears to have severed the links between Mary and the rest of her family, mirroring the lack of communication between Bennett and his father.

The young married couple then seem to have embarked on a career based on fraud. They would purchase cheap violins through the *Exchange and Mart* for around 4s 6d, which they would then re-advertise. Mary would pose as a distraught and poverty-stricken clergyman's daughter or a widow. She would sometimes claim that her husband was a gifted, professional musician who had suddenly died, leaving her with the only option of selling his most treasured possession, the violin. After all, she had small children to feed and no other means of income. In this way she would sell the violins for one or two guineas each. In October 1898 Mary gave birth to a daughter, Ruby, who became a part of the charade.

It seems very clear that the couple made a considerable amount of money from the sale of these violins, because in early 1900 Bennett was able to buy a grocers shop in Westgate-on-Sea. Bennett was able to pay £375 of the £450 asking price for the business in cash. It is here that accounts begin to diverge. Either Bennett kept the shop for just eight days, or, in other accounts, two months. What is certain is that the grocery business was completely destroyed by a mysterious fire. Bennett had taken the sensible precaution of insuring it with the Kent Insurance Company. He managed to make a tidy sum despite the fact that his insurance claim was originally turned down. It is probable that he received over £200 for the building in addition to the £450 he received for the loss of his horse, cart, stock and piano. Most of the stock had been purchased on credit and had not yet been paid for.

The couple seem to have used the proceeds to purchase tickets on a steamer bound for

Cape Town. They left Ruby with Bennett's grandfather in Gravesend with the story that they were going to North America. Bennett purchased the tickets in the name of Mr and Mrs Hood on 7 March; he paid for a single fare costing around £45 for the two-berth cabin on SS *Gaika*. Strangely, he also purchased in London a false moustache and wig for himself and a blonde wig for Mary. Exactly why the couple went to Cape Town is unknown, but Bennett's defence counsel in the trial, Sir Edward Marshall Hall, told the court that Bennett had gone to South Africa as he had been engaged as a spy for the Boers. Whatever actually happened in South Africa does not seem to have come to a great deal as they only stayed in Cape Town for four days before heading back on another ship, returning to London on 9 May. Initially they moved into 64 Wickham Lane, Plumstead, which was a boarding house owned by Emma Elliston, the wife of a police constable. The rooms were originally booked by Mary, and Bennett only arrived later in the evening. Mary then left to collect Ruby and the three of them were installed by 12 May. Mrs Elliston later testified that she believed the couple to be on particularly bad terms with one another. She described Bennett as being aggressive towards his wife and on at least one occasion Mary had told her that her husband had struck her. Indeed, when Mary had arrived with the child Bennett was angry that she had taken so long. Mary was heard to say 'You knew the time I should come. Why did you not come and meet me? What with carrying the baby and the luggage, I could not get here any sooner.' Elliston testified that Bennett replied 'Damn you, and the baby too'. Throughout their stay Elliston claimed that Mary always appeared to be affectionate and kindly towards her husband, although she did once hear Mary say to Bennett 'Herbert, I shall always follow you for the sake of the child and if you are not careful I will get you fifteen years.' Bennett was heard to reply 'I wish you were dead. And if you are not careful you soon will be.' Elliston also heard Bennett tell Mary to find a house in Bexleyheath. 'I have a berth at Woolwich. From tonight I do not wish to live with you again.'

Whatever the truth behind the quarrels, it is clear that by the middle of June both had left Mrs Elliston's house. It seems that the couple and their child then stayed with a Mrs MacDonald at 10 Woolwich Road, but by 12 June, Bennett, posing as a bachelor, also lived at 41 Union Street, Woolwich. In July, Mary and the child moved into 1 Glencoe Villas, Izane Road, Bexleyheath. She paid three months' rent in advance to take possession of a semi-detached house, also producing a reference signed by W.A. Phillips. It had actually been written by Bennett himself, who, after spending three weeks working for the Co-operative Society in Woolwich, leaving their employment on 29 June, had been temporarily unemployed until 16 July, when he began working as a labourer at the Woolwich Arsenal for some 30s a week. At this time he was living in Union Street, Woolwich, in a house owned by a landlady called Mrs Pankhurst.

Bennett did not make many visits to Glencoe Villas to see his wife and child. Money was an immediate problem; not only was he paying for the rent on the house in Izane Road but he was also having to find money for Mrs Pankhurst and he was, by then, seeing another woman. He had met Alice Meadows on 1 July when he accompanied a friend and fellow lodger called Stevens to London. Alice was a friend of Stevens's fiancée. She was a parlour maid employed by a family near Hyde Park and was immediately smitten by Bennett. He told her that he had been a grocer's assistant and was single, independently wealthy through inheritance and now a profitable second-hand violin tradesman. He told Alice that his cousin Fred lived with his wife and child in Bexleyheath and that on occasion he would have to go and visit them. They exchanged a number of affectionate letters and saw one another regularly on Thursdays and Sundays.

Bennett wanted to take Alice away during her fortnight's holiday and was keen to take her to Ireland. In the event she finally agreed to go to Great Yarmouth with him for a weekend. One of Alice's work colleagues knew the addresses of some respectable accommodation in Great Yarmouth and Bennett wrote to Mrs Rudrum in order to enquire whether she had any vacancies. As it was a bank holiday weekend she replied in the negative, so on Saturday 4 August they travelled first class by train to Great Yarmouth and stayed in separate rooms at the Crown and Anchor Hotel. What is particularly significant about this weekend is that it not only allayed Alice's fears about going to Ireland for a fortnight with Bennett, but he also revealed that he was particularly scathing about the 'Rows' area of the town. At the time there were 129 narrow lanes where the houses were so close together that you could reach across the alleyways and touch the buildings on either side. Bennett told Alice that he was extremely pleased that they had not chosen to stay in number 3, Row 104, which was Mrs Rudrum's house.

They arrived back in London on the Sunday. On Thursday 9 August Alice sent Bennett a telegram wishing him many happy returns as it was his birthday, but that day he also received another telegram, which was delivered to his lodgings. It was opened by Mrs Pankhurst and it read 'Try to come home M very ill'. It had been sent by Mary's next-door neighbour. Mrs Pankhurst took the telegram directly to Bennett at the Woolwich Arsenal and he explained to her that M was his cousin who lived in Bexley. That night he visited Glencoe Villas by bicycle and returned to Woolwich the following morning with a woman's umbrella and no bicycle. Bennett told Mrs Pankhurst that his cousin was ill with influenza and that it was not expected that she would live much longer.

Bennett continued his affair with Alice Meadows and on 28 August they left for their fortnight's holiday in Killarney in Ireland. It seems that Bennett was flush with cash as they travelled in first class, stayed in respectable hotels and wined and dined every night. When they returned to England on 11 September Alice was the proud possessor of a diamond and ruby ring, given to her by Bennett as a token of his love and intention to marry her the following June. At all times during the holiday it appears that Bennett was the perfect gentleman who never forced his attentions on Alice, content only to be in her company. Bennett even introduced Alice as his fiancée to Mrs Pankhurst. The pair returned to work happy.

On Friday 14 September Bennett visited Glencoe Villas, and it seems that plans had been made with his wife as she hurriedly went shopping with her neighbour, Lillian Langman, for clothes which included a blouse and a veil. Bennett was a busy man that day, as he also managed to tell Alice Meadows that he would not be able to see her on Saturday 15 because he had to travel to Gravesend to see his ailing grandfather.

On Saturday 15 September Bennett again visited Glencoe Villas, having told the Woolwich Arsenal that he was ill. Soon after he left, Mary also left the house, telling her neighbour, Lillian Langman, that she was going on holiday with her husband. She said 'My old man is going to take me after all, we're going to Yorkshire'. Mrs Langman was sure from what she had said that she was going to Leeds. After asking her neighbour to look after her dog, Mary locked up the house and took Ruby, a brown bag and a brown paper parcel away with her. Mrs Langman also noted that Mary was wearing her treasured gold chain.

At 9pm that Saturday night Mary arrived at Mrs Rudrum's house in Great Yarmouth, using the name Mrs Hood. Mrs Rudrum distinctly remembered seeing a man walk into the Row with Mary, but when she opened the door only Mary and Ruby were there. Mary settled into the room and put the child to bed, immediately leaving on her own and not returning until nearly midnight. Mrs Rudrum saw that she was rather drunk on her return, and it was at this stage that Mary told her that she came from York, was a widow and that her husband had died three months before her child had been born. She told Mrs Rudrum that she had been drinking with her brother-in-law and that he was a jealous man who tended to follow her around. The same night Bennett had checked into the Crown and Anchor Hotel in Great Yarmouth but had left early the following morning, catching the 7.30am train, which arrived in London at 11.30am. At noon he visited Alice Meadows's mother's house at 22 York Road, Stepney and spoke to Mrs Lenston, who also lived there.

On the Monday Bennett was back at work at Woolwich Arsenal and at some point during that week he encountered two friends that had worked with him at the Co-operative Stores. They asked after his wife and child and he tearfully explained to them that they had died in South Africa from the fever. Bennett said 'Don't say much about it, as I feel it very much. She was my right hand'. On Wednesday Bennett made the journey to Glencoe Villas and asked if anyone had been to visit the house. On Thursday he told a disappointed Alice that he would not be able to see her on the following Sunday because his grandfather in Gravesend had worsened and he was honour-bound to see the old man. It is probable that Bennett was in London until at least the afternoon of Saturday 22 September, because Mrs Pankhurst saw him in Union Street, carrying a railway timetable and wearing a light grey suit. Also on Saturday Bennett rearranged plans by telephone with Alice, confirming that he would not be able to meet her and her brother on the river on Sunday but would, instead, see her outside her place of work at 3.30pm.

Meanwhile, in Great Yarmouth, Mary had been returning to Mrs Rudrum's house at around 9pm each evening. When she went out on Friday 21 September she told Mrs Rudrum that she was expecting to receive a letter that day. Mary did not return until 10.45 that night and Mrs Rudrum's daughter, Alice, was sure that she had seen a man standing with her at the bottom of the Row. She even claimed to have heard the man say to Mary 'You understand, don't you, I am placed in an awkward position just now.' This was followed by a kissing sound. There was indeed a letter waiting addressed to Mrs Hood, or Mary. It was postmarked in Woolwich and simply said 'Meet me under the big clock and put your baby to bed.' It was signed 'Hood'. Mary explained to Mrs Rudrum that the letter had come from her brother-in-law, who had been trying to find her a house in London.

On the following day Mary went out for the morning but was in Mrs Rudrum's home throughout the afternoon, only leaving again at 6.30pm. Mrs Rudrum testified that Mary was wearing her gold brooch, her long, gold chain, five rings and, as it would later turn out, her treasured silver watch. She had a considerable sum of money in her purse. Alice Rudrum met Mary outside the Town Hall at around 9pm, and she was also seen by a witness called Mr Borking, who managed the South Quay Distillery pub in Great Yarmouth. He was later able to identify both Mary and the man who accompanied her, Bennett. This was at about 10pm and Mr Borking was somewhat surprised to see two strangers in a pub that was normally only used by fishermen and their wives. He described the man as having a large moustache which he kept stroking. The man drank whisky and the woman gin. At some point Mary's male companion looked at a railway timetable and they stayed in the pub for some time, leaving together. Mr Borking was the last person to see Mary alive, apart, of course, from her murderer.

At around 11pm a man whose name was either Alfred Marks or Mason was enjoying a courtship with his girlfriend, Blanche Smith, on the south beach at Great Yarmouth. The night was dark, dry and warm and they distinctly heard scuffling noises nearby and assumed it was another courting couple. They also heard a woman's voice moaning 'Mercy, mercy'. About 10 minutes later they left the beach and happened to pass a man and woman. The man looked up and glared at them and they could see that the woman was lying on her back on the sand.

Just before midnight, or at 11.30pm according to the testimony of Mr Reade, a waiter, a dishevelled and out-of-breath man arrived at the Crown and Anchor Hotel. Reade recognised him as the same Mr Bennett that had stayed there before. The man explained that he had just missed the last tram from Gorleston and that he would have to leave early on the Sunday morning to catch the 7.20 train to London. Whether this was Bennett or not, a man in a light-grey suit and a soft trilby hat was later seen by a local newsagent, Mr Headley, standing beside the open door of a third-class compartment at the station. Mr Headley also described the man as being rather nervous and agitated. If this was Bennett, he probably had good reason to be both.

At around 6am on Sunday 23 John Lawton left his home at 36 Boreham Road and walked along Barrack Road towards the seafront. He was a bathing hut boy and when he reached the South Denes area of the beach he angled off towards the bathing huts. It was then that he noticed what appeared to be a woman asleep on the sand. He met his employer, Mr Briers, and mentioned that he had seen a sleeping woman. Mr Briers suggested that as this was not really the done thing, and in any case the local council frowned upon using the beach as a bedroom, that Lawton should go and wake her up.

As Lawton approached the sleeping woman he could see that she was lying on her back and just as he was about to shake her shoulder, it became clear that the woman was dead. She had been strangled with a mohair bootlace. It had been drawn so tight around her neck that it was embedded in the flesh. What was peculiar was the knot, which was a reef knot with a granny knot above it. The woman's face was bruised and scratched, her fingers were clenched, her skirt and petticoat had been dragged up over her knees and there were bloodstains on her underclothes. Lawton had seen enough and ran into town, where he happened upon PC Manship. The constable described the woman as wearing a light grey skirt and jacket which was trimmed with white braid, and a white blouse and a green tie. Beside the body was a sailor's hat with a black band as well as a black veil with white spots. He found a pair of kid gloves in the pocket of her jacket. PC Manship described the woman's hair as being titian in colour and noted that she was wearing five rings, three on her left hand and two on her right. There was no other jewellery on the body.

Mrs Rudrum had already reported the fact that one of her guests was missing. Very quickly the local police were able to link the two incidents and Inspector Lingwood made haste to investigate the disappearance of Mrs Hood. Lingwood searched Mrs Hood's bedroom, finding little of immediate significance, except one half of a first-class railway ticket from Liverpool Street Station, a gold brooch with the word 'baby' engraved on it, a small purse containing a latch key and two pieces of baby's clothing with a laundry mark which read '599'. Significantly Lingwood also discovered a photograph of the mysterious Mrs Hood and her baby that had been taken by a beach photographer the Thursday before. The photograph clearly showed her gold chain, which had not been found on the body. The watch that Mrs Rudrum had seen the last time Mary left the house was also missing.

The police circulated the photograph of Mrs Hood and set police forces all around the country to discover the identity of the laundry mark. However, by the end of October no progress had been made and at the coroner's inquest the jury agreed on a verdict of 'wilful murder by person or persons unknown'.

Mary Jane Clark was buried as Mrs Hood at St Nicholas's Church, Great Yarmouth, witnessed by a huge crowd of sightseers.

Bennett, wearing his grey suit and a bowler hat, encountered Alice Meadows in Hyde Park at 1pm on Sunday 23 September. She was amazed to see him as she believed him to still be in Gravesend. He explained that all of his relatives were there, and that he had come specifically to see her as he would have to return to Woolwich as soon as possible. He declined the offer of having either lunch or dinner at Alice's mother's house. Bennett did go to Woolwich, where he was seen by Mrs Pankhurst, who commented on the fact that he was wearing the same suit that he had worn the previous day. That night or the following day he wrote a letter to Alice, which read:

My own darling Alice,

I received your kind and loving letter this evening, and was quite pleased to hear from you, as it cheers me up. I arrived home quite safe but was not at all happy. I am glad you had somebody to pass the time away with, dearest, as you would have felt very miserable after seeing me as you did. I shall be very glad indeed, my darling, when you do not have to leave me at all, for I feel quite miserable now that I have had to wait so long to see you.

I shall be up on Thursday evening, dearest, all being well, as I am now on day work, and I hope I shall keep at day work as it is much better.

I have been to Bexley tonight, dear, and am sorry to tell you that grandfather passed away this morning, at 3.30 am and is to be buried on Monday next, when I shall not be able to attend as I must not lose any more time at present.

I hope you are feeling better, darling, and I shall be glad to see you out of the place altogether. Give my love to mother and all at home when you write. Hoping they are all quite well, I must now close, my dearest, as it is getting late. Hoping to see you on Thursday when I shall have lots of news.

With kindest love and kisses, I remain your most loving and affectionate

Herbert

Bennett followed up the 'disposal' of his grandfather, as far as Alice was concerned, with a similar treatment of his cousin in Bexley. He told Mrs Pankhurst that he had given his cousin, Fred, £15 to take his family to South Africa.

On Wednesday 26 September Bennett visited Glencoe Villas, terminated the tenancy in writing to the landlord, explaining that he was emigrating to America and, at the same time, told Mrs Langman that his wife was ill in Yorkshire. While at Glencoe Villas he collected some of Mary's clothes, which he later gave to Alice, saying that they were his cousin Fred's wife's clothes and that she would not need such warm garments in a warmer climate. When he saw Alice on that Wednesday he also told her that he wished to move the date of their wedding forward to Christmas. He also gave her a gold brooch in the shape of a pickaxe and shovel which had belonged to his wife Mary and explained that he had arranged to buy his cousin Fred's furniture so that they could settle down as soon as they were married.

As for the Glencoe Villas lease, Bennett was told by the agents that he would have to give three months' notice. It was finally agreed that he should pay £4 10s in settlement and he told the landlord and house agents that his wife had left the house for health reasons.

On Sunday 30 he again met Alice Meadows, who joyfully agreed to marry him at Christmas. Bennett gave her a blue coat and skirt in which she could be wed, a sealskin cape, some lace, a tablecloth, a silver brooch and some dress material. All of these items had belonged to his wife.

Sometime in early October, Bennett bumped into a man called Mr Parritt who vaguely knew Bennett and asked after his wife and child. Bennett gave the stock answer that they had died of a fever in South Africa and that he was too distraught to talk much about the matter. On 6 October he returned again to Glencoe Villas to collect his wife's dog, and told Mrs Langman that his wife was still seriously ill and had asked him to collect her dog and take it with him to Leeds. On 17 October Alice Meadows gave up her job as a parlour maid and was taken to Charlton by Bennett to see a house which he thought would be a suitable matrimonial home. Bennett paid a deposit on the house to secure it for his future wife.

It is not entirely clear how by early November the police had finally made a link between Mrs Hood and Woolwich. It appears that Mrs Rudrum and her daughter Alice had remembered that the letter Mrs Hood had received the day before she had been killed had a Woolwich postmark. By all accounts no one was using 599 as their laundry mark but enquiries in the Bexleyheath area revealed the fact that on 5 November a Mrs Bennett was reported missing. The link was quickly made between the laundry mark and Glencoe Villas. Neighbours were shown the beach photograph and it quickly emerged that Mrs Hood and Mrs Bennett were indeed the same woman. Chief Inspector Leach of Scotland Yard was told that Bennett worked for the Co-operative Stores and eventually spoke to a friend and co-employee of Bennett's called Robert Allen. He, too, was able to identify the photograph as being of Mrs Bennett and her child. Allen recounted to the chief inspector that sometime in the previous month he had met Bennett by chance and agreed to buy a bicycle from him. He had agreed to meet Bennett at Glencoe Villas, which Bennett had explained was his cousin's house. Bennett also showed him a piano which he also offered for sale. Allen claimed to have asked 'Is your wife here?' to which Bennett had replied 'She is not here. She is down home.' Later, he told the chief inspector, Bennett had said 'I have no wife, but I am about to be married'. Allen was confused; he had met a woman with Bennett who he was sure had been introduced to him as Bennett's wife. In the event, Allen had agreed to pay £23 for both the bicycle and the piano. Curiously Bennett had produced a receipt for 15 guineas, telling Allen that this was what he had paid for the bicycle. Allen checked the price with the manufacturers, who told him that this was a grossly inflated price and not the recommended retail price. He accused Bennett of forging a receipt for the bicycle and refused to pay him more than £6 for it.

Leach was very interested in meeting Mr Bennett and Allen was able to furnish him with his current address. On 8 November Leach waited for Bennett to leave his job at the Woolwich Arsenal. Allen introduced Leach as a Mr Brown. As he put his arm around Bennett's shoulder, he told Bennett 'I am a police officer and I arrest you for the murder of Mrs Hood on Yarmouth beach'. Bennett was stunned and replied 'I do not understand what you mean'. Bennett was taken by Leach and a police sergeant to Woolwich Police Station where he was formally arrested, to which Bennett replied 'I have not been to Yarmouth. I have not lived with my wife since January, when I found a lot of letters from another man in her pocket'. When shown the beach photograph Bennett told the two police officers that he did not recognise the woman or the child.

The police's next move was to search Bennett's room at 18 William Street under the watchful eyes of Mrs Pankhurst. They found a portmanteau with a label from the *Avondale Castle*, presumably the return ship that Bennett and his wife had used when returning from South Africa. In it they found a false moustache, a man's and a woman's wig, a revolver and cartridges, a receipt for Glencoe Villas, collars marked 599, two pearl necklaces and 14 letters from Alice Meadows. The most damning evidence not only linked Bennett with Great

Yarmouth but also with the mysterious Mrs Hood. In triumph Leach pulled out not only a receipt from the Crown and Anchor Hotel in Great Yarmouth for the period that Bennett had stayed there with Alice, but also a long gold necklace and a silver watch.

In due course, the Rudrums were shown the watch and chain and were able to identify them as those worn by Mrs Hood. They were also asked whether the name Bennett meant anything to them. Not only could they produce Bennett's letter asking for lodgings back in the early summer, but they could now positively assert that it was the same handwriting that they had seen on the letter sent to Mrs Hood on the day before her death.

By 17 November the newspapers were full of stories regarding the case and certainly the feeling against Bennett in Great Yarmouth was very ugly. When Bennett was brought before the Great Yarmouth Magistrates at the Town Hall a mob tried to lynch him. However, Bennett remained relaxed and throughout the whole of the four-day hearing he was happy to smile for the newspaper cameramen. The *Evening News* reported 'His thin lips nervously twitched as the charge against him was read.' The *Daily Mail* said of him 'He has a good forehead, with wavy, dark brown hair, a long nose which is straight except for a slight tilt at the end, brown eyes which are a trifle near together, large unshapely ears and a slightly receding chin. He had neglected to get his hands clean before coming to court.' Characteristically Bennett pleaded not guilty; he only showed a moment of concern when the magistrates committed him to trial for the murder.

The *Evening News*, it is said, prejudiced the case against Bennett before he came to trial on 26 February 1901 at the Central Criminal Court at the Old Bailey. The newspaper had interviewed Allen, Mrs Elliston and one of Bennett's former landladies, Mrs Cato. Mrs Cato could throw light on Bennett's fraudulent sale of violins and even said, when talking about a murder, that Bennett had suggested 'There is only one way to do a job of that kind. Strangle them. It is quick and silent'. As far as the *Evening News* was concerned Bennett was guilty. They even managed to organise an interview with Alice Meadows. The reporter, in the most flowery prose, described Alice as 'Prostrated with grief and hesitating between love and duty, doubtful as to whether to screen the man she loves from the merciless clutches of the law, or whether to aid justice in its demand that the woman done to death on the sands at Yarmouth be avenged'.

Originally the trial was to be held in Norwich at the Norfolk County Assizes. However, Bennett's solicitor, the Tunbridge Wells based E. Elvy Robb, would not agree to a trial in Norfolk as his client would be disadvantaged due to the local feeling against him. It also made sense that since a large number of the witnesses were London-based that the case should be transferred to the Old Bailey, to heard before the Lord Chief Justice Lord Alverstone.

Bennett's defence counsel was the famed advocate Marshall Hall and the prosecution was led by Charles Gill. Marshall Hall clearly believed in his client's innocence and in one conversation with Thorn Drury, a junior counsel, the young man said 'My God, I believe that man's innocent'. Marshall Hall replied 'Of course he is innocent'.

From the outset of the trial Marshall Hall made strenuous efforts to undermine the testimony of each of the prosecution witnesses. It was clear that the most damning evidence was the watch and chain. He was also concerned about the Mrs Pankhurst and Mrs MacDonald at the trial.

evidence related to Bennett's visits to Great Yarmouth and the callous way that he had disposed of his wife's assets after her death. Above all, Bennett had a motive; his affair and proposed marriage to Alice Meadows. On the other hand, as far as Alice was concerned, Bennett was a perfect gentleman. Marshall Hall faced a huge list of prosecution witnesses but was able to use the fact that so much information had been given in the newspapers to his advantage. When he cross-examined Mrs Elliston about the evidence she had given regarding Bennett's behaviour towards his wife, Marshall Hall held little back:

Marshall Hall: Do you read the *Evening News* and the *Daily Mail*?

Elliston: I have been worried too much to do so lately.

MH: Did you see a statement of yours about November last?

Elliston: I saw it in the papers.

MH: Did you read the statement as an account of what you knew about this case in the *Daily Mail* of November 12th?

Elliston: I saw it in some evening paper.

MH: Were you one of the first people to recognise the photograph of the deceased as being Mrs Bennett?

Elliston: Yes.

MH: Were you much visited by people representing newspapers?

Elliston: There were only one or two.

MH: Did you speak freely to them?

Elliston: I did not say much to them.

MH: Did you tell them this, that when Mrs Bennett arrived at your house she was richly dressed and wearing a quantity of jewellery?

Elliston: I did not say she was wearing a quantity of jewellery; I said she was dressed well, but not richly dressed. I said her bodice was lined with silk but not her dresses. I said she had a lot of jewellery. She had gold spectacles, ornaments in her hair, a gold bracelet and rings.

MH: Did you say her underwear was covered with lace?

Elliston: I saw her underclothes were good and had lace on them.

MH: Did you say to the reporter that her purse was observed to be well filled with gold.

Elliston: Yes. She had plenty of money.

Mrs Elliston and Mr Marshall Hall, QC.

The prisoner and Mr Hall, QC.

Judge: What were they paying you a week?

Elliston: Ten shillings a week for the apartments.

MH: Did you tell the press that you did not believe the story that they had come from South Africa?

Elliston: I did not say I did not believe it.

MH: Did you say they did not look like people who had come off a sea voyage?

Elliston: I do not remember.

MH: That must have been an invention of the gentlemen of the press?

Elliston: I suppose so.

MH: Did you see an account, purporting to be an account of what you had said to a reporter, in an evening paper?

Elliston: I read something in an evening paper, but I do not know when it was.

MH: Did your husband actually go to the police station to see Bennett the night he was arrested?

Elliston: Yes, he went there to identify him.

MH: Knowing that on 6th November this man had been arrested on the charge of murder, on 11th November you were gossiping about this case to a newspaper man?

Elliston: I did not think it would do Bennett any harm.

MH: (holding up a copy of the *Evening News*) And you as a woman will say that you did not tell the man what appeared in the paper?

Admittedly, Mrs Elliston's husband was a police constable so he would have been able to have given an unimpeachable identification of Bennett. Nevertheless, damage had been done to this witness's testimony. There was amusement too during the trial, particularly when Bennett's grandfather, William Simmons was called by the prosecution to deny that he was dead. He was asked by Gill 'And is it not true that you were to be buried on September 24th?'

Mrs Pankhurst could not be shaken from her testimony that Bennett had not slept at his lodgings on 22 September. She even told the court that her son had gone upstairs with a cup of tea for Bennett on Sunday morning, but had returned with it undrunk as Bennett was not there. Bennett's two friends from the Co-operative Stores, Mr Cameron and Mr Parritt, similarly resisted all of Marshall Hall's attempts to induce them to change their story that Bennett was with them on the evening of 29 September, as Bennett had claimed that it was in fact the night of the 22nd when he was with them.

Marshall Hall tried a different tack with Robert Allen, beginning with the statement that Allen owed Bennett money from the bicycle and piano transaction:

MH: You owe him £17.

Allen: There is that to pay over the piano and bicycle transaction.

MH: Have you said that if Bennett worried you for the money you would prosecute him for fraud?

Allen: No.

MH: Did you say the cycle receipt was forged?

Allen: Yes.

MH: Do you want to have your revenge on this man who had swindled you over the bicycle by having him arrested in the street?

Allen: I had no idea of having revenge.

MH: You got the piano and the bicycle and you propose to keep them?

Allen: I have them still, and I do not know what I shall do with them. I had an expert to examine the piano and he said it was not worth the price.

MH: And yet you agreed to buy it?

Mr Borking, the pub landlord in Great Yarmouth, the waiter at the Crown and Anchor and the newsagent on Great Yarmouth railway station all testified that they recognised Bennett as having been in the town both on 22 and 23 September. A Mrs Gibson, the wife of a fisherman who was in the South Quay Distillery pub on the Saturday night, was actually slightly unsure that the man sat with Mary was Bennett. This was largely on account of the fact that the man that she had seen had a heavier moustache. Marshall Hall accused Mr Reade, the waiter at the Crown and Anchor Hotel, of only having come forward to identify Bennett after having seen articles in the press. As far as the newsagent was concerned, Marshall Hall managed to convince the man to admit that the person that he had seen standing in the doorway of the third-class compartment only looked like Bennett. All of these witnesses had told the court that Bennett was wearing a trilby hat. In fact Bennett only ever wore a bowler hat and indeed he was wearing the self-same hat when he met Alice Meadows that Sunday afternoon.

Mrs Rudrum's testimony could have proved to have been decisive in either acquitting or condemning Marshall Hall's client. She told the court that the letter that Mrs Hood had received on the Friday before her death had been postmarked from Woolwich, and that she had produced a letter from Bennett enquiring about a room earlier in the summer. She had also found a petticoat in a drawer in her house which had been missed by the police. It was marked with ink and bore the word 'Benet'. Marshall Hall then began to direct his line of enquiry to prove the fact that the petticoat evidence had been created by Mrs Rudrum herself. First he asked her to spell the name Bennett and she replied 'Bennet' and then said that the name should have another 't' on the end of it. The defence counsel could smell blood and pursued his cross-examination:

MH: You said one t first, then two; which is it?

Rudrum: I meant two ts.

MH: Will you write it down?

Rudrum: I cannot unless you tell me how to spell it. I am a very bad speller.

MH: Where did you find the petticoat?

Rudrum: Hanging up by the bed. It was afterwards put in a drawer and not produced again till I was asked for it.

MH: Just look at this petticoat. It has been torn or cut after it was marked, because the ink has gone through onto the piece which has been cut off.

Rudrum: Yes.

MH: You knew the police were searching everywhere to establish the identity of the woman?

Rudrum: Yes.

MH: Do you mean to tell me that the petticoat was hanging up in the woman's room when Lingwood came on 23rd September?

Rudrum: Yes. He saw it I think.

MH: Did you not see that he was searching for all the clothes he could find?

Rudrum: You must remember that I was in a very excited state that morning.

At this point the Judge interceded and asked Mrs Rudrum:

'Can you explain how the petticoat, which was hanging up on a peg in the woman's room, was not discovered on the morning the search was made?'

Rudrum: No my Lord.

With this Marshall Hall seems to have been content that the jury would at least consider the fact that Mrs Rudrum had created this piece of evidence at some point after his client had been charged with the murder.

Marshall Hall was also concerned with Mrs Rudrum's evidence about the watch and link chain, as if it was established that her Mrs Hood had owned both of these items, the fact that they were found in Bennett's portmanteau would surely hang his client. The only positive evidence aside from Mrs Rudrum and her daughter's testimony that Mrs Hood had these two items was the beach photograph taken by a man called Mr Conyers. During Mrs Rudrum's cross-examination she claimed that she was certain that Mrs Hood had been wearing a link chain but was not absolutely sure about the watch. Initially, when the police had shown her the chain that they had found in Bennett's portmanteau, she was not sure that it was the same one that she had seen previously.

Rudrum: I was told by the police that they had found the chain.

MH: And you believed it, Mrs Rudrum?

Rudrum: No. One does not know what to believe.

MH: But you are now prepared to say it was the same chain?

Rudrum: Yes.

MH: Are you prepared to back your opinion against your honest doubt. Did you ever realise the meaning of the words, 'I identify the watch and chain produced'?

Rudrum: I never had the chain in my hands.

MH: Though you had doubts before, now that you have been cross-examined are you positive?

Rudrum: Yes, I am.

MH: Are you equally positive as to the watch?

Rudrum: No.

MH: What made you doubt when you first went into the box?

Rudrum: It was the light.

MH: But the (beach) photograph has made you certain?

Rudrum: Yes.

MH: Are you as sure of that as everything else?

Rudrum: Yes.

Mr Conyers, the beach photographer, had been in the photographic trade for 35 years and was shown an enlargement of the snap that he had taken of Mary and Ruby. The first copy was poor but the second he agreed was a reasonable enlargement of the picture that he had taken. He admitted that it was difficult to state whether the chain in the photograph and the actual chain were the same item on account of the fact that the chain in the picture was out of focus. Even Alice Rudrum when she was cross-examined agreed that it was not clear from the photograph or from her recollections of having seen the chain whether the item produced in court was the same.

When Marshall Hall finally had the opportunity to present his defence case he continually focussed on the fact that many of the witnesses had been given large sums of money by the newspapers for their stories, implying that this had coloured their testimony against his client. However, the main plank of his defence was to try and establish that the watch and chain found in Bennett's portmanteau had nothing to do with the two items that had clearly been taken from the deceased's body. Experts were called to testify that the chain in the photograph was a rope or Prince of Wales design and was nothing like the link chain found in Bennett's lodging room. Marshall Hall also called Mrs Cato, who told the court that Mrs Bennett actually had two watches and two chains. The one that she was wearing was an imitation gold chain and the one in the photograph could well have been this imitation one. For good measure she also added that Bennett had always treated his wife well.

This time it was Gill's opportunity to destroy one of the witnesses. Mrs Cato had told the *Evening News* that 'Mrs Bennett was a lovable little creature, and if ever a woman was fond of a man she was fond of him. He treated her in a way to crush the love of any woman.' Gill pointed out to the court that her two widely differing views and comments about Bennett were not compatible.

Marshall Hall had an ace up his sleeve in the shape of Douglas Sholto Douglas, who claimed that he had seen Bennett between 6 and 7pm at Lee Green on 22 September. Douglas described walking back to his house in Hither Green at around 6pm on Saturday 22. He was accosted by a man who asked for a match; the stranger was wearing a grey suit and a bowler hat and they walked along the road together for a while. The man told Douglas that he worked at the Woolwich Arsenal, had been to Ireland and that he travelled around the country quite a lot. They went into the Tiger public house in Lee Green, Douglas drinking beer and the other man drinking spirits. When they came out of the pub the man pointed to the house next door to the drinking house and told Douglas that a namesake of his lived there. Douglas could see the name plate which read 'F.K. Bennett'. Knowing that Gill would inevitably want to know why Douglas had not come forward until this time, Marshall Hall began to ask the questions himself and started by asking him why he had not come forward until November.

Douglas: About the middle of November I saw the reports of the Yarmouth murder trial.

M.H: What occurred?

Douglas: Well, when I found that the name of the man charged with the murder was Bennett, when I read of the light grey suit, and that the man worked at Woolwich, I took him for the same man I saw when I was out for a walk on that Saturday, 22nd September. I thought I was justified in making further investigations. I learned afterwards that the prisoner had been in Ireland. All this made me think it was my duty to communicate with the police.

MH: Did you see the prisoner?

Douglas: Yes, I went to Norwich and saw him in prison. I did not speak to him nor he to me. I had a good look at him, both full face and profile.

MH: And what was your opinion?

Douglas: I had no doubt that the prisoner was the man that I met in the lane on 22nd September.

MH: Have you any doubt?

Douglas: I have not a shadow of the doubt about the man or the date.

MH: Have you the smallest interest in this case?

Douglas: No. The suggestion is perfectly absurd.

Gill did try to undermine Douglas's evidence but failed to shake him on a single issue. Douglas added that he knew the date was 22 September because he had been potting plants both on 15 September and 29 September as the plants had dates on them. He had no pots with the date 22 September, and was therefore certain that this was the day that he had encountered the man that he later recognised as Bennett. One has to ask the question why Bennett did not mention the fact that he had had a drink with a man in Lee Green to either the police, his solicitor or defence counsel. Only by chance did Douglas choose to come forward when he did.

Bennett chose not to go into the witness box himself. On the one hand, it is claimed that Bennett actually refused to give evidence, while on the other it is said that he was considered to be so unreliable that whatever he had said would have put the noose around his own neck. Marshall Hall, in a letter to his friend Sir Arthur Pinero, which was, admittedly, sent after the trial, explained the situation:

When I saw that wretched man Bennett on Friday morning alone I said to him this: 'If you will only go into the box and admit everything except the actual murder, I can get a verdict, but of course you must admit that when you saw the papers on the day after the murder you knew it was your wife, but that you were afraid to communicate for fear of losing Alice Meadows'. His reply was: 'I cannot say that, because I was not in Yarmouth on the 22nd, and I never knew that the murdered woman was my wife till I was arrested'.

I pointed out that this was hopeless, and he declined to give evidence at all.

Gill, in his summing up, told the jury to consider the fact that there was no real answer to where Bennett had been on the nights of the 15 and 22 September. He suggested that Douglas's testimony could have been cobbled together from what had been read in the newspapers.

Marshall Hall's closing statements were interrupted by the arrival of a telegram from Lowestoft. It was from a stationer called O'Driscoll and it read 'Have Lowestoft police made report if not communicate at once most important'. The information was indeed interesting. O'Driscoll said that on Wednesday 26 September a man had come into his shop in the evening and O'Driscoll saw that the man had scratches on his face and, significantly, one of his boots was laced and the other was not. The man asked O'Driscoll for a newspaper that had a good report on the murder in Great Yarmouth. When the man paid the shopkeeper O'Driscoll also saw that the man's hands were scratched. O'Driscoll added that the man read the newspaper in the shop, groaning as he did so. The man then became aware that O'Driscoll was staring at him and ran out of the shop. All of this evidence was relayed in person by O'Driscoll to a stunned courtroom. Clearly the Lowestoft police had ignored the fact that O'Driscoll had been able to describe the man and the circumstances of his encounter with him. The doctor who had examined Mary's body was recalled and asked whether he had discovered any skin or blood under her fingernails. He had replied in the negative, but had added that the sand could have erased all trace of this.

In the event, Lord Alverstone's summing up was distinctly against Bennett, although he did make a reference to O'Driscoll's testimony and told the jury that 'They ought not to allow such evidence as this to weigh upon their minds if in the end they were satisfied of the guilt of the prisoner'.

With the arguments completed the seven-day trial was at an end and all that now remained was for the jury to consider their verdict. It appears that they had little difficulty in making their decision and were back in court after just 35 minutes. Inevitably the verdict was guilty. Lord Alverstone had no choice but to don the black cap and pronounce the sentence of death on Herbert John Bennett. He would return to Norfolk for one last time to be hanged in Norwich on 21 March 1901 by James and Thomas Billington. As the black flagstaff was hoisted to signal the impending execution, it snapped, which led many to believe in the superstition that Bennett was in fact innocent.

Much of the evidence seemed overwhelming, and from what the jury saw and heard, the evidence against Bennett was almost conclusive. However, there were too many questions left unanswered. To begin with, why did Bennett choose to stay at the Crown and Anchor Hotel twice, once with Alice Meadows and once on the night that he had murdered his wife? Surely he must have realised that he would have been recognised? Who was the man that the Rudrums claimed that Mrs Hood had spoken to and kissed the night before her death? Why would Bennett wish to sexually assault his wife before murdering her on the beach? Where had Bennett's money for all of these trips come from? How had he afforded to support his wife and child and finance his relationship with Alice Meadows? Above all, why did Bennett wait a week before murdering his wife? Every moment that Mary stayed with the Rudrums ran the risk of her revealing to them her real name. And why, in any case, had Mary registered herself with the Rudrums as Mrs Hood? What was Mary doing during the week she spent in Great Yarmouth? Where was she each evening and who was she drinking with?

It is quite possible that Mary had become involved quite willingly with one of Bennett's scams. It is perfectly possible that Bennett had selected someone to either carry out a fraud against, or perhaps blackmail. Perhaps the man that Mary had been seen with on that Friday night was the intended victim. Following this train of thought, the climax of the scam must have inevitably been on Saturday 22 September. Something inevitably went hopelessly wrong. Even if Mary was involved in some kind of criminal activity with Bennett and that was the purpose of her subterfuge in Great Yarmouth, then it is also reasonable to suspect that Bennett may have intended to have absconded with all of the proceeds of the crime and run off with Alice Meadows anyway.

If we assume that Mary wished to implicate some married or well-connected Great Yarmouth man, then would it not be the perfect thing to be discovered in the act by her husband on the beach at Great Yarmouth? Perhaps the man, sexually pent up after having spent a week with a flirtatious woman, failed to control himself and attempted to sexually assault Mary. In the event, he strangled her and fled the scene. This still leaves many questions unanswered. Were the watch and chain the same as those that the Rudrums claim Mary had worn? More damning is the fact that Bennett, straight after his wife's death, and despite the fact that he had claimed to be unaware of it, began to make gifts of his wife's possessions to Alice Meadows.

Twelve years after the brutal murder of Mary Bennett another woman was found at virtually the same spot on the South Beach at Great Yarmouth. This time the victim had been strangled with her own bootlace.

Dora May Grey was 18 and lived near the cattle market in Great Yarmouth and worked in a Manby Road boarding house. On 14 July 1912 she had told a friend that she had been to Lowestoft with gentleman and that she had arranged to meet him again that evening. She was last seen alive by a witness walking towards South Beach. The only other major difference between this case and the Bennett murder was that it appears that Dora Grey was not actually murdered on the beach and that her body was dragged there by the killer.

Could it be that the same murderer, more than 11 years after having brutally done away with Mary Bennett, reprised his crime on the unfortunate Dora Grey and that Bennett, after all, was an innocent man? Or was it a copycat killing by someone who knew the story? These questions remain unsolved.

Finally, poor Ruby Bennett, who had lost her mother so tragically in Great Yarmouth and her father on the gallows, was still only two years old and an orphan. Herbert John Bennett's parents willingly adopted their granddaughter and the money received from a newspaper appeal assured her of a comfortable existence into her own adulthood.

CHAPTER FIVE

MADELEINE'S LOVE LETTERS

The Trial of Madeleine Smith – Glasgow, 1857

Unflattering portrait of Madeleine Smith.

FOR 10 days in the summer of 1857, while the 'winds of change' raged across the Indian sub-continent in the violent and protracted uprising of Bengal soldiers, the country's eyes were glued to newspaper reports of a trial in Glasgow. The defendant stood charged with the wilful murder of a Channel Islander and the nation was gripped by the revelations and disclosures that they read.

Magdalene (later Madeleine) Hamilton Smith was born on 29 May 1835 at 167 Regent Street, Glasgow. She was the eldest child of James Smith and Jane Hamilton Smith, being followed by two further daughters and two sons. The only unfortunate blip on the Smith's horizon in the early years of Madeleine's life was the winding up of the Glasgow Marine Insurance Company, of which John Smith, her paternal grandfather, was a director. The losses had been so huge that Madeleine's father, his brothers and their own father had to file for bankruptcy in 1843. Unfortunately Madeleine also lost her maternal grandfather, David Hamilton, in the same year; he had been an eminent architect and was well-respected.

By the 1850s the Smiths had recovered financially and in 1853 Madeleine returned to Glasgow having completed her education at a finishing school in London. By all accounts Madeleine soon became one of the most eligible young women in Glasgow. She was described as being attractive, confident and stylish, with grey eyes and dark hair. The family lived in India Street and had a country house called Rowaleyn at Rhu on Gare Loch off the Firth of Clyde. Madeleine's father was now a wealthy man once more, as an architect with considerable influence.

Back in 1841, at the age of 18, Pierre Emile L'Angelier had arrived in Scotland for the first time. He was born in Jersey in 1823 and was of French extraction. It seems that Emile, as he was known, was something of a restless soul and had returned to the Channel Islands and France at various times before finding himself in Edinburgh in 1851. His situation was entirely different from Madeleine's; he was living in the Rainbow Tavern and it is, perhaps, prudent to give some indication of his character, as witnessed by the people that he lived with at the time.

> L'Angelier's circumstances were very bad; he was living on Mr Baker's bounty waiting there till he got a situation. I thought him a quiet sort of person but he was very easily excited and, at times, subject to low spirits. I have often seen him crying at night. Latterly, before he went to Dundee, he told me he was tired of his existence and wished himself out of the world. He said so on more than one occasion. I remember on one occasion he got out of bed and went to the window and threw it up. I rose out of bed and went to him, and he said that if I had not disturbed him he would have thrown himself out. The windows of the Rainbow are about six stories from the ground. He was very cool, collected and did not seem at all agitated when I spoke to him. I thought he was in earnest. He had talked about it so often before. He would often get up at night and walk up and down the room weeping very much. I happen to know that he had, at this time, met with a disappointment in a love matter. It was about some lady in Fife. He was in distress about not having a situation in order to enable him to keep to his engagement with her. We sometimes talked together, in the morning, before business began. One morning, we had walked to Leith Pier and he said he had a great mind to throw himself over because he was quite tired of his existence. I have seen him reading newspaper accounts of suicide, and I have heard him say that here was a person who had the courage that he should have had, that he wished he had the same courage, or something to that effect.
>
> *Nephew of George Baker, owner of the Rainbow Tavern, Edinburgh.*

Other guests and acquaintances at the tavern described Emile as being a vain, boastful liar. It seems he was much taken to crying and introversion. Despite this he seems to have been a reasonably competent worker when he was in employment. After his short stay of between six and nine months in Edinburgh, he moved in January 1852 to work for a seed merchant, William Laird, in Dundee. Laird described Emile as often looking unwell, changeable in temper and somewhat melancholy. It seems that his suicidal tendencies reached a climax when he discovered that the woman that he had hoped to marry in Fife had announced her engagement to another man. This was despite the fact that Emile was on fairly intimate terms with at least two women in Dundee. There is also another significant fact about Emile's time in Dundee which was recounted by David Hill, who also worked for Laird at the time. Apparently Emile confided in Hill that he regularly took arsenic. This is corroborated by William Ogilvie, who worked in a Dundee bank and was the secretary of the Floral and Horticultural Society in Dundee. He also claims to have had a conversation about arsenic with Emile:

> He mentioned another effect of arsenic, which was that it improved the complexion. I inferred from his remarks that he took it for that purpose. He did not exactly say so, but I understood that it was one of the reasons why he took it. He also said that he complained of pains in his back and had a little difficulty in breathing and he said it had a good effect in that way. I am not sure he ever showed me arsenic I rather think he did on that occasion that he opened his desk and showed me a paper containing something white. I have seen him on more than one occasion eat poppy seeds in large quantities – in handfuls – in the shop. I remarked this the first occasion I saw him. Some person had come into the shop for it, and when they went away he ate some of it. I expressed surprise, and he said that, so far from being dangerous, it was much better than filberts, and that he took it in large quantities. He said he had taken the poppy seeds in such quantities that he had got quite giddy with them.

It seems that Dundee did not suit Emile's vision of life as in September 1852 he once again made a move, this time to Glasgow. Soon the worlds of the east and west end would collide, but for now Emile had to be content with 10 shillings a week as a packing clerk for Huggings and Co. in Bothwell Street.

Before turning to the meeting of Madeleine and Emile, another strange and revealing story casts additional light on the young Channel Islander's nature. It was Christmas Day 1853, and the Glasgow merchant, William D'Esterre Roberts, invited Emile to his home. He knew Emile as he sat next to him in church every Sunday.

> When the ladies retired L'Angelier became very ill, and wished to leave the room. I went with him, and came back to the dining room and remained some time. I wondered why he did not come. I opened the dining room door, and heard a groan as of some person vomiting. I found him very ill – vomiting and purging. A good many gentlemen came out of the room and saw him. I sent for cholera mixture, and gave him a good deal of it. He nearly emptied the bottle. I got very much frightened, as cholera had been in the town shortly before. After a time, one of the gentlemen took him in a cab to his lodgings. He called on me the next day or the day after that, to apologise for his illness. He was nearly two hours, ill in my house.

Emile was determined to raise his station in life and needed to capture the heart of a wealthy woman. Whether he had seen Madeleine prior to his conversation with Charles Baird or not is unknown. However, his repeated requests to be introduced to the very eligible Miss Smith wore Baird down, culminating in an introduction on Sauchiehall Street in April 1855. It seems that Madeleine found the Frenchman very charming and they began a clandestine relationship. Madeleine's parents discovered that their daughter was seeing a wholly inappropriate and unsuitable young man and forbade her to see him again. From the outset Madeleine's letters to Emile were gushingly romantic and by December 1855 she was already signing her letters 'Mimi L'Angelier'. Letters between the pair were delivered back and forth by Mary Perry, a friend of Emile, and it seems that by the spring of 1856 they were physical lovers, as it is clear that Emile had met Madeleine secretly at Rowaleyn.

By the summer Madeleine was beginning to be tired of Emile and was already receiving the attention of an older, but far more eligible suitor, in the shape of William Minnoch. He was a partner in Houldsworth and Co., a cotton-spinning business. Minnoch's salary was £4,000 per annum, while Emile's was just £52.

In the winter of 1856 the Smith family moved into 7 Blythswood Square and Minnoch was their next-door neighbour. He could offer many attractions, including wealth, which Emile could never match. With Minnoch Madeleine could socialise, be seen in public and enjoy the benefits of her station in life. With Emile all she could ever look forward to was clandestine meetings in the dark, exchanges of letters and silently making love when the rest of the household was asleep.

Despite the cooling of Madeleine's feelings, it is clear that she was still pursuing a relationship with Emile in 1857, as on Sunday 25 January she wrote:

> Emile, my beloved, you have just left me. At this moment my heart and soul burns with love for you. What would I not give to be your fond wife? My nightdress was on when you saw me. Would to God you were in the same attire. We would be happy. I have never felt so unhappy as I have done for some time past. I would do anything to keep sad thoughts from my mind, but whatever place, some things make me feel sad. A dark spot is on the future. What can it be? Oh God keep it from us. I weep now, Emile, to think of our fate. If we could only get married, all would be well, but alas, I see no chance, no chance of happiness for me. I must speak with you.

On the following Wednesday, 28 January, Madeleine accepted William Minnoch's offer of marriage. It became clear to Madeleine that she had better ensure that Emile returned her letters. They would not only undermine her relationship and proposed marriage to Minnoch if discovered, but if Emile chose to show them to anyone then she would risk a scandal that would rock her whole family. On the same day as her acceptance of the marriage proposal she wrote again to Emile:

> I trust to your honour as a gentleman that you will not reveal anything that may have passed between us. I shall feel obliged by your bringing me my letters and likeness on Thursday evening at 7. Be at the area gate, and the maid, Christina

Haggart, will take the parcel from you. On Friday night, I shall send you all your letters and likeness etcetera. I trust you may yet be happy, and get one more worthy of you than I.

You may be astonished at this sudden change, but, for some time back, you must have noticed a coolness in my notes. My love for you has ceased and that is why I was cool. I did once love you truly, fondly, but, for some time back, I have lost much of that love.

There is no other reason for my conduct, and I think it but fair to let you know this. I might have gone on and become your wife but I could not have loved you as I thought. My conduct, you will condemn but I did, at one time, love you with heart and soul. It has cost me much to tell you this – sleepness nights – but it is necessary you should know.

If you remain in Glasgow or go away, I hope you succeed in all your endeavours. I know you will never injure the character of one you so fondly loved. No, Emile, I know you have honour and are a gentleman. What has passed you will not mention. I know, when I ask you that, you will comply.

It was soon to be clear that Emile was not a gentleman. He certainly had a conversation about Madeleine's latest letter with Thomas Kennedy, a work colleague, and told him that he could not bear the thought of Madeleine marrying another man, adding that she would be the death of him. Kennedy advised him to give back the letters and to try and get over the infatuation. Any day now the engagement notice would appear in the press and Madeleine was getting desperate.

As far as Emile was concerned, if he had to return the letters then it would be into the hands of Madeleine's father. Madeleine wrote to Emile again on 9 February:

Emile, I have just had your note. For the love you once had for me, do nothing till I see you. For God's sake, do not bring your Mimi to an open shame. Emile, I have deceived you. I have deceived my mother. I deceived you by telling you she still knew of our engagement. She did not. She, poor woman, thought I had broken off with you last winter. This I now confess and as for wishing any engagement with another, I do not fancy she ever thought of it.

Emile, write to no one, to Papa or any other. If Papa should read my letters to you, he will put me from him, he will hate me. And my poor mother. It would break her heart. It would bring shame to them all. Emile, it will kill my mother. She is not well.

Oh, Emile, be not harsh to me. I am the most guilty, miserable wretch on the face of the Earth. Do not drive me to death. When I ceased to love you, believe me, it was not for another. I am free from all engagements at present.

Please do nothing till I see you on Wednesday night – be at the Hamilton's at 12, and I shall open my shutter, and then you come to the area gate, and I shall see you. One word, tomorrow night, at my window, to tell me, or I shall go mad. Emile, you did love me. I did fondly, truly love you too. Oh, dear Emile, be not harsh to me.

I cannot ask forgiveness. I am too guilty for that. I have deceived. It was love for you, at the time, made me say Mama knew of our engagement. I will tell you that only myself and our maid, Christina Haggart, knew of my engagement to you. Mama did not know since last winter. Tomorrow – one word, and on Wednesday, we meet.

I would not again ask you to love me, for I know you could not. But, oh, Emile, do not make me go mad. Hate me, despise me, but please, please do not expose me. Pray for me, for a guilty wretch, but do nothing. I cannot write more.

Emile was determined that his chance in a lifetime to marry into a wealthy family should not be cast aside by unnecessary thoughts of honour. It seems from this date Emile determined that he would wreak his revenge upon Madeleine. Simultaneously Madeleine was also looking for a way out and to this end it is believed that she sent a house boy out to get some prussic acid in order to commit suicide should there be no other alternative.

If Emile's plan to ruin Madeleine had any hope of working he would have to lay a trail of evidence leading to her door. He began to compile entries in a pocket book which it seems clear he began on 11 February.

Wednesday 11th: Dined at Mr Mitchells. Saw M at 12 pm in CH room.

Friday 13th: Saw Mr Phillpot, saw Mimi, dined at 144 Renfrew Street.

Saturday 14th: a letter from M.

Monday 16th: wrote M.

Thursday 19th: saw Mimi a few minutes. Was very ill during the night.

Friday 20th: passed two pleasant hours with M in the drawing room.

Saturday 21st: don't feel well.

Sunday 22nd: saw Mimi in drawing room promised me French bible. Taken very ill.

Tuesday 24th: wrote M.

Wednesday 25th: M wrote me.

The rest of the diary entries continue in a similar vein and were clearly devised to link his bouts of illness to his frequent meetings with Madeleine. At the same time he was attempting to create a whole range of witnesses who could attest to his illnesses and meetings with Madeleine. When he visited Mary Perry he told her that he was very ill and had fallen over. A week later he said 'I can't think why I was so unwell after getting that coffee and chocolate from her.' He was, of course, referring to Madeleine. At that same meeting with Mary Perry he confided 'If she were to poison me, I would forgive her'. On 16 March he told Mary Perry's sister about his health and the coffee and cocoa that had made him ill and that he believed he had been poisoned.

As it was, Madeleine had been buying arsenic. She had signed the poison register at Murdock's in Sauchiehall Street when she purchased an ounce. She gave the reason for the purchase as being for use in the garden in the country house. Again, on 6 March, Madeleine went into Currie's and purchased some indigo-stained arsenic; she was accompanied by her friend Mary Buchanan. A second purchase was made from the same store on Wednesday 18 March.

Emile L'Angelier arriving home ill.

What on earth can we make of these coincidences? What we do know is that gradually Emile was building up a body of evidence to suggest to many people that he was being poisoned. There were still letters being sent by Madeleine pleading for the return of her letters.

By 19 March Emile had taken a leave of absence from work and left for the Bridge of Allan, which was a favoured haunt of the Smith family. Before leaving he made it plain that he was expecting a letter from Madeleine. While away Emile wrote to Mary Perry and a William Stephenson, telling them that he would be home on Wednesday. Emile in fact returned to Glasgow on Sunday 22, making it clear that he had arranged to meet Madeleine. Emile arrived at his lodgings at 7.30pm and told his landlady when he left the house at 9pm that he needed the pass key because he would be returning home late. At 2.30am on the Monday morning his landlady was awoken by the door bell and found Emile slumped against the door frame, holding his stomach. Emile was very ill throughout the night and at 7am his landlady, Mrs Jenkins, called in Dr Steven. At no time did Emile mention poisoning. At 9am, on the verge of death, Emile asked that Mrs Perry come to his bedside as she alone could tell the doctor why he was so ill. Just before 11.15am Emile passed away and Mrs Perry did not arrive until noon.

A post-mortem was carried out on the body and it was found to contain no fewer than 82 grains of arsenic in the stomach; undoubtedly this was the cause of death. When Madeleine's letters finally fell into the hands of the police it was inevitable that Madeleine should find herself charged with murder. The charge came on Tuesday 31 March and Madeleine spent the next three months in prison, awaiting her trial. Shortly after she was arrested she made the following declaration:

My name is Madeleine Smith. I am a native of Glasgow; twenty-one years of age; and I reside with my father, James Smith, Architect, at No 7 Blythswood Square, Glasgow. For about the last two years I have been acquainted with Emile L'Angelier, who was in the employment of W.B. Huggins & Co., in Bothwell Street, and who lodged at No.11 Franklin Place. He recently paid his addresses to me, and I have met with him on a variety of occasions… I had not seen M. L'Angelier for about three weeks before his death, and the last time I saw him on a night about half past ten o'clock. On that occasion he tapped at my bedroom window, which is on the ground floor, and fronts Main Street. I talked to him from the window, which is stanchioned outside, and I did not go out to him, nor did he come in to me…

He was in the habit of writing notes to me, and I was in the habit of replying to him by notes. The last note I wrote to him was on the Friday before his death, viz. Friday the 20th March current. I now see and identify that note, and the relative envelope. In consequence of that note, I expected him to visit me on Saturday night, the 21st current, at my bedroom window in the same way as formerly mentioned, but he did not come and sent no notice. There was no tapping on my window said Saturday night, or on the following night, being Sunday. I went to bed on Sunday night about ten o'clock, and remained in bed till the usual time of getting up next morning, being eight or nine o'clock.

M. L'Angelier was very unwell for some time, and had gone to the Bridge of Allan for his health; and he complained of sickness, but I have no idea what was the cause of it. I remember giving him some cocoa from my window one night some time ago, but I cannot specify the time particularly. He took the cup in his hand, and barely tasted the contents; and I gave him no bread to it. I was taking some cocoa myself at the time, and had prepared it myself. It was between ten and eleven pm when I gave it to him…

I have bought arsenic on various occasions. The last I bought was a sixpenceworth which I bought in Currie, the apothecary's, in Sauchiehall Street, and, prior to that, I bought two other quantities of arsenic, for which I paid sixpence each – one of these in Currie's, and the other in Murdoch, the apothecary's in Sauchiehall Street. I used it all as a cosmetic, and applied it to my face, neck, and arms, diluted with water. The arsenic I got in Currie's shop I got there on Wednesday the 18th March, and I used it all on one occasion, having put it in the basin where I was to wash myself. I had been advised to the use of arsenic in the way I have mentioned by a young lady, the daughter of an actress, and I had also seen the use of it recommended in the newspapers. The young lady's name was Guibilei, and I had met her at school at Clapham, near London. I did not wish any of my father's family to be aware that I was using the arsenic, and, therefore, never mentioned it to any of them; and I don't suppose they or any of the servants ever noticed any of it in the basin. When I bought the arsenic… I am not sure whether I was asked or not what it was for, but I think I said it was for a gardener to kill rats or destroy vermin about flowers, and I only said this because I did not wish them to know that I was going to use it as a cosmetic.

For several years past, Mr Minnoch, of the firm of William Houldsworth & Co., has been coming a good deal about my father's house, and about a month ago Mr Minnoch made a proposal of marriage to me, and I gave him my hand in token of acceptance, but no time for the marriage has yet been fixed, and my object in writing the note before mentioned was to have a meeting with M. L'Angelier to tell him that I was engaged to Mr Minnoch…

I never administered, or caused to be administered, to M. L'Angelier arsenic or anything injurious. And this I declare to be the truth.

In the event she was charged on three counts of administering poison to Emile, resulting in his death. Lord Justice-Clerk Hope and Lords Ivory and Handyside presided at the High Court in Edinburgh. The prosecution was led by the Lord Advocate, James Moncrieff, who was supported by the Solicitor General, Edward Frances Maitland. Madeleine's defence counsel was led by the Dean of the Faculty of Advocates, John Inglis, supported by George Young and Alexander Moncrieff.

The Lord Advocate attempted to sum up on at least two occasions the complex nature of the relationship between Emile and Madeleine:

She saw the position she was in; she knew what letters she had written to L'Angelier; she knew what he could reveal; she knew that, if those letters were sent to her father, not only would her marriage with Mr Minnoch be broken off, but that she could not hold her head up again. She writes in despair to him to give her back her letters; he refuses. There is one interview; she attempts to buy prussic acid. There is another interview; she had bought arsenic. There is a third interview; she has bought arsenic again. On the 12th March she has been with Mr Minnoch making arrangements for her marriage in June; she buys arsenic on the 18th; on the 21st she invited L'Angelier, with all the ardour of passion, to come to see her; L'Angelier dies of poisoning on the morning of the 23rd.

It was clear that Madeleine was in an awkward position. Throughout the trial she was continually referred to as 'this miserable girl', 'this unfortunate lady' or 'this poor creature'. Understandably the prosecution had to convince the jury that despite the fact that the defendant was a young woman from a wealthy and educated family, she had the necessary characteristics to carry out the crime. At times Moncrieff described her as being in a 'depraved moral state of thought and feeling' or in 'an entire overthrow of the moral sense'. Surely, he contended, the language used in her letters must show her uninhibited feelings and actions. The prosecution went on to examine Madeleine's sexual morals; after all, had not she said in her own words that she had been sleeping with Emile? The jury was asked to examine 'the mental and moral state to which she had reduced herself'. The prosecution said that they had to do this so that the jury 'will then be better able to appreciate the course which ultimately she was led to pursue'. As far as the prosecution was concerned the fact that she had shown a distinct moral defect in having pre-marital sex was sufficient to show that she was capable of another moral defect, that of murder. Throughout the prosecution contended that Madeleine had every reason to wish that Emile could disappear. 'She knew that she was completely in L'Angelier's power'. They went on 'she was so committed that she could not extricate herself'. Again they pressed home the point:

Some extrication or other was inevitable if she hoped to save her character, and, with a strength of will which I think you will see she exhibited more than once, she resolved she would not go back to L'Angelier; she had accepted the love of another and had determined to marry that other.

Did Madeleine not have another way out? Could she not have ignored the fact that Emile still had the letters? Could she not have ignored his threats to expose her? Certainly the prosecution made no comment on Emile's conduct; after all he was blackmailing Madeleine, but this was not the concern of the prosecution. They admitted that it was a dishonourable threat but, as they said themselves:

There is much that is dishonourable in this case, but not that. It would not have been honourable to allow the prisoner to become the wife of any other man. I do not see how L'Angelier, as a man of honour, could allow this marriage with Mr Minnoch to take place and remain silent.

In order to secure a conviction, the prosecution had to prove that Madeleine had either murdered or tried to murder Emile. It was certain that she had bought arsenic; it was also certain that she had bought prussic acid, but why? In contradiction to the reasons that she had given the chemists when purchasing both substances, Madeleine had claimed in her statement that they were for cosmetic reasons. Medical experts denied that they had ever heard of prussic acid being used for the hands; equally they warned of the dangers of using arsenic. The prosecution hammered home the point that the defendant had claimed that she had had at least three arsenic washes within a month. 'Again, do you really think that it did her complexion so much good the time before that she came back for more of it?' he asked the jury. Was there really a credible reason for Madeleine's possession of arsenic?

The prosecution then turned to the possibility that Emile had either accidentally poisoned himself or that it had been a deliberate act of suicide. It seemed obvious that they must convince the jury to discount both possibilities. Several witnesses, as we have already seen, could testify that Emile had used arsenic, poppy seeds and laudanum. They also told the court that Emile often suffered from depression and that he often spoke of taking his own life. In fact at least two witnesses testified that they had been with Emile when he was on the verge of actually carrying out the act. The prosecution asked the jury to reject these aspects of Emile's character as he claimed that on both occasions, in the Rainbow Tavern and at Leith Pier, a man committed to the idea of suicide would not have a companion with him to divert him from his purpose. As for the arsenic poisoning, and the possibility of suicide, the prosecution discounted this entirely:

> Is it conceivable, that, without having gone near her house [on the Sunday night] he committed suicide? No, that is beyond the bounds of probability. There is a possibility, no doubt, that when he went to see Miss Smith, she told him she was going to give him up, and this had a great impression on his mind. But if she saw him, what comes of her declaration that she did not see him on that night? And if she did see him on that night, is there any link wanting in the chain of evidence that I have laid before you? I can conceive no possibility of it being a case of suicide that does not imply that they met, and if they met then the evidence of her guilt is overwhelming.

The 'if' question was a gaping hole in the prosecution's case. There were three vital things that they could not prove. There was no conclusive evidence that on the three crucial nights of 19 February, 22 February and 22 March Madeleine had seen Emile. The prosecution then began to try to fill in these holes. Mrs Perry told the court that Emile had eaten with her on 17 February, and it was then that he had told her that he had arranged to see Madeleine on the 19th. Emile, in a conversation with a fellow lodger on the 20th, told him that he had seen Madeleine the night before. The prosecution drew evidence from one of Madeleine's letters, which was probably written on 25 February, 'You did look bad Sunday night'. They took this to mean that she had seen him on the 22nd. The third date was far more critical; this was the night when, by some means, the arsenic had got into Emile's body. There were only inferences to be made. Emile had certainly been at great pains to tell as many people as possible that he was going to see Madeleine but did the meeting actually take place? This was what the jury, so the prosecution told them, had to infer from the combination of events and conjectures.

The prosecution, having carefully laid the foundation in the jury's mind that Madeleine was an unfortunate woman who had been driven to murder Emile, simply because there was no other way out of her situation, left the defence with the difficult task of re-establishing her honour and credibility. When John Inglis stood up to address the jury as he opened the defence case, he said:

Gentlemen of the jury, the charge against the prisoner is murder, and the punishment for murder is death, and that simple statement is sufficient to suggest to us the awful solemnity of this occasion which brings you and me face to face.

Inglis began by attacking the character of Emile. He described him as 'an unknown adventurer' who 'intruded himself into the society of this young lady' and, what was more, 'insinuated himself into her confidence'. Having established Emile as a blackmailer and intruder into the polite society that Madeleine inhabited, Inglis then turned his attention to building up the character of his client:

All past experiences teaches us that perfection, even in depravity, is not rapidly attained. It is not by such short and easy stages as the prosecution has been able to trace in the career of Madeleine Smith that a gentle, loving girl passes at once into the savage grandeur of a Medea, or the appalling wickedness of a Borgia. There is and must be a certain progress in guilt.

Inglis then attempted to unravel the chain of events, coincidences and assumptions that had been made by the prosecution. He began by stating that:

First, the means of committing the crime must be in the prisoner's hands; the possession of poison is absolutely necessary. Second, on each occasion the deceased must have been ill from the consequences of the poison, and on the third occasion must have died from the same cause. But, it would be most defective of all proofs of poisoning to stop at such facts as these. One person may be in possession of poison and another die from the effects of poison and yet that proves nothing. You must have a third element: opportunity. You must have the opportunity of the parties coming into contact. And we shall see how far there is the slightest room for such a suspicion here.

Systematically Inglis attacked the key dates. He told the court that there was no evidence, apart from hearsay, that his client had met the deceased on 19 February. In any case, by her own admission, his client had not been in possession of arsenic until the 21st:

I say to a certainty for this reason – because when the prisoner went to buy arsenic afterwards, on February 21st and on March 16th and 18th, she went about it in so open a way that it was quite impossible for her to escape observation if it came to be enquired into. How could that be? Why, one could imagine that a person entertaining a murderous purpose of this kind might go on increasing in caution as she proceeded; but how she should throw away all idea of caution upon the second, and third, and fourth occasions if she went to purchase so secretly on the first, I leave it to you to explain to your own minds.

Since the prosecution had not suggested that Madeleine had purchased arsenic prior to the 21st as they had no evidence to support this, Inglis pressed the point home to the jury:

Am I not struggling a good deal too hard to show you that the possibility of purchasing arsenic before the 19th is absolutely disproved? That is no part of my business. You are bound to allow me to assume that arsenic was not administered on the 19th by the prisoner.

Inglis now turned to the exact nature of Emile's illness on the 20th, and said:

Was L'Angelier ill from the effects of arsenic on the morning of the 20th? I ask you to consider that question as much as the prosecutor has asked you. If you can come to the conclusion, from the symptoms exhibited, that he was ill from the effects of arsenic on the morning of the 20th, what is the inference from that? That he had arsenic administered to him by other hands than the prisoner's. If you are to hold that the symptoms of that morning's illness were not such to indicate the presence of arsenic in his stomach, what is the inference from that? The result of it is to destroy the whole theory of the prosecutor's case – a theory of successive administrations, and to show how utterly impossible it is for him to bring evidence up to the point of an actual administration. I give my learned friend the opposition of being impaled on one or other of the horns of that dilemma. I care not which. Either L'Angelier was ill from arsenical poisoning on the morning of the 20th, or he was not. If he was he had received arsenic from other hands than the prisoner's. If he was not, the foundation of the whole case is shaken. So much for the first charge. I have disposed of the first charge in a way which I trust you won't forget in dealing with the remainder, because I think it enables me to take a position from which I shall demolish every remaining atom of this case.

Inglis then attempted to establish a clear chronology of the events. He said it was clear that Emile had been ill from at least 22 February to 2 March, as he had been confined to his rooms. On 5 March there was an exchange of letters between Emile and Madeleine. From 6 to 17 March she was at Bridge of Allan and meanwhile from 10 to 22 March Emile had only paid one visit to Glasgow, on the night he died, and was either in Edinburgh or Bridge of Allan during the rest of the period:

You will now see, gentlemen, the reason why I wanted these dates well fixed in your minds, for from the alleged purchase of poison to the end of the tragedy there is no possibility of contact or of administration – unless you think you have evidence that they met on one or other or both of those Sundays, February 22nd and March 22nd.

Inglis then proposed to discount 22 February. By Emile's landlady's testimony the court had learned that he had not gone out that Sunday; indeed, a fellow lodger had confirmed this.

Now, gentlemen, I must say that to conjecture in the face of this evidence that L'Angelier was out of the house that night is one of the most violent suppositions ever made in the presence of a jury.

It was Inglis's contention that the letter that they had alleged Madeleine to have written on 25 February, referring to Sunday 22nd, could not be accurately dated. The letter itself was undated and the post mark was indistinct.

> The only date that the letter bears is Wednesday, and it may be, so far as the letter is traced, any Wednesday in the whole course of their correspondence.

Inglis felt that it was erroneous to suggest that this letter referred to Sunday 22 February. 'There is no internal evidence in this letter, nor in the place where it was found, nor anywhere else, to fix the date'.

Skilfully Inglis had all but demolished the first two key dates in the prosecution's case; he now moved on to attack 22 March, which, after all, was the most significant aspect of the whole trial. By now, of course, Madeleine had purchased three lots of arsenic, so, at the very least, she had the means by which to poison Emile. But did she have the opportunity to administer it? What was not necessarily contested was the fact that Emile had left his lodgings at 9pm. He had visited Terrace Street to see a friend in a lodging house at 9.20pm; he had left moments later because he had been told that his friend was not in. Crucially Terrace Street was but five minute's walk from Blythswood Square and Madeleine. Inglis hoped to prove to the jury that despite Emile's return to Glasgow he had neither hoped for nor expected a meeting with Madeleine. There had been two letters from Madeleine which the prosecution had contended pointed to the fact that there was a meeting between the two on that Sunday. The first letter from Madeleine, asking Emile to meet her, had been returned unopened. The second, which had a post mark of Saturday morning, could be interpreted one of two ways. Madeleine had the habit of writing her letters in the evening and having them posted the following morning. When she wrote 'I shall wait again tomorrow night', Inglis argued that this referred to Saturday night and not to Sunday. In the event, Emile did not receive the letter until Sunday. In a letter, written from the Bridge of Allan on Friday to Mrs Perry, Emile wrote, 'I should have come to see someone last night, but the letter came too late so we were both disappointed.' Inglis summed up the implications to the jury:

> If he had wanted to have a meeting on a evening subsequent to that on which it was appointed, he could have been in on Friday. The circumstances were the same. And yet on Sunday, when there was far less facility for putting his purpose into execution, when he required to walk a considerable part of the way instead of going by rail, he is represented as having done this on purpose to keep a meeting that had been appointed for the previous night. I say this is not a reasonable proposition.

Why then did Emile cut short his visit to the Bridge of Allan in the certain knowledge that he had already missed the opportunity of meeting Madeleine? Inglis had found a reason and was able to refer to a letter written by Emile to a fellow lodger on 16 March: 'I have received no letters from Mr Mitchell; I should like to know very much what he wants with me.' Inglis was only too happy to explain this:

> We don't know anything of Mr Mitchell and the crown has not told us; but apparently L'Angelier was expecting letters from this Mr Mitchell when he was in Edinburgh. He

was anxious to receive them, and anxious to know what Mitchell wanted; and who can tell what letters he received at Bridge of Allan on that Sunday morning? Who can tell that there was not a letter from this Mitchell, and, if so, who can tell what it contained?

The prosecution had not a shred of evidence that the meeting between Emile and Madeleine had taken place on Sunday 22 March, and Inglis had given the jury every reason to believe that Emile's arrival in Glasgow had a completely different explanation. He went on:

> From half past nine till past two o'clock – at least five hours – he is absolutely lost sight of. I was startled at the boldness of the manner in which the Lord Advocate met this difficulty. He says that it is no doubt a matter of conjecture and inference that in the interval he was in the presence of the prisoner. Good heavens! Inference and conjecture! I never heard such an expression from the mouth of a crown prosecutor in a capital charge before, as indicating or describing a link in the chain of the prosecution case. It is absolutely new to me. I have heard it many a time in the mouth of a prisoner's counsel – and I dare say you will hear it many a time in mine yet before I have done – but for the prosecutor himself to describe one part of his evidence as a piece of conjecture and hypothesis is to me an entire and most startling novelty.

In his conclusion Inglis asked the jury to seriously consider that the deceased had committed suicide. He denied that Madeleine had a true motive for the murder and he asked the jury to consider why she had bought arsenic on 6 March and, on that day, left Glasgow and the man that the prosecution claimed she had wished to murder. It was preposterous to suggest that she had bought it on the off-chance that Emile would turn up at the Bridge of Allan. Why did she buy more arsenic when there was no opportunity to give it to Emile?

> Ponder well before you permit anything short of the clearest evidence to induce or mislead you into giving such an awful verdict as is demanded of you. And dare any man hearing me – dare any man here or elsewhere say that he has formed a clear opinion against the prisoner? Will any man venture for one moment to make that assertion? And yet, if on anything short of clear opinion you convict the prisoner, reflect – I beseech you, reflect – what the consequences may be. Never did I feel so unwilling to part with a jury, never did I feel that I had said so little as after this long address. I cannot explain it to myself, except by a strong and overwhelming conviction of what your verdict ought to be. May the spirit of all truth guide you to an honest, a just, and a true verdict.

What, then, could be the conclusions drawn by the jury as a result of the evidence that they had heard? Was there any proof that Emile and Madeleine had met on the crucial dates of 22 February and 22 March? If they believed that this had been the case, then they had to accept the fact that the undated letter referring to the first Sunday had been received by Emile on Wednesday 25 February. In the event, the prosecution claimed that they did have additional evidence, but that it had not been put before the jury. The Lord Advocate now asked the court to consider the use of Emile's pocket book diary. Inglis was entirely against this. The jury was asked to leave. The pocket book had several entries which alluded to meetings with Madeleine and, on 19 and 22 February, Emile's handwriting testified that he was ill after they had seen one another. In the event, the three judges decided by a majority that the pocket book was inadmissible evidence, so how it might have affected the jury's decision will never be known. The main ground for Inglis's objection was that the entries could not be independently tested. One of the judges is quoted as saying:

A man might have threatened another, he might have hatred against him and be determined to revenge himself, and what entries might he not make in a diary for this purpose?

One of the other judges swiftly replied with a very credible answer:

Vanity might lead to statements being made that were wholly imaginary, with a view to the subsequent exhibition of the book; and were its admissibility as evidence set up by death, it might become a fearful instrument of calumny and accusation.

The second major question was whether the jury accepted the series of coincidences identified by the prosecution and the huge leaps of logic and surmise that they had made throughout their case. On the one hand how could it be explained that Madeleine was in possession of arsenic and that Emile had died from arsenical poisoning? Was it reasonable to suggest that despite the fact that Emile had in his hands the power to ruin her, that this was not the reason for her purchases of arsenic? Did the link between the two parts of the story hang together?

Madeleine could not give evidence herself so she could not, beyond her declaration, answer or explain the series of coincidences that had brought her to the court on a charge of murder. In the end it seemed that Inglis's logic, experience and eloquence convinced the Scottish jury that there was more than an element of doubt. Two of the 15 jurors, however, cast their votes in favour of a guilty verdict. Some of the jury later confided that others thought Madeleine guilty but were not prepared to take the responsibility of condemning the woman to death. In the event, to wild applause and cheering, the jury returned a verdict of 'not proven'. This left Madeleine free, but with suspicion still hanging over her head.

It seems that Inglis had convinced the jury of four key facts. Firstly, that from his own admission by word and by his handwriting in the pocket book, Emile had suspected that Madeleine was poisoning him. Regarding the second point, Inglis had said to the jury:

We are asked to believe that he took, from her hand, a poisoned cup in which there lurked half an ounce of arsenic and this, with all his previous suspicion that she was practising on his life. There is not a case on record in which it has ever been shown that a person administering poison to another ever succeeded in persuading him to swallow such a quantity. It is the most difficult thing to conceal a vehicle in which it could be given. Even supposing he did swallow all this arsenic in a cup of cocoa, as is suggested, it is, at least, next to impossible that, with all the gritty powder passing over his throat, he should not become aware that he had swallowed something unusual.

Inglis had clearly demonstrated to the jury that it was improbable that the arsenic had been given to Emile by anything other than his own hand. As for the third point, this relates to the arsenic itself. Madeleine had purchased arsenic mixed with indigo from Mr Currie and the arsenic bought at Murdoch's was mixed with soot. How then could the prosecution explain the fact that white arsenic was found in Emile's stomach? The final point was a telling one too. Given the fact that Madeleine wished Emile to return her letters, surely she must not have been stupid enough to assume that his death would end the matter? Clearly someone would go through his personal effects, discover the letters and make the link between Emile and Madeleine. The whole purpose of the murder would have been pointless, as not only could she be implicated in at least prompting the suicide of Emile, but also the dreaded letters, which she so hoped would remain a secret, would be revealed.

Some questions still surround the case. Emile's name does not appear in any poison book in either Glasgow, Stirling or Bridge of Allan, so how did he come by arsenic if he killed himself? Did he purchase it under an assumed name? Also, there is reason to believe that he had been taking arsenic for some time, but why was there no arsenic found in his possession after his death? Did he know that Madeleine was also buying arsenic? Did he intend to either kill himself or make himself ill to frame Madeleine as revenge? Alternatively, did he start taking increasing amounts of the poison in order to attract her attention and win her back? If Emile took his own arsenic what happened to Madeleine's arsenic? Is it reasonable to assume that she used it for cosmetic purposes?

Madeleine Smith was taken from the court and she changed into a brown, silk dress, a bonnet with a dark veil and then wrapped herself with a cloak. She exited the court building through a side door with her brother and took a train to Glasgow, where a cab was waiting to drive her to Rowaleyn, where she arrived at 10pm. Four days later she wrote a letter to Miss Aitken, the matron of Edinburgh prison:

Dear Miss Aitken,

You shall be glad to hear that I am well – in fact I am quite well, and my spirits are not in the least down. I left Edinburgh and went to Slateford, and got home to Rowaleyn during the night. But, alas, I found Mama in a bad state of health. But I trust in a short time all will be well with her. The others are all well. The feeling in the west is not so good towards me as you kind Edinburgh people showed me. I rather think it shall be necessary for me to leave Scotland for a few months, but Mama is so unwell we do not like to fix anything at present. If you ever see Mr C. Combe, tell him that the panel was not at all pleased with the verdict. I was delighted with the loud cheer the court gave. I did not feel in the least put about when the jury were considering whether they would send me home or keep me. I think I must have had several hundred letters, all from gentlemen, some offering me consolation, and some their hearths and homes. My friend I know nothing of. I have not seen him. I hear he has been ill, which I don't much care. I hope you will give me a note. Thank Miss Bell and Agnes in my name for all their kindness and attention to me. I should like you to send me my Bible and watch to 124 St Vincent Street, Glasgow, to J. Smith. The country is looking most lovely. As soon as I know my arrangements I shall let you know where I am to be sent to. With kind love to yourself and Mr Smith, ever believe me, yours sincerely,

Madeleine Smith

In the event, Madeleine did indeed leave Scotland. She travelled to London under the assumed name of Lena Smith. She married the artist and designer, George Wardle, who was a close friend of William Morris. As Lena Wardle she enjoyed a rich and varied social life and even met George Bernard Shaw. He was later to describe her as being a good-humoured, attractive woman and not in the least sinister.

By the time she had reached her mid-seventies, she moved to New York as Mrs Sheehy, having married again. Her son Tom lived in New York and it was there that she lived out the last years of her life. At the ripe old age of 93, while being looked after by her grand-daughter, she died on 12 April 1928. Madeleine was buried in Mount Hope Cemetery and the inscription on her gravestone simply reads 'Lena Sheehy'.

CHAPTER SIX

THE BLIND KILLER

The Impossible Death of Thomas Farrant – Bristol, 1867

GILES CLIFT was a 53-year-old blind man who kept a lodging house at 1 Little Street, St James's, in Bristol. He had been married for either four or 12 years; records are unclear. It seems that the marriage was not a happy one and Clift often quarrelled with his wife. Finally, after visits to the magistrate's court, it was agreed that they should live separate lives. His wife left and moved in with Thomas Farrant, Giles Clift's great-nephew.

Thomas Farrant was a fruit seller aged around 25. Clift's wife and Farrant lived together at the Colston's Arms in Hotwell Road, Bristol. Clift was particularly angry about the fact that his wife had taken things that belonged to him and was co-habiting with one of his relatives. On Thursday evening, 26 December 1867, at around 6pm, Clift was accompanied to the Colston's Arms by Mr Lyons, a young man who lived with him at the lodging house. Clift proposed to confront Farrant and his wife, and when they arrived at the public house Lyons chose to remain downstairs while, presumably rather tentatively, Clift went upstairs to find the room where his wife, their three-year-old daughter and Farrant were living. Lyons later said that he heard a lot of noise and screaming from the room above and concluded that a quarrel had erupted between the adults. Lyons ran up the stairs and barged into the room, where he saw Giles Clift beating his wife with the leg of a bedstead. Bravely he rushed to protect the woman and ushered her downstairs to safety. However, Mrs Clift ran straight up the stairs again to retrieve her child, and there were more screams and scuffles.

It was at this point that passers-by in the road saw a man fall head-first from a top window of the building onto the ledge above the window of the basement and then slump onto the pavement. The body was that of Thomas Farrant. It is not clear whether Farrant was already dead when he hit the paving slabs or died later, but given the extent of his injuries he could not have survived for very long. Witnesses reported that blood was pouring from his head and other wounds and in the space of a couple of minutes there was a considerable pool of blood around his body.

A boy was sent to Clifton Police Station to report that a man had been thrown out of the window of the Colston's Arms in Hotwell Road. Police Constable Dawes and another constable were sent to the scene by the officer in charge, an Inspector Attwood. The constables took a stretcher with them and when they arrived they could see that the man was bleeding from the mouth, nose and ears and was either dead or very close to it. They manhandled him onto the stretcher and brought him back to the Clifton Police Station. Still there was blood pouring out of his body. Inspector Attwood had Thomas Farrant placed in front of a fire and his face was bathed with warm water. The police surgeon, Mr Bernard from Victoria Square, was sent for, along with a medical officer of the Clifton Union, a Mr Steele. When the two doctors arrived they examined Thomas Farrant's now dead body and concluded that the cause of death had been a dislocated neck.

Meanwhile, a police constable had gone up to the room to investigate the window from which Thomas Farrant had fallen. He measured the distance from the windowsill to the pavement, concluding that it was at least 27 feet 10 inches. He also noted that there had been a struggle in the room and various items of furniture and ornaments were damaged. Very soon afterwards Giles Clift was arrested by PC 179 Fletcher who was on plain-clothes duty. Clift was taken to Clifton Police Station and locked in one of the cells.

The initial interrogation revealed little. Clift claimed that he had not physically assaulted Thomas Farrant and in fact had not even spoken to him. The argument and fracas had been between Clift and his wife and he added that Farrant had not tried to intercede or make any comment. It was his view that Farrant had actually tried to get away from him and in so doing had fallen through the two-foot square window.

Thomas Farrant's uncle attacks his wife.

We should bear in mind at this point that Thomas Farrant was a hale and hearty 25-year-old, seemingly in the prime of life. On the other hand, Giles Clift was over 50 years of age and was described as being thin and apparently weak, as well as blind. In Clift's defence, however, the police could find not a single bruise or mark on his entire body. Could it really be the case that Farrant was so frightened of his blind relative that in desperation to escape his clutches he had dashed his brains out on the pavement nearly 30 feet below?

Giles Clift was incensed by the fact that his wife was living with Farrant, her nephew by marriage, and that Clift's three-year-old daughter was also living with them. Mrs Clift claimed that her husband had screamed at Thomas Farrant 'Thee, I'll break thee neck out of the window'. Since she was the only other person in the room that could reliably give any kind of evidence, this complicated matters. She may have had a vested interest in implicating her husband. On the other hand, her lover was dead and the fear of the implications of this may have swayed her evidence in one direction or another.

The following day Mr M. Alman, Giles Clift's solicitor, appeared before Mr S. Hare and Mr W. Wills, the sitting magistrates. He asked whether his client would be brought before them that day as he was in jail, charged with the murder of Thomas Farrant. The solicitor was told that the case would first be considered by the coroner and that if the jury proposed a verdict that Giles Clift should appear before the magistrates on that charge, and they would consider the matter in due course. Unfortunately the deputy coroner, Mr H. Wasbrough, was not available, so the inquest could not take place until Saturday 28 December at the earliest. Mr Allman also asked the magistrates whether his blind client could be bailed or released, given the fact that he would suffer hardship from being held in jail for another day. The magistrates refused and told Allman that one day should not make a great deal of difference. Later in the day the deputy coroner informed the magistrates and Mr Allman that the inquest would be held at the Hope and Anchor public house, Jacob's Wells, on Saturday afternoon. He proposed to call four witnesses: Mrs Clift, Mr Lyons, a man who lived in the basement of the Colston's Arms and another man who had seen Thomas Farrant fall out of the window.

In actual fact Mr H. Wasbrough held the inquest at Clifton Police Station on Brandon Hill. This was a reasonable change of venue since the body of Thomas Farrant was still at the police station and undoubtedly the jury would want to have a closer look at the corpse. Thomas Farrant was described by the deputy coroner as an itinerant fruit vendor whose death occurred under mysterious circumstances in the Hotwell Road. Having minutely examined the body, the jury was then conveyed to the Colston's Arms and taken into the room where the fight between Giles Clift and his wife had taken place. There were still signs of the scuffle and the room was still wrecked from the thrashing about and struggle that had occurred two days before. It was, however, apparent that the room had been interfered with and items had been removed. Whether this was done by the police or some other individual was unknown. The most important consideration was to look at the window from which Thomas Farrant had either fallen or been pushed. On closer examination the two-foot square window was, in fact, far more inhibiting than the police had originally assumed. When the sash was raised there was a gap of only 17½ inches. The jury, the deputy coroner and the others present seemed to agree that it would have been impossible for Farrant to have accidentally fallen out of such a small space. On the outside ledge of the window there were marks, which it was suggested were fingerprints. The assumption was that Thomas Farrant wriggled through the small gap and then held onto the ledge in order to gently drop himself down onto a wider and more stable platform below. It seemed that this was the most reasonable solution to Thomas Farrant's fall and that he had been trying to avoid the clutches of Giles Clift and had unfortunately fallen to his death. The assembled crowd also noted that there was a heel print or mark on the ledge over the lowest front window of the public house. It was clearly marked in the lead flashing.

The jury and attendant investigators reconvened at the Hope and Anchor in order to hear the testimony of the witnesses. During the three hours that the proceedings took to complete Giles Clift was described as appearing nervous. Throughout the testimony he listened very carefully, apparently still handcuffed to a constable. The first testimony was given by Henry Lyons. He was the man that had accompanied Clift to the Colston's Arms in order to confront Mrs Clift and her lover.

Lyons was a carpenter by trade and it must be remembered that he actually lived in the same house as Giles Clift. He told the inquest that he had gone up the stairs to Mrs Clift's room with Giles Clift. They encountered Mrs Clift coming out of a room with a candle in her hand. When she saw her husband she ran back into the room and slammed the door. Clift had opened the door and gone in and Lyons had stayed outside. A few minutes later, after hearing cries and screams for help, he too entered the room to investigate the commotion. Lyons saw Giles Clift rolling around the floor with his wife. Lyons extracted Mrs Clift from the struggle and she ran down the stairs. Lyons told the coroner that Thomas Farrant was not in the room at the time but the window was open. He helped Giles Clift collect belongings which they intended to take back with them, which took several minutes. Someone then came up the stairs and told them that Thomas Farrant was lying prostrate on the pavement below. Lyons claimed that Giles Clift said 'Well, I didn't do it, for I didn't see him or hear him. I didn't know he was here'.

Lyons knew a considerable amount about the Clifts but much less about Thomas Farrant, the deceased man. He told the court Giles Clift had actually been married for about four years and that the 53-year-old blind man quarrelled with his wife throughout the time that they were living together. He recounted that on Christmas Eve Giles Clift's 28-year-old wife had appeared at 1 Little Street and broken seven panes of glass in the windows of the house. He claimed that he had never heard Giles Clift threatening Thomas Farrant and that all he knew was that Farrant was Clift's great-nephew and that, much to his great-uncle's disgust, he had been co-habiting with his wife for six weeks.

The coroner then called Eliza Evans. She was a widow and lived in rooms directly beneath those that had been taken by Thomas Farrant and Mrs Clift and her daughter. Mrs Evans claimed to have heard scuffles emanating from the rooms above her, which she believed came from the area to the front of the building, near the window. She had heard Mrs Clift coming down the stairs and after that the noises had ceased. She also said that she had not heard the window being opened, which she could normally hear.

Mr Butler and a Mr Griffin both saw Thomas Farrant fall from the window onto the pavement below. Mr Butler was walking along Hotwell Road when Thomas Farrant emerged from the window. He described to the inquest how he had seen the man fall out of the window and that he saw the man's heel strike the lead of the ledge over the front window. He had seen the body fall onto the pavement.

Dr Charles Steele was the medical expert that carried out the post-mortem on Thomas Farrant. He was able to explain the cause of death quite explicitly, stating that it was due to a fractured skull. He went on to describe the state of Thomas Farrant's body and told the inquest that he had found a bruise under the deceased's chin and that the man's teeth had cut a deep wound in his lower lip. Farrant's front teeth in his upper jaw had been forced up into their sockets. His conclusion was that Thomas Farrant had hit his chin heavily on the windowsill while getting out of the room. He concluded that Thomas Farrant must have been attempting to exit the window in haste, had emerged legs first and had then hung onto the windowsill with his fingers. Unfortunately his fingers had slipped and his chin had violently struck the windowsill. The shock and pain caused him to fall onto the pavement below. He also suggested that unfortunately he had struck the ledge below him with his feet, which forced his body away from the building. It was for this reason that Farrant had such severe damage to his head, as this had been the part of his body that had hit the pavement first.

After PC Fletcher had simply stated that he had been the constable that had arrested Giles Clift, it was the task of the deputy coroner, Mr Wasbrough, to sum up on behalf of the jury. He concluded that it was almost certain that Thomas Farrant had tried to escape Giles Clift's violent and unexpected arrival by trying to escape through the window. In doing so, tragically, he had slipped and fallen to the ground.

The jury did not take long to consider their verdict. It was their contention that Thomas Farrant had, indeed, been extremely unwilling to be confronted by his great-uncle and become embroiled in an argument. It was suggested that Thomas Farrant would have been well aware of Giles Clift's wrath. As a result the verdict of the jury was that there was no murder charge for Giles Clift to answer and that unfortunately the deceased, Thomas Farrant, had inadvertently caused his own death.

What remains unclear about this case is why a strong 25-year-old man would choose to try to squeeze through a 17½-inch by 24-inch gap, which he knew was some 30 feet above the pavement. Why did he not simply side step the older man and leave through the door? What did Thomas Farrant really have to fear from the blind 53-year-old? Surely it would have been a simple matter to have restrained the older man or at least to have avoided any blows that he sought to strike? Is it possible then that Giles Clift, with the assistance of Henry Lyons, man-handled the unfortunate Thomas Farrant, legs first out of the window, just as his wife had said?

CHAPTER SEVEN

SHE SHOULD TELL US HOW SHE DID IT

The Murder Drama of Adelaide Bartlett
– Victoria, London, 1886

A DELAIDE BARTLETT was born Adelaide Blanche de la Tremoile in Orléans, France in 1856. It is said that her father was a wealthy Englishman, perhaps a member of Queen Victoria's party when she toured France in 1855. On Adelaide's marriage certificate she gives her father's name as Adolphe Collot de la Tremoile, Comte de Thouars d'Escury, and her date of birth as 20 December. Since the state visit had occurred the previous August, it is unlikely that an Englishman was her father. It has also been suggested that her mother was not French at all and that her name could have been Clara Chamberlain. Her mother was unmarried and so, to leave behind the comparative disgrace of being born out of wedlock, Adelaide came to England at the age of 17. She moved into a house in Richmond with her guardian, then later, in 1875, she went to stay in Kingston-upon-Thames with her maternal aunt and uncle, Mr and Mrs William Chamberlain. Here accounts of the story diverge. Either a local removal man, Charles Bartlett, knew the Chamberlains, or Adelaide stayed for a while in Charles Bartlett's home as a companion for his 16-year-old daughter. In any event, Charles Bartlett introduced Adelaide to his brother, Edwin, who immediately fell in love with her.

By all accounts Adelaide was a strikingly attractive woman with dark, curly hair, a full mouth and a perfect complexion. Edwin was 29 and was a partner in a grocery and provision concern with an Edward Baxter. It seems that events moved very quickly and Edwin proposed to the young girl. Adelaide's relations seemed reasonably happy that the match was a good one and that the marriage should proceed.

From the outset Edwin had explained to Adelaide that he intended their relationship to be platonic and did not propose that the marriage needed to be a physical one. There was no honeymoon; instead, to prove his good faith directly after the marriage, Edwin sent Adelaide to a ladies' finishing school in Stoke Newington. She only lived with Edwin during the school holidays. These arrangements were maintained for two years, with Edwin living above one of his shops in Station Road, Herne Hill. After a brief stay at a convent finishing school in Brussels, Adelaide joined her husband in London in 1878.

Edwin Bartlett *(Police News)*

Edwin bred Newfoundland dogs, which seems to have taken up most of his precious spare time. Adelaide, meanwhile, occupied herself with music, needlework and helping her husband with the dogs.

The Bartlett's rooms were also occupied by Edwin's younger brother, Frederick, and life in the household seemed fairly routine, without friction. Things were to change abruptly. Edwin and Frederick's mother died, and they invited their father, also called Edwin, to live with them. Very soon it became apparent that the old man was a bad-tempered and unpleasant character who had taken a severe dislike to Adelaide. Not content with making her life a misery, the old man also accused his younger son Frederick of sleeping with her. Either shortly before or around the time of this accusation Adelaide ran away from home, only to be coaxed back by her husband. Edwin took Adelaide's side completely against his father and even went to the extreme of requiring his father to sign an apology that had been drawn up by a solicitor. His father had no desire to be made homeless so, at least on the surface, the household returned to normal.

In 1881 two events affected the Bartletts' future. Adelaide began to make it clear to her husband that she wanted to have a child. Given that this meant a radical change in their relationship, a certain degree of preparation was necessary. It appears, somewhat unusually, that Edwin gave Adelaide a book to read, entitled ***Esoteric Anthropology (the Mysteries of Man: A***

Edwin Bartlett's father, also named Edwin. *(Police News)*

Comprehensive and Confidential Treatise on the Structure, Functions, Passionate Attractions and Perversions, True and False, Physical and Social Conditions and the Most Intimate Relations of Men and Women), a snappily titled volume by T.L. Nichols, MD. Adelaide was to learn from the book exactly when in the lunar cycle it would be ideal to have much-delayed sexual relations with her husband. The act took place on a Sunday afternoon and, although it was later said that this was the only time that Edwin and Adelaide ever had sex, it resulted in Adelaide falling pregnant. However, according to Annie Walker, who was engaged as a midwife in the latter stages of the pregnancy, Adelaide confided to her that this had not been the only time that she and her husband had had sex. On the contrary, although it had not been a regular event, on the other occasions they had taken precautions. Indeed, what are we to make of the fact that a pocket full of condoms was found in Edwin's clothes after his death? Some have suggested that considering the fact that Victorian London was awash with prostitutes, and that Edwin moved freely around the capital with his work, abstaining from having sex with his wife would not have been too great a strain.

The second major event in 1881 was that Edwin had a nervous breakdown, which his father oddly associated with laying a floor in the house. It is probably worth pointing out that Edwin was something of a hypochondriac. Many years before, as a young man, he had decided to have a full set of dentures fitted on the grounds that they would be better and more efficient than his

> ESOTERIC
>
> # ANTHROPOLOGY
>
> (THE MYSTERIES OF MAN):
>
> A COMPREHENSIVE AND CONFIDENTIAL TREATISE ON THE STRUCTURE, FUNCTIONS, PASSIONAL ATTRACTIONS, AND PERVERSIONS, TRUE AND FALSE PHYSICAL AND SOCIAL CONDITIONS, AND THE MOST INTIMATE RELATIONS OF MEN AND WOMEN.
>
> ANATOMICAL, PHYSIOLOGICAL, PATHOLOGICAL, THERAPEUTICAL, AND OBSTETRICAL;
>
> HYGIENIC AND HYDROPATHIC.
>
> *From the American Stereotype Edition, Revised and Rewritten.*
>
> By T. L. NICHOLS, M.D., F.A.S.,
> Principal of the American Hydropathic Institute; Author of "Human Physiology the Basis of Sanitary and Social Science."
>
> MALVERN:
> PUBLISHED BY T. L. NICHOLS.

Cover of *Esoteric Anthropology*.

real teeth. Consequently, he had all of his teeth sawn off at the gums to facilitate the fitting of the dentures. It also appears that he was taken to ingesting various medicines and potions to improve his health, some of which we now know to be poisonous.

To return to Adelaide's pregnancy, towards the end of her confinement Edwin had arranged, through the good Dr Nichols's wife, that the already mentioned Annie Walker, a qualified midwife, should be on hand to assist at the delivery. In the event it was a very difficult birth and Annie begged Edwin to call a doctor. Here we have further evidence of Edwin's strange attitudes towards the relationships of men and women. Edwin refused to call a doctor in on the basis that he did not want 'any man interfering with her'. Unfortunately by the time Edwin had been persuaded to change his mind the baby was dead. Annie Walker

Bartlett's shops at Herne Hill.

stayed in the household for about another three weeks, gradually becoming close friends with Adelaide. It is interesting that even after the Bartletts no longer needed Annie, she continued to visit and stay at the house as a friend, rather than an employee. It was during this period that Annie Walker witnessed and was confided in many of the more secret aspects of the Bartlett's relationship. As she was able to recount much later, Annie found the Bartletts to be an affectionate couple who invariably offered a united front. Adelaide confided in Annie that one of the only things that concerned her was that Edwin's will expressly stated that he would leave everything to her only if she never remarried. She may well have had reason to complain, as a good deal of the ready cash and assets of Edwin's business had been derived from the dowry he obtained by marrying her.

In 1883 they moved into rooms above another of Edwin's shops in Lordship Lane, East Dulwich, jettisoning Edwin's father in the process on the grounds that this was a smaller house. Edwin arranged for his father to rent a property of his own. It was here that Adelaide met the wife of George Matthews, one of Edwin's business associates. Alice Matthews would remain close to Adelaide for the next few years.

They moved again in 1885 to Merton Abbey, near Wimbledon, where, one Sunday morning, they went to the Wesleyan Chapel. George Dyson was the preacher that day, a slightly built man with a receding hairline and a black moustache. He was about 27 years old, and soon after meeting the Bartletts, called at their house. During the conversation, which seems to have been predominantly with Edwin, Dyson explained that he was going to study for a degree at Trinity College, Dublin, which obviously impressed Edwin. Edwin asked Dyson to make sure that he visited them again when he returned from Dublin. Although the three did not know it, their future friendship would have catastrophic effects on all of their lives.

George Dyson (*Police News*)

Edwin Bartlett's will.

At some point, presumably before the Bartletts moved again, George Dyson had been persuaded to tutor Adelaide in history, geography and Latin. It seems that the lessons did not begin until the Bartletts had moved back into London and were living in Claverton Street, Pimlico. For hours Adelaide and George would spend time together with the curtains closed and pinned together. As Dyson was only earning £100 a year, the additional income from this personal tutorship was most welcome. It was later claimed that Adelaide would sit at Dyson's feet with her head on his knee. Even Edwin appeared to be happy for them to hold hands and even kiss one another in his presence. Nevertheless, it seems that Edwin had complete faith in this clergyman and he seemed very keen to include George in Adelaide's future should something happen to him. Not only did he make Dyson an executor of his will, but he told Dyson that he hoped the two of them would 'come together'. At some time around this period the Bartletts went to Dover for a month. Edwin was keen that Dyson should go with them and offered him a first-class season ticket so that he could join them whenever he had the chance. From a letter written in Dover to Dyson we can see that Edwin was already more than reliant on the clergyman.

14 St James Street
Dover, Monday

Dear George,

Permit me to say I feel great pleasure in thus addressing you for the first time. To me it is a privilege to think I am allowed to feel towards you as a brother, and I hope our friendship may ripen as time goes on, without anything to mar its future brightness. Would that I could find words to express my thankfulness to you for the very loving letter you sent Adelaide today. It would have done anybody good to see her overflowing with joy as she read it whilst walking along the street, and afterwards as she read it to me. I felt my heart going out to you. I long to tell you how proud I feel at the thought I should soon be able to clasp the hand of the man who from his heart could pen such noble thoughts. Who can help loving you? I felt I must say two words: 'thank you', and my desire to do so is my excuse for troubling you with this. Looking towards the future with joyfulness, I am yours affectionately.

Edwin

George Dyson's reply was equally as gushing and affectionate.

My Dear Edwin,

Thank you very much for the brotherly letter you sent me yesterday. I am sure I respond from my heart to your wish that our friendship may ripen with the lapse of time, and I do so with confidence, for I feel that our friendship is founded on a firm, abiding basis – trust and esteem. I have from a boy been ever longing for the confidence and trust of others. I have never been so perfectly happy as when in possession of this. It is in this respect, among many others, that you have shown yourself a true friend. You have thanked me, and now I thank you; I ought to confess that I read your warm and generous letter with a kind of half fear – a fear lest you should ever be disappointed in me and find me a far more prosy, matter-of-fact creature than you expect. Thank you, moreover, for the telegram; it was very considerate to send it. I am looking forward with much pleasure to next week. Thus far I have been able to stave off any work and trust to be able to keep it clear. Good old Dover! It will ever possess a pleasant memory for me in my mind and a warm place in my heart. With very kind regards, believe me, yours affectionately,

George

Reading these two letters with the benefit of hindsight, we could be forgiven for believing that it was not George and Adelaide that had fallen in love, but George and Edwin. There is no evidence that Edwin and George ever had a physical relationship, but Edwin's letter, together with his strange physical relationship with his wife, could suggest that he was a latent homosexual. It also appears that Edwin travelled up to Putney during that month and persuaded Dyson to spend the night with them in Dover.

Edwin's season ticket offer to George continued when he and his wife returned to Pimlico, as he supplied the clergyman with a ticket so that he could travel to their house from Putney at any time. By now, Dyson had his own church in Putney and the Bartletts were safely established in their new home, which was owned by Frederick Doggett, who was a registrar of births and deaths. Dyson had his own slippers and jacket at the Bartlett home, but it appears that he was becoming rather too fond of Adelaide. He told Edwin of his feelings, and said that he felt that he ought to stop seeing the Bartletts. Edwin, however, assured Dyson that his wife had become a better woman as a result of their friendship. The visits continued, Mrs Doggett noting that the window curtains were both drawn and pinned together whenever Dyson was alone with Adelaide.

It was probably on 8 December 1885 that Edwin first became ill. He was suffering from sickness, diarrhoea and haemorrhaging of the bowels. Adelaide immediately called Dr Alfred Leach, who examined Edwin. Edwin also complained to the doctor that he had severe toothache and was feeling depressed and very sick. Leach looked into Edwin's mouth and suggested that he had taken mercury, as there was a blue line around his gums. This observation would later be mentioned in court. At the time it was believed that mercury was a means by which a patient could be treated for syphilis. Perhaps, if Edwin had caught syphilis from a prostitute at some undefined time in the past, it could be a very good reason why he abstained from sexual relations with Adelaide. Equally, given the fact that syphilis was almost inevitably terminal, it would explain why he was so keen to push Adelaide into Dyson's arms. This is all, of course, pure speculation, because, until the very end of his life, Edwin refused to admit that he had 'a pestilent disease'. Edwin's own explanation for the apparent mercury poisoning was that he had found a pill in the drawer and taken it. He did not know what the pill was, but it is unlikely that a single pill containing mercury would have produced the blue line around his gums.

Edwin's bizarre dental decision as a young man had obviously come back to haunt him. At the time, whoever had sawn off the teeth at the gums had literally done just that. The roots were still in his gums, presumably never cleaned, as they were covered by the dentures. Leach noted the decomposition of Edwin's gums and another dentist was called in to extract no fewer than 15 roots and stumps. It is perfectly possible that a small dose of mercury, coupled with the sulphides produced by the rotting teeth, created mercuric sulphide which accounted for the blue line.

Dr Leach continued to treat the patient, but it seems that during the next few days Edwin remained depressed and had fits of hysteria and delusions, although physically he did begin to improve. Edwin's father came to visit his son on several occasions, but was only allowed to see Edwin three times because Adelaide did not want her husband upset by the old man's ill-nature. It was clear that Edwin's father had grave suspicions about Adelaide even then. It should be remembered that he was sure that his younger son, Frederick, had already slept with her and he was now coming to the conclusion that she was being regularly bedded by the Reverend Dyson.

By 19 December Dr Leach wanted Edwin either to go away for a while to convalesce without his wife, or to call in another doctor for a second opinion. Adelaide apparently told Leach 'if Mr Bartlett does not get better soon, his friends and relations will accuse me of poisoning him'.

A second medical opinion was sought from Dr Dudley, who found Edwin very depressed, unable to sleep and with gums that were still very spongy and inflamed. His opinion was that Bartlett should get out of his bed and take a constitutional every day to improve his health.

On Christmas Day Edwin discovered to his horror that he had passed a roundworm and from then on was convinced that he could feel worms wriggling in his throat and in his bowels. The sudden appearance of a roundworm seems to have tipped Edwin's mind over the edge, and bizarrely, at around this time, he suddenly developed a desire to recommence sexual relations with Adelaide. As far as Adelaide was concerned, however, not only was her husband an unattractive physical and mental wreck, but she had also, to all intents and purposes, been promised to George Dyson.

On 27 December Adelaide asked George Dyson to buy a large quantity of chloroform for her. She explained to him that she had previously been able to get chloroform from Annie Walker, which was untrue, as her friend had been living abroad for some time. George duly complied with her request and collected three bottles of chloroform from three different chemists, lying about the reasons for its purchase, claiming that he was intending to use it to remove grease spots from clothes. Chloroform was a controlled substance and not normally given to anyone unless on prescription, but Dyson was a minister and the chemists had no reason to suspect that he was lying. George dutifully put all of the chloroform into one bottle and gave it to Adelaide. She explained to him that her husband was suffering from a painful complaint and that it could only be treated by chloroform. She did not explain to Dyson how the chloroform was to be used but confidentially she told him that this other complaint that her husband suffered from was unknown to the doctors.

On 31 December Dr Leach arrived to check on the patient, who had eaten six oysters and a large portion of jugged hare for his breakfast. Adelaide and Leach managed to get Edwin out of bed and into a cab, and the pair accompanied him to see the dentist. It was not good news;

the dentist suggested that Edwin's gums were in a state of necrosis, meaning that they had rotted to such an extent that the blood no longer flowed into them. It was decided that at least one more tooth would have to be extracted; consequently the dentist administered gas to Edwin and carried out the operation. However unpleasant the operation may have been, it did not seem to dent Edwin's appetite and he ate more jugged hare, oysters, cake and chutney for his dinner. He also ordered a large haddock for his breakfast the following morning. At some point shortly after Edwin and Adelaide had returned to Pimlico, there was a conversation with Mrs Doggett about chloroform. Mrs Doggett had told Adelaide that when she had had an operation some years ago that she had found taking chloroform 'nice and pleasant'. Mrs Doggett said that Adelaide told her that she often administered chloroform to her husband to help him to sleep.

Although it was New Year's Eve and there were celebrations going on at the Doggetts', Adelaide dutifully sat beside her husband's bed throughout the evening. The Doggetts retired at 12.15am, only to be awoken at 4am by Adelaide banging on their bedroom door, shouting 'Go and fetch Dr Leach. I think Mr Bartlett is dead!' She claimed to have fallen asleep holding her husband's foot, which she claimed soothed him, and had awoken to feel his skin cold in her hand. She had immediately tried to revive him by pouring brandy down his neck. Adelaide added that she had already sent the Doggetts' maid to fetch Dr Leach.

When Dr Leach arrived he could see no immediate reason why Edwin had died. Adelaide claimed that when she had woken up she had seen Edwin twisted on his side, with his face downwards, and had given him the brandy. Certainly there was a smell of brandy on Edwin's chest and a half-full glass was on the mantelpiece beside the bed. When Leach smelt the glass it had the unmistakable aroma of chloroform, or ether. Edwin's father had also been informed of what had happened to his son and came into the bedroom and kissed Edwin's face, immediately saying to Dr Leach 'We must have a post-mortem'. Leach asked Adelaide 'Could he have taken poison?' to which she replied no, how could her husband have obtained poison, having been confined to bed for such a length of time. Edwin's father was convinced that his daughter-in-law had poisoned his son but there was a bottle of chlorodyne on the mantelpiece which Edwin had rubbed into his gums. Could this not be, Adelaide suggested, how her husband had died?

Dr Leach was wavering about signing the death certificate, but Adelaide insisted that a post-mortem be carried out. 'Spare no expense', she added.

The post-mortem was carried out on 2 January by Dr Green at Charing Cross Hospital. The examiners were unable to discover any natural cause of death; consequently they sent Edwin's stomach away for further examination. Meanwhile, in order to avoid the suspicions surrounding her, and Edwin's unpleasant father's accusations, Adelaide went to stay with her friends, the Matthews.

By now, even before the full post-mortem results were made public, George Dyson was beginning to panic. If it was proved that Edwin had died as a result of chloroform poisoning, then surely the fact that he had purchased the substance would implicate him in the death.

The results of the examination of Edwin's stomach revealed that there was chloroform present in the organ, but what the doctors could not work out was how it got there. Not only is chloroform extremely unpleasant to taste and would induce vomiting, but there would certainly be some traces of it in the lungs, which the post-mortem had not revealed.

As soon as Dyson was certain that the death had been caused by the chloroform, he immediately rushed to see Adelaide at the Matthews' house. Mrs Matthews overheard Dyson saying to Adelaide 'You did not tell me Edwin was going to die soon'. Adelaide denied any involvement, to which Dyson replied 'My God, I am a ruined man'. Dyson warned Adelaide that he was going to make a clean breast of it, and she begged him not to make any mention of the chloroform. Dyson also demanded the return of poems that he had written to her, as he felt that people would misinterpret their relationship if they were read. He was particularly keen on getting back the following verse:

> Who is it that hath burst the door,
> Unclosed the heart that shut before,
> And set her queen-like on her throne,
> And made its homage all her own?
>
> My Birdie

Adelaide realised that Dyson would probably implicate her in the death of Edwin. She found solace in talking to Dr Leach, to whom she confided the real reason for obtaining the chloroform. She explained that in Edwin's more lucid moments in the last month of his life he had begun to demand more intimacy with Adelaide than he had done in the preceding 11 years. She went on to explain that in her own mind she had already been promised to Dyson and thus, in an odd way, it would have been unfaithful for her to have sex with her husband. As a result she had persuaded Dyson to obtain the chloroform for her so that she could put drops of it on a handkerchief and knock her husband out if he became too passionate. On the night of Edwin's death, she confessed that she had admitted this practice to Edwin and given him the bottle. They had talked amicably about it for a little while and he had placed the bottle on the mantelpiece. Edwin was rather sulky and had turned over in his bed and gone to sleep. At some undisclosed point in this evening of confession to her husband, she had removed the bottle of chloroform and put it in the drawer of her dressing table. There the bottle had lain until after her husband's death, when the police had carried out their search of the room. She then confessed to having thrown it from the window of a moving train into a pond somewhere between Victoria and Peckham Rye. There are several holes in Adelaide's story, not the least of which was the fact that the pond was frozen over at the time. Leach told her that he was surprised that a few drops of chloroform had been sufficient to knock Edwin out, to which Adelaide had no reply.

By late January a Home Office analyst had confirmed the exact nature of Edwin Bartlett's death. What remained outstanding was an explanation of how the chloroform had got into his stomach. Just before this confirmation, probably on 16 January, Adelaide and Dyson met for the last time before they would be joined together in utterly different circumstances.

Adelaide apparently told Dyson that he was upsetting himself unduly and that provided he did not incriminate himself he could be assured that she would not incriminate him. There may have been another meeting on around 19 January at the Matthews' house, where Adelaide confided in Dyson the facts of how she had disposed of the chloroform.

The inevitable coroner's inquest was held in February and Dr Leach told the assembled crowd, as the case had by now received a great deal of public interest, of the confidential conversations that he had had with Adelaide. She did not give evidence, but George Dyson did. He explained to the coroner that he had been deceived and thrown into the company of a wicked woman by her own husband. He said that he had panicked when he had discovered that the cause of Edwin's death was chloroform, and had disposed of the three small bottles by hiding them under different bushes on Wandsworth Common. The coroner's jury had no alternative but to return a verdict of wilful murder, prompting Adelaide's immediate arrest. If Dyson had expected that 'making a clean breast of it' would have absolved his presumed involvement in the death of Edwin Bartlett, then he was wrong, because on 13 April, before Mr Justice Wills, he found himself standing next to the 'wicked woman' in the dock at the Old Bailey. At the very last minute, however, Dyson managed to avoid the indignity of the charges against him, as although he had admitted to having obtained the chloroform, there was no other direct evidence to implicate him in the murder. Adelaide then stood alone in the dock.

She was ably defended by one of the greatest advocates of the time, Edward Clarke QC MP. His task was not an easy one; on the face of it he had to convince a male, Victorian jury that a French adulteress had not murdered her doting and gullible husband. The key factor in Adelaide and Clarke's favour was that no one could explain how the chloroform had ended up in Edwin Bartlett's stomach.

Clarke had had plenty of time to consider the defence of his client, having been engaged just two days after the coroner's inquest. At some point on 20 February he was approached to defend Adelaide Bartlett; presumably the funds for the defence had come from Adelaide's own mysterious family. Certainly, Adelaide could not have afforded to have paid Clarke's bills.

Unlike the coroner's inquest, Adelaide could not give evidence in a murder trial. In any case, it was probably as well that she could not take the witness stand, as she would have had to face cross-examination by the Attorney General, Sir Charles Russell.

Since 20 February Clarke had spent several days in the British Museum Library, studying chloroform. It appears that he was so taken with the prospect of

Caricature of Sir Edward Clarke.

defending this appealing French woman, coupled with the unlimited funds available for her defence, that he dropped every other case that he was working on. This gave Clarke a massive advantage over his adversary, Russell, which he was to take full advantage of throughout the trial.

Each day, throughout the whole trial, Clarke arrived at the court early and gave maximum support to Adelaide. As we have seen, the first major sensation was the Crown's withdrawal of the charges against George Dyson. In the event, the Crown's decision actually played into Clarke's hands; now the jury could see a solitary female, and Dyson would have to appear as a witness against his client. Sometime later in his memoirs, Clarke wrote:

> Having admitted that he [Dyson] was innocent, the Attorney General could not help calling him as a witness, and so offering him for my cross-examination. That would not be hostile, but friendly and sympathetic, for the more closely I could associate his actions with those of Mrs Bartlett, the more I should strengthen the instinctive reluctance of the jury to send her to the hangman's chord, while he passed unrebuked to freedom.

However, this was all for later in the trial as it was now time for the prosecution to begin to set the agenda and the direction in which they wished the jury to consider the case. The key was the chloroform in the stomach. Russell suggested to the jury that there were just three explanations. The first was suicide and Russell explained that there was no evidence to suggest that Edwin Bartlett wished to take his own life. The second was that the chloroform had accidentally got into Edwin Bartlett's stomach; surely he suggested, this could not be the case,

Bartlett trial.

for as the jury would discover, chloroform had an extremely unpleasant nature and caused pain both when taking it and after it was ingested. The third explanation, Russell claimed, was the only one which adequately encompassed the facts as they were known. Somehow Adelaide Bartlett had used chloroform to render her husband unconscious, before, quite simply, pouring the remainder down his throat.

Russell's first witness was the unwelcome figure of Edwin's father. He told the court of his very real suspicions against his daughter-in-law, but, as he was to concede in cross-examination, he had no real grounds for any accusations against Adelaide. Clarke ripped Edwin Bartlett's testimony to shreds, citing the solicitor's apology when the old man had accused his son, Frederick, of sleeping with Adelaide, but worse, he forced the old man to admit that he was trying to have his son's will contested as he believed under the circumstances that the estate should have gone to him. It was, perhaps, a very foolish move for the prosecution to call Edwin Bartlett senior at all, as the jury was now clear that the old man had an ulterior motive for his accusation and that, in any event, he had resented the presence of Adelaide from the outset.

On the second day of the trial it was the turn of the Reverend George Dyson to give his long-awaited evidence to the court. At every turn Dyson made strenuous efforts to distance himself from Adelaide's thoughts and actions, appearing to be very hostile to her in an attempt save his reputation at her expense. Clarke needed to use Dyson's own words to give the jury cause to doubt whether Adelaide had actually murdered her husband. During the cross-examination Dyson admitted that Edwin Bartlett had some very strange ideas, and that he was a hypochondriac who was convinced that he was going to die. Dyson went on to admit that Adelaide had never asked him to conceal the purchase of the chloroform, and that he had thrown away the chloroform bottles purely on account of the fact that they might have implicated him in Edwin's death.

Dr Leach was the next major witness and was able to shed some light on Edwin's medical history. He had also been present at the post-mortem. He told the court that Adelaide had appeared calm and devoted to her husband at all times. Leach described Edwin as being on the verge of insanity. He described his deceased patient as being eccentric, unbalanced, invariably neurotic and occasionally hysterical. Clarke, when cross-examining him, ensured that Dr Leach told the judge and jury that it had been Adelaide who insisted on the post-mortem, when Dr Leach was considering whether it was necessary or not, and also questioned Leach about the use of chloroform. He asked him whether it was possible for Adelaide to have rendered her husband unconscious and then poured a larger dose down his throat. Leach said that in his opinion this was impossible. Given the fact that Edwin Bartlett had eaten a large meal, vomiting as a result of the administration of the chloroform would be inevitable and he had seen no sign of such vomiting.

The chief medical expert called by the prosecution was the Professor of Medical Jurisprudence at Guy's Hospital, a Dr Thomas Stevenson. He was a well-known, if not internationally recognised, expert toxicologist. Even his evidence was inconclusive; when asked whether it was possible to pour liquid chloroform down someone's throat, he explained that although this was not beyond the realms of possibility, that inevitably there would be signs of it in the windpipe. A post-mortem had established the fact that there was no chloroform in the windpipe; so Stevenson was at a loss to explain how the chloroform had arrived in Bartlett's stomach. He was also asked whether he knew of any murder that had been committed in a way in which the prosecution maintained had occurred in this case. He replied that to the best of his knowledge he was unaware of one. This rather inconclusive evidence completed the prosecution's case and it was now the turn of Edward Clarke to begin to systematically undermine what little Russell had proven. He began by addressing the jury directly:

> It is a marvellous thing that you are asked by the prosecution to accept. You are asked to believe that a woman who for years had lived in friendship and affection with her husband, who during the whole time of his illness had striven to tend him, to nurse him and help him, who had tended him by day, who had sacrificed her own rest to watch over him at night, had spent night after night without going to her restful bed, simply giving to herself sleep at the bottom of his couch that she might be ready by him to comfort him by her presence, who had called doctors, who had taken all the pains that the most tender and affectionate nurse possibly could, that by no possibility should any chance be lost of the doctor's ascertaining what his trouble was, and having the quickest means to cure it; you are asked to imagine that that woman on New Year's Eve was suddenly transformed into a murderess, committing crime not only without excuse, but absolutely without any object; you are asked to believe that by a sort of inspiration she succeeds in committing that crime by the execution of a delicate and difficult operation – an operation which would have been delicate and difficult to the highest trained doctors that this country has in it.

As we will see from Clarke's concluding statement to the jury, he wanted the jury to believe that Edwin Bartlett was an eccentric man who had literally given his wife to George Dyson and was happy with the prospect of them marrying after his death. He claimed that Edwin and Adelaide's marriage was essentially a platonic one and that they had only ever had sexual intercourse on one occasion, which had resulted in the pregnancy that ended with the death of their child. Unaccountably, in the last days of Edwin's life, his desire for Adelaide had been rekindled, but Adelaide, fearing the imminent death of her husband, had already mentally wed George Dyson. This was why, Clarke claimed, that she had persuaded Dyson to obtain the chloroform; she intended to use it solely to avoid an act that she felt would have been unfaithful to Dyson. Whether she had actually gone through with using the chloroform on her husband or not was a matter of conjecture, but in any event, she could not keep her intent from Edwin. It seemed probable, that on the last evening of his life, she had told him of her dilemma and given him the bottle. As far as Clarke was concerned, although Edwin would have grudgingly accepted what his wife had told him, he would nevertheless have been hurt by it. The bottle of chloroform had been placed on the mantelpiece and, somehow, as his dutiful wife dozed, holding his foot, he had reached for the chloroform and swallowed it. Whether this was a deliberate act to get back at his wife, or simply to attract her attention and concern, would never be known. Clarke asked the jury to believe that Adelaide was so virtuous that she would not even allow her own husband to have sexual intercourse with her after he had promised her to George Dyson. The matter of the contraceptives in Edwin's pocket was never raised by either the prosecution or the defence. We can only draw our own conclusions. Edwin may have had them so that he could make love to Adelaide without infecting her with syphilis, which he may have believed that he had. Alternatively, the condoms could have been there for some time and have been intended to prevent Edwin contracting syphilis from other women. The post-mortem did not reveal that Edwin Bartlett had syphilis, but we should not necessarily be swayed by this piece of evidence, since, as a hypochondriac, Edwin may well have believed that he was infected.

To return to Clarke's final summing up, which was listened to by a crowded court, filled with the public and barristers hanging on his every word, he said:

This woman has not had the happiest of lives. She has been described to you as one who had no friends. But she had one friend – her husband. He did stand by her, strange as his ideas may have been, disordered as it would seem from some things that have been said, his intellect in some respects must have been. Yet in his strange way he stood by her and protected her. He was affectionate in manner, and when her reputation was assailed, he defended it as only the husband could defend it. And to her at this moment it may seem most strange that he to whom she had given this persistent affection, even during years of such a life, should be the one of whose foul murder she now stands accused. And if he himself could know what passes among us here – how strange, how sorrowful it might seem to him – how strange that such an accusation should have been formulated and tried in court, in spite of the efforts which he endeavoured to make to prevent it – the precautions which perhaps by his own rash despairing act he too defeated. Gentlemen, that husband has gone. But she is not left without a friend. She will find that friend here today in the spirit which guides your judgement and clears your eyes upon this case. The spirit of justice is in this court today to comfort and protect her in the hour of her utmost need. It has strengthened, I hope, my voice. It will, I trust, clear your eyes and guide your judgement. It will speak with the evidence which I hope and believe has demolished and destroyed the suspicion which rests on her. And that spirit will in firm, unfaltering voice when your verdict tells the whole world that in your judgement Adelaide Bartlett is not guilty.

Despite Edward Clarke's unequivocal call to the jury to acquit his client, he could not have accounted for the fact that the judge, Justice Wills, was absolutely positive that Adelaide Bartlett was guilty. He did not attempt to conceal his belief that Adelaide had sought to dispose of an inconvenient husband and that she had already committed adultery with George Dyson, possibly on account of the fact that she had been allowed to read the

Adelaide Bartlett in court.

'outpouring of impurity' found within the pages of Dr Nichols's book.

It seems, however, that the jury were far more impressed with Edward Clarke's summing up than with either what Justice Wills or Sir Charles Russell had told them in court. They took two hours to reach their verdict, which the foreman delivered to a hushed court.

Although we think there is the gravest suspicion attaching to the prisoner, we do not think there is sufficient evidence to show how or by whom the chloroform was administered.

It was therefore the jury's decision that Adelaide Bartlett was not guilty of murdering her husband.

At this decision the court erupted into applause, which further irritated the judge. Edward Clarke broke down and cried as he watched Adelaide Bartlett being led to freedom.

A week later Edward Clarke received a letter from Adelaide, which read:

66 Gresham Street
April 24th

Dear Sir

Forgive me for not earlier expressing my heartfelt gratitude to you. I feel that I owe my life to your earnest efforts, and though I cannot put into words the feelings that fill my heart, you will understand all that my pen fails to express to you.

Your kind looks towards me cheered me very much, for I felt that you believed me innocent. I have heard many eloquent Jesuits preach, but I never listened to anything finer than your speech.

My story was a painful one, but sadly true. My consent to marriage was not asked, and I only saw my husband once before my wedding day.

I am much gratified that Dr Stevenson has written to say that he concurs in the verdict, he wrote so kindly of Miss Wood who has been a true friend. I received great kindness at Clerkenwell [where Adelaide had been held prior to the trial] from the governor to the lowest, they did their best to comfort me.

Assuring you that I shall always remember you with feelings of deepest gratitude, I am, sincerely yours,

Adelaide Bartlett

It seems from Adelaide's letter that the hand of her father was ever-present, even in Clerkenwell prison. The Miss Wood to whom she refers in the letter was the sister of her solicitor, at whose house she stayed for several weeks following her acquittal.

Regardless of the verdict, there were many that still believed that Adelaide Bartlett had carried out the premeditated murder on her hypochondriac husband. Even Queen Victoria's surgeon at St Bartholomew's Hospital, Sir James Paget, was quoted as saying 'Now the case is over, she should tell us in the interests of science how she did it'. The debate continued to rage. Dr Leach, who wrote an article about the case in *The Lancet*, said that Edwin took the chloroform himself 'out of sheer mischief, with the intention of alarming by his symptoms the wife who an hour or two before had talked about using it in an emergency'. Edward Clarke, her defence counsel, believed that Edwin had actually committed suicide and had heard the dentist on the last day of his life tell Dr Leach and Adelaide that he had necrosis. Clarke felt he had taken the chloroform in order to avoid a much more lingering death.

Over the years since the case was heard at the Old Bailey more theories have come to light, as well as a possible solution, but none fully explain how or by whom the fatal dose was administered.

Writers on the case have drawn inferences from a supposed conversation between Adelaide and Dr Leach, when she asked him about hypnotism. This has led some to suggest that Adelaide hypnotised Edwin and then induced him to drink the chloroform. This does still not explain why there was no trace of chloroform in Edwin's body apart from the amount found in his stomach. Perhaps the fact that there was a considerable amount of alcohol found in the stomach as well can help us understand how the chloroform was delivered.

The late detective writer, Christianna Brand (1909–1988) may have discovered exactly how the chloroform managed to get into Edwin's stomach. Brand poured some chloroform into a glass of brandy and was amazed to see that it hung suspended in the alcohol 'like a yolk in the white of an egg'. If Edwin had then drunk the contents of the glass, the chloroform could have been delivered into the stomach without leaving any trace of its journey in the mouth, oesophagus or windpipe.

If we accept this experiment to be a reasonable explanation then any one of the three possibilities which were outlined at the beginning of the prosecution's case could still be viable. Edwin may have inadvertently reached out and drunk the brandy, not knowing that by some mischance it had been mixed with chloroform. Alternatively, given that both the chloroform bottle and the glass of brandy were within his reach, he could have stretched out his arm and taken both of them, mixing the cocktail himself without awakening Adelaide. The effects would not have been immediate and he could have replaced the two items on the mantelpiece and lain down in his bed and died. These actions could either have been suicide, or carried out in the mistaken belief that the concoction would not kill him. The final alternative, although ruled out by Clarke, Leach, the jury and Adelaide, was that his wife mixed the fatal cocktail, either as a deliberate act of murder, or in the mistaken belief that the chloroform would in some way ease her husband's pains.

Adelaide returned to Orléans, although alternative reports suggest that she emigrated to America. In either case, she left the controversy to the pundits and disappeared into obscurity, presumably supported by both Edwin's estate and her family.

CHAPTER EIGHT

WHAT ART CAN TURN HIM INTO CLAY

The Poisoning of Charles Bravo – Balham, London, 1876

FLORENCE CAMPBELL was the daughter of a wealthy merchant who lived in Buscot Park, Berkshire and owned a town house in Lowndes Square, London. Her father, Robert Tertius Campbell, and his wife, Anne, had been delivered of the attractive, gentle and self-possessed Florence in 1845. She was described as being a small and pretty girl with blue eyes and a shock of red-gold to bright chestnut hair.

In 1863, or by some accounts, the following year, Florence, at the age of 19, visited Montreal and met a wealthy young guards officer, Captain Ricardo. He was 23, very wealthy and an eligible potential husband. Alexander Lewis Ricardo was the son of the late John Lewis Ricardo, MP and the great-nephew of the economist David Ricardo. His paternal family were millionaires and his mother, Lady Catherine Duff, was the sister of the 5th Earl of Fife.

They were married at Buscot Church on 21 September 1864 and travelled to the Rhine for their honeymoon. Ricardo had ensured that Florence would want for nothing and had taken out a £40,000 life assurance policy in order to protect her future should the unthinkable happen. Their wedding, officiated at by the Bishop of Oxford, Samuel Wilberforce, was a glittering social occasion and their marriage seemed blessed.

The couple moved into the leased Holkham Hall in Norfolk, but as Captain Ricardo's social life revolved around London, they soon moved to the capital. Unfortunately, despite the fact that he had a new bride, Ricardo not only kept a mistress but also could not stop himself from continuing his hard-drinking, bachelor life. Florence found that her husband's attitudes to his lifestyle and to her fluctuated. At times he would be remorseful and repentant about his drinking, promising to reform and attempting to reconcile himself to her, despite the effects on their marriage, while at other times he would disappear for days, only to return the worse for wear.

Florence's reaction was unusual for a woman of her background and upbringing; she too turned to alcohol. She had admitted to friends that 'when he was sober, we were happy together', although often the pair were both neither sober nor happy. By spring 1870 Florence was reduced to a nervous and physical wreck. Ricardo, meanwhile, was still drinking as heavily as before, and she decided at length that something must be done.

Since 1842 Malvern had been establishing itself as the 'Metropolis of the Water Cure'. Thousands of people had made their way to the spa to put themselves into the guiding hands of doctors Wilson and Gully. Wilson had introduced the concept of hydrotherapy from Bavaria, while Gully was the practical business mind of the partnership. He had created systems that would use the curative powers of water in the form of foot baths, plunge baths, douches and compresses. His apparatus had attracted the glitterati of the period, including Tennyson, Bulwer Lytton and Bishop Wilberforce, who had married Florence and Ricardo. Gully was not only a shrewd business man, he also had an impeccable medical background and great charisma. Florence knew of the Malvern set up as she had been taken there as a child. It was her view that since she was both miserable and ill, Dr Gully's scientific understanding and sympathy would cure her of her malaise. A discussion apparently took place between Florence and her husband and he agreed to join her at Malvern, thinking that he too might benefit from hydrotherapy.

For Florence, Dr Gully represented everything that her husband was not; he was calm and kind and provided everything that Florence needed in her poor mental and physical state. She admired Gully and was very grateful for his attentions, and at some stage this admiration began to change into love. Gully, to her, was not only a father-figure, but also a stabilising and dependable influence which was lacking in her marriage. As far as her parents, the Campbells were concerned, their daughter's need to seek medical attention was undoubtedly the fault of her husband.

Dr Gully. (*Vanity Fair, 1876*)

The couple signed a deed of separation in March 1870, which was actually witnessed by Dr Gully himself. Ricardo moved to Cologne, having unsuccessfully attempted to get Florence to forgive him and have him back. Florence received £1,200 a year under the terms of the life assurance policy after the separation, but she became considerably richer when her husband died in 1871, increasing her pay-out to £4,000 per year.

At this time Florence was still at Malvern with Dr Gully, and it seems that she was determined to 'catch' him. His income from the practice was around £10,000 a year and, although he was married and his only son was grown up, his wife had been separated from him for 30 years and was living in an asylum. Gully was 63 years old and the 26-year-old Florence was completely infatuated with him. Her family disapproved and broke off contact with her, feeling that her interest in Dr Gully was indiscreet. This left Florence bereft of friends and social contacts and consequently she moved in to the house of her solicitor, Mr Brooks, on Tooting Common. Brooks had three daughters who were cared for by their governess, Jane Cannon Cox. She was a middle-aged widow with scraped-back dark hair; she wore spectacles and was thin of frame. Her husband had been an engineer in Jamaica but had died, leaving her to care for her three young sons. She was a self-possessed and efficient woman, but she had been assisted financially by a wealthy friend, Joseph Bravo. Following his advice she had invested what little money she had in a furnished house in Lancaster Road, Notting Hill. While she received rent from the tenants of this house, she supplemented her income with her salary as governess to the Brooks children. Her three boys attended a school in Streatham. Very soon Jane Cox would become an indispensable companion for the friendless Florence Ricardo.

In 1872 Dr Gully retired and sold his hydrotherapy practise. In a vast civic reception he was thanked by the worthies of Malvern for the prosperity he had brought to the town over 30 years. Amazingly, Gully eventually settled in a house on Tooting Common, directly opposite the Brooks's home.

Florence desperately wanted to become part of a social circle and enjoy the lifestyle she had experienced in Malvern and before her marriage. She still lived with the Brooks family, and it was not long before she realised that Jane Cox could provide her with the means by which to set up a home herself, as she was experienced in household management and the direction of servants. Florence found Jane sympathetic, affectionate, tactful and, above all, very interested in swapping the humdrum life of a poorly paid governess for the more exciting prospect of running a household for her new-found rich and self-indulgent friend. Although their relationship, strictly speaking, was one of employer and servant, in fact they considered one another equal and called each other by their

Drawing of Jane Cox.

Christian names. At the Brooks's Jane was not badly paid by contemporary standards; although she only received £100 a year, all her expenses, clothing and other incidentals meant that the total bill for the Cox family must have been closer to £400. The Brookses were also very supportive of Jane's three children.

However, these good terms did not stop Jane from leaving the Brooks family in 1872 when the widow Ricardo moved into a house in Leigham Court Road, Streatham Hill. Florence immediately renamed the house 'Stokefield' in memory of the house that she had lived in while in Malvern. Dr Gully also purchased a house directly opposite in Leigham Court Road. He and Florence ate at one another's houses, often visited London together and were often seen by servants embracing and kissing. Outwardly the relationship remained discreet and when they stayed in London they not only took servants with them but also booked separate rooms. Jane Cox described the doctor as being 'a very fascinating man, likely to be of great interest to women'. Jane was also aware of the fact that technically Gully was still married.

In the summer of 1872 Florence and Dr Gully went to the German spa town of Kissingen. They travelled under their own names and occupied separate rooms in the hotels they stayed in. However, while they were on the continent they were intimate and Florence fell pregnant. When she returned to England she miscarried the child, after which she was nursed by both Jane and Dr Gully. Later, Jane would state that she was unaware that Florence's illness was on account of a miscarriage until around 1875. At the time Florence claimed that it was a severe internal derangement which had been brought on by the baths in Kissingen.

The Priory.

In 1874, with the leases on the houses in Leigham Court Road due to expire, Florence decided to move to a 10-acre estate called the Priory, in Balham. Dr Gully had found a semi-detached house situated between Balham station and the common, which he ultimately called Orwell Lodge. Florence's new home had been built in the early 1800s; it was an airy and graceful building with an arched doorway and crenellated roof, with an ancient oak tree in the middle of the front lawn. It was exactly what Florence had been looking for and she spent a great deal of money purchasing Venetian glass and other luxuries to fill the house. As a keen gardener she was delighted with the green-house, strawberry beds, vegetable garden, grape house and melon pit. She built a fernery, paying as much as 20 guineas for some of the plants. The gardens were filled with flowers and perfectly kept at all times of the year. Florence was a keen carriage driver and kept her own landau and horse.

Close up of Priory Court.

Meanwhile, on Bedford Hill Road Dr Gully had furnished his house, engaged servants and seemed happy in his retirement. He was ably assisted by his butler, Pritchard. Dr Gully was a frequent visitor to the Priory and even had his own set of keys. One of the parlour maids later said 'I never opened the door to him, but I have found him in the house'.

Sometime around 1875 Florence had a new lodge built to open up her estate on the Bedford Hill Road side. She installed her coachman, Mr Griffiths, and his wife in the new building. Griffiths would often take Dr Gully home from the Priory and on other occasions would drive the couple into London or around the Tooting Common countryside. It seems that although the arrangement was a comfortable one, their relationship had become rather staid. Some accounts claim that they quarrelled.

Soon Dr Gully's monopoly of Florence's affections was sorely tested by the arrival on the scene of Charles Bravo. Jane's friends, the Bravos, lived on Palace Green in Kensington. Charles Bravo was Mrs Bravo's son by a previous marriage but had chosen to take his stepfather Joseph Bravo's name. He was a dark-haired, round-featured, generally good-looking young man, who had been educated with the view to becoming a barrister. Unfortunately, despite the advantages of his upbringing, it does not appear that Charles was a particularly good lawyer and now, at the age of nearly 30, he did not devote a great deal of time to his calling nor profit greatly from his work. Nevertheless he still went to his chambers every day and it seems that his stepfather was perfectly happy to subsidise and indulge him.

Portrait of Charles Bravo.

Charles had a mistress; in fact they had been partners for at least four years. It seems that Charles did not consider marriage as he was perfectly happy with his arrangements.

Destiny threw Florence Ricardo and Charles Bravo together. One day Florence went on a shopping trip to London by carriage, taking Jane Cox with her. They had arranged that Florence's driver would drop Jane at the Bravos' house in Kensington. Florence would then do her shopping and pick Jane up before returning to Balham. When Florence's carriage arrived to pick up her friend the door was opened by Mrs Bravo, who asked the young woman in to take some refreshment. Florence was shown into the drawing room, where Charles Bravo greeted her. At the time they did not take much notice of one another, and the visit was short and formal.

Later in the year Dr Gully decided to go on a trip with some of his family to Europe and as a result, in order to fill in the time while Dr Gully was away, Florence and Jane went to Brighton. However, the visit simply bored Florence. By chance, on one of their constitutionals in the town, they bumped into Charles Bravo. In stark contrast to their first meeting, it appears that Charles and Florence were now instantly attracted to one another. Jane found herself something of a 'gooseberry' and it seems that Florence was ready to jettison the elderly Dr Gully in favour of a relationship with a man of her own age. She was an independent widow with her own money. These were obvious attractions for Charles Bravo. It soon became clear that Charles was not only very attracted to Florence but that he would also soon propose marriage. They seemed a good match.

When Dr Gully returned to England in October he visited Florence in Brighton. Rather than tell him the truth about her relationship with Charles, she gave him a completely different explanation for terminating their relationship. Gully had been a useful prop for Florence after the harrowing experience of her first marriage but now he was surplus to requirements. She told him that she grieved for the loss of her family and that while she maintained her relationship with him they would not countenance communication with her; she yearned to be reunited with them and had lately been informed that her mother was unwell and this had brought the matter to a head. Although Gully was shocked, he was a gentleman and reluctantly agreed that parting would be the best course of action. He was to say later 'I was very much attached to her at the time, and I had thought that she was fondly attached to me.'

With Gully disposed of it seems that Florence must have made it perfectly clear to Charles Bravo that she was available. Consequently, when he asked her to marry him in November, she immediately accepted. The news did not take long to get to Dr Gully, who was angered, having made many difficult decisions over the last five years with Florence in mind. He had given up his Malvern practice, social circle and public acclamation. He had pandered to Florence's whims and now she had deceived him and abandoned him.

Dr Gully wrote an angry letter to Florence, and one can understand his bitterness. He was considerably older than her and found himself facing a solitary retirement. In retrospect he found Florence demanding and spoilt, and prone to drinking too much.

Conversely, Florence's family were delighted at her decision and welcomed her and her fiancé back into the family. Not only had she put an end to what they considered her immoral relationship with Dr Gully, but she had chosen a man that was suitable in terms of character, wealth and age. As far as the Bravos were concerned, it was Charles's mother that presented the most serious stumbling block. Her possessive nature would not have found any match for her son acceptable, but Florence was utterly unthinkable in her eyes. Had she had her way the relationship would have been terminated immediately. She saw the aspects of Florence's character that had so attracted her son to be the most serious flaws in the woman's nature. Florence was a worldly woman who had already been married and, what is more, she was independent both financially and in her outlook on life. As for Florence's few friends and associates, their reaction was mixed, particularly since they knew little of Charles Bravo and much about Florence's own character.

In Florence's defence, however, it appears from the outset that she was more candid and open with her fiancé than could reasonably have been expected under the circumstances. She told Charles about her tragic marriage to Captain Ricardo and of her relationship with Dr Gully. Charles admitted that he too had a less than clean past and told Florence about his mistress. They both agreed that they would put these matters behind them and never speak of them again.

Charles Bravo also discussed Florence quite openly with Jane and asked her opinion about whether Florence would be capable of sustaining a married relationship and not be tempted by the lure of another man. It seems that they agreed that although Florence had made her mistakes in the past, she dearly wanted a loving and open relationship now. Jane, knowing of Charles's mother's antipathy towards Florence, actually suggested to him that he tell his mother about her past. In this way, she argued, everything would be open and his mother would never be able to discover Florence's past independently and use it as a weapon to drive a wedge between the couple. Charles obviously knew his mother far better than Jane, or, at the very least, he was terrified of her reaction, and refused to even think about doing Jane's suggestion. He maintained that their collective pasts were a matter for Florence and himself and no business of his mother's.

The date for the marriage was set for 7 December 1875. However, a certain degree of unpleasantness occurred in the indecently short period between the proposal and the wedding date. First, we must bear in mind that the Married Woman's Property Act was not in place and that on marrying all of a woman's assets would pass into the control of her husband. The only loophole to avoid this was if the woman had been prudent enough to secure her assets by settlement prior to the marriage. In search of the riches that Florence would bring him, Charles visited her solicitors. It was a frosty meeting, sparked off by Charles's reaction to the solicitor's congratulations on the impending marriage. He replied 'Damn your congratulations! I have come about the money.' Charles Bravo wanted everything assigned to him as was his right, without the need for a settlement. Florence's solicitor, on the other hand, wanted to secure his client's income from her husband's insurance, the Priory and all her effects. Charles demanded that the house and furniture should become his property when they married, but he allowed himself to be persuaded that the £4,000 pay-out should remain the property of his future wife. Following this meeting with the solicitor it seems that Florence and Charles had their first major difference of opinion. On the one hand, Charles refused to countenance the prospect of sitting on a lounge sofa that did not belong to him, in a house that was not his property. On the other hand, Florence, mindful of her previous experience of marriage, was keen to ensure that should her relationship with Charles break down, she would not be left homeless and penniless. As far as she was concerned, her jewellery, carriage, furniture and, above all, the Priory, should remain hers for as long as she lived. Charles rather callously told her that unless she acceded to his wishes, he would break off the marriage. It is not difficult to understand the situation from Charles's perspective. His generous stepfather had always provided everything that Charles owned. It is therefore not unreasonable to suggest that although his behaviour towards Florence and her solicitor was overbearing and cold, he simply did not wish to continue his life as a kept man.

Who could Florence turn to for advice, apart from Dr Gully? Despite the fact that Florence had told him unequivocally that she would no longer see him, he readily acceded to her request to meet with him immediately on a matter of great urgency. They met in her coachman's lodge on the Priory estate. It seems that the meeting was formal, if not cordial, and Gully told Florence that Charles's reaction was perfectly understandable and she should

not risk breaking off the marriage on account of the disagreement. He advised her to submit to Charles's demands, kissed her hand, wished her happiness and left.

After the end of Florence's relationship with Dr Gully, he had done the best he could to smooth over the ruffles of the break-up. She remained aloof and did not contact him. He, without prompting, returned his key to the Priory, told his staff that neither Florence nor Jane was welcome at Orwell Lodge, and did his best to avoid any accidental contact with them.

When Florence left her parents' home in Lowndes Square on 7 December 1875 she hoped that she was beginning a fresh life and a happy marriage with a man who both loved her and supported her. Mrs Bravo, Charles's mother, seems to have been unable to

Florence Bravo on her honeymoon.

countenance the idea that her son was about to be married and refused to attend the ceremony. Apart from this unfortunate decision, it seems that the wedding went off reasonably well and soon the newly married couple were happily ensconced at the Priory. However, it became clear very soon that Charles Bravo was a violent and arrogant man.

Charles's stepfather gave him a £20,000 settlement when he married, followed later by another £1,200. All Charles paid for from this income was the upkeep of the stables at the Priory. Everything else was paid for by Florence. She spent money freely, but lived always within her means. However, it was not in Charles Bravo's nature to allow money to be spent without his knowledge, permission and control. He was described by friends and enemies as being somewhere between careful and mean. He could simply not understand that his wife would be prepared to spend 20 guineas on a plant. Charles was determined to cut back any unnecessary expenditure in the household and unfortunately turned to his mother for advice on how to achieve this. This was the woman's opportunity to strike back at Florence, who had taken her son away from her, and she and Charles proposed a series of swingeing cuts to curtail the outflow of cash. Florence did not need three gardeners to maintain the Priory's acreage. Four horses were also considered excessive. Charles's mother was not finished, and also suggested that now Florence was married she no longer needed the companionship of Jane Cannon Cox. Over a period of time it is clear that Charles and Florence discussed many of the matters relating to cost-cutting that had been brought up by Charles's mother. Florence was initially unhappy to lose any of the gardeners but gradually conceded that some of the flower and vegetable beds could be turfed over to reduce the amount of work. As for the horses, Charles initially lost his argument as Florence was so attached to the animals. Clearly Charles spent a considerable amount of time calculating and recalculating the costs and probable savings that he hoped to introduce. It was when he discovered that if he included Jane Cox's salary, board and expenses that the total cost was around £400 that he became determined to try to trade Jane's loss for Florence's beloved horses.

During all of this Mrs Bravo had not restricted her interference to priming her son, but had been actively canvassing Jane Cox to consider leaving her daughter-in-law's employ. She carefully suggested to Jane that she should consider the huge advantages of moving back to Jamaica with her children. After all, Jane had an aunt still living in Jamaica who could easily provide accommodation and support for her niece and her children. Whatever conversations occurred between Charles's mother and Jane, however, Jane adamantly refused to even contemplate Mrs Bravo's suggestions.

Whatever Jane Cox would decide about moving to Jamaica could be rendered irrelevant if Charles could convince Florence that they no longer needed her services. Charles decided to take a longer view of this and of the horses. It seems clear that Florence was beginning to understand the character of her husband. While she complied with his wishes and everything was going his way he was perfectly content, but in achieving this he would countenance no opposition to his views. Faced with an impenetrable barrier, Charles would become morose, argumentative and, on occasion, violent. One such occasion was witnessed by Mary Anne

Keeber, who saw Charles strike Florence in what she termed a moment of 'passion and anger'. She was later to describe Charles as being petulant to the point of childishness. For the most part, however, it seems that despite their differences regarding the household, they were mostly happy and affectionate.

Later, both Florence and Jane would testify that Charles Bravo gradually developed a pathological hatred and jealousy of Dr Gully. It seems that beyond anything thoughts of his wife's relationship with 'that man' angered him to the point of violence, and he was not averse to recounting what Florence had told him about her relationship with Gully in order to press a point home or gain the upper hand in an argument. In retrospect, given the circumstances that both Florence and Jane were to find themselves in, it is not beyond the realms of possibility that they were prepared to lie about Charles's violent reactions. However, given the fact that Charles had neither seen nor spoken to Dr Gully, and could therefore not imagine his wife with him, it is not unusual that his imagination should have been working overtime since learning that Florence had once been the doctor's mistress. Little by little Charles's jealousy grew and he often referred to Dr Gully as a 'wretch' and on occasion threatened to kill him.

Regardless of these problems, Florence miscarried another child in January 1876, one month after they were married. In February she decided to go to Brighton to convalesce. Throughout her stay there Charles wrote to her every day and clearly showed his concern and devotion, coupled with the fact that he was missing her. However, one such letter, dated 15 February and written at Palace Green, was later used as evidence to support Florence and Jane's assertions that Charles was a violent man.

My darling wife,

Looking back on the weeks of our marriage I feel that many of my words, although kindly meant were unnecessarily harsh. In future my rebukes, if it is necessary to say anything, which God forbid! shall be given with the utmost gentleness. I hold you to be the best of wives. We have had bitter troubles, but I trust that in times to come the sweet peace of our lives will not be disturbed by memories like these. I wish I could sleep away my life until you return. Come back as well as you can to your devoted husband, Charles.

Of course the letter could either refer to their arguments about Florence's relationship with Dr Gully or could simply be a reference to Florence's miscarriage.

While neither Florence nor Charles had seen Dr Gully it is clear that Jane Cox had seen him on more than one occasion. There were ample opportunities for an accidental meeting; Jane would visit her boys at St Ann's school, attend to business at her own house on Lancaster Road or simply be out shopping. It was outside the Army and Navy Stores in Victoria Street that she met Dr Gully and he took the opportunity of asking her to return a book that he had lent Florence. On a second occasion, when Jane met Dr Gully, again by chance, at Balham station, she asked him whether he would send her a prescription. He promised to do so, adding that he would post it to the Priory. It was the arrival of this letter that would reveal perhaps another more secretive aspect of Charles Bravo's character. Firstly Charles would make it his business to be at hand when the postman arrived; he would collect the mail and then open all of the correspondence, no matter to whom it was addressed, before passing it on to either his wife or one of the servants. When the letter containing the prescription arrived from Dr Gully, in the absence of his wife, Charles asked Jane whether he should open the letter as it was in Dr Gully's handwriting. Jane demurred but consented to opening the letter in front of Charles Bravo, showing him that it was simply a prescription from Dr Gully and that the envelope contained nothing else. How did Charles possibly recognise Dr Gully's handwriting? Or, indeed, was he simply pretending that he was able to? The answer to these questions has never come to light, but it may suggest that he had already intercepted a letter from Dr Gully to his wife and could, therefore, recognise the handwriting.

Briefly we should return to the question of Charles Bravo's mother suggesting that Jane should move to Jamaica. It is probable that she was perfectly aware of the fact that Jane had received a letter from her aunt in April 1875, asking her to return to the island. Although Jane had refused to consider this as an option in her conversation with Charles's mother, it does appear that Jane and her aunt had been corresponding about the matter for almost a year. A letter received on 8 March 1876, written by a friend of Jane's aunt, asked: 'Could you not leave the boys and come for a few months? Mrs Cox thinks it would be to your advantage to be here as you understand business so well. Decide quickly.'

Jane's aunt Margaret had even offered to send out the necessary funds to pay for what she hoped would be a one-way trip to the West Indies. It seems that Jane was giving this serious consideration but she was concerned that she would lack the means to return to England as her aunt's friend had suggested. Rather practically, she needed to write a tactful letter asking her aunt to forward sufficient money for a return trip before she committed herself. In the event, and in the absence of Florence, she turned to Charles's father, Joseph, for impartial advice. Joseph Bravo was later to testify:

> I expressed a very strong opinion as to the propriety of her going at once to the island.
> She urged that it would be inconvenient that she did not know what to do with her
> boys. I told her that it was for her boys' future welfare that she should go; that it was
> her duty to her boys as well as to her aunt that she should go. But all in vain.

Was Jane considering going to Jamaica? It seems that we must assume that she was as the prescription that was in Dr Gully's envelope was a homeopathic treatment for Jamaica fever.

Although we are somewhat jumping ahead in time, on 11 April Jane received another letter from her aunt, asking her to come to Jamaica immediately as she was ailing. The letter also said that Joseph Bravo would be asked to advance her outward fare and that money for the return trip would be deposited with Bravo's partner, Mr Solomon.

By this time Florence was back from Brighton and Jane immediately read the letter aloud to her. They then gave the letter to Charles Bravo who, having read it, said 'It seems you will have to go. I will take care of the boys while you are away and I shall be happy to see you on your return.'

In the light of this exchange and in the almost certain knowledge that her way was clear to go to Jamaica and to return, it seems that Jane could not be implicated in the future death of Charles Bravo. Given the assurances of not only looking after her children and a welcome back to the Priory from Charles, why should she wish him dead? If he was to die before she was due to leave, it would impede her ability to make the trip. This factor is probably worth bearing in mind when we consider the events of the next few months.

Returning to matters after the opening of the envelope containing the prescription from Dr Gully, in either late March or early April Florence returned to the Priory from Brighton. On 6 April she miscarried again. This time the situation was far more serious as far as her health was concerned. She was confined to bed for 10 days, in great pain, extremely weak from loss of blood and unable to sleep. In deference to his wife's condition Charles moved into the spare room on the same landing and Jane vacated her bedroom and shared the bed with Florence.

During the period that Florence was confined to bed Jane happened to meet Dr Gully, who was on his way to Bayswater to stay with his son and daughter-in-law. Jane explained to the doctor about Florence's condition and asked him whether he could recommend treatment. Dr Gully knew that most conventional pain killers had an adverse affect on Florence, and said that he would try to discover a sedative that would not have side effects. Mindful of his hydrotherapy treatments, he also suggested that Florence be given cold baths and have her spine washed; he claimed that this would ease the pain and make her more relaxed. Jane was concerned that a communication from Dr Gully with a prescription would immediately be intercepted and misinterpreted by Charles and, given the condition that Florence was in, this was no time to have a re-emergence of the argument between the couple. She therefore asked Dr Gully to send the prescription to her home in Lancaster Road. Since she made regular visits, presumably to collect rent from the tenants, she would be able to pick up the envelope and then cash the prescription. In the event, Dr Gully actually sent the medicine rather than a prescription. It was in a green half-ounce bottle and contained laurel water. Gully knew that this would be a mild enough sedative not to produce any complications.

By 14 April, Good Friday, Florence was sufficiently well to get up for a short period in the middle of the day. It was a holiday period, and Charles had taken advantage of the time to stay at the Priory and not attend his chambers. In an attempt to allay her parents' fears for her health, Florence wrote a letter to her mother:

We hope Papa is gaining strength and that he will soon be quite well [Florence's father had taken ill after returning from a trip to Rome]. Auntie came over yesterday and is looking blooming. Uncle and Peggy are coming tomorrow, and Charlie is looking forward to a game of lawn-tennis. I never saw him look so well. The country is life to him, he walks about with a book under his arm as happy as a king. We leave here on Thursday for Worthing, and hope to return to welcome you and Papa here, and then Ernie and Tot. I am getting stronger, but it is a long business. It seems ages before one feels really well, but by dint of sitz baths and spinal washes I have wooed sleep back, one of the most important steps to recovery.

It seems clear that Charles managed to get sight of this letter. Florence, after wandering around the house for some time, went to her bedroom to lie down. Charles followed her and wanted to talk. He ignored her polite requests to let her sleep and she had to order him to leave the room. Jane Cox witnessed the argument and claimed that Charles had said 'She's a selfish pig. Let her go back to Gully'. It transpired that Charles was actually suffering from another bout of neuralgia, and with soothing words from Jane went to his bedroom where she brought him a hot mixture of brandy and lemon. Whether Charles thought he had an ally in Jane is unclear but he told her that the quarrel was not anything to do with her, and said 'You are a good little woman' and kissed her cheek.

On Easter Saturday Florence was sufficiently well to accompany Jane Cox to Streatham to collect the three boys and bring them to the Priory for the weekend. The headmaster told them that they could only leave school on Easter Monday. The women arranged to pick them up on the Monday and then drove back to the Priory. By the time they had returned Charles had already set up the tennis court and was playing a game with the butler. Everything was set for Mr Orr and Peggy, Florence's uncle and aunt, and Jane's children to be entertained on 17 April. It seems they all had a pleasant day but what is particularly interesting about events is that after Charles had agreed to meet Mr Orr at the St James Hall Restaurant in Piccadilly the next day for lunch, he had a conversation with Mary Anne Keeber. She encountered him slumped in a chair beside a fire, with his face in his hands. From the evidence of Keeber later, the conversation ran thus:

Charles: Mary Anne I feel very cross.

Keeber: Do you, sir? What is the matter?

Charles: I have toothache, like you do sometimes. What do you take for it?

Keeber: What are you doing for it sir?

Charles: I rub my gums with laudanum, and sometimes chloroform.

The next day, Tuesday 18 April, the decision appears to have already been made that Florence could do with the sea air in order to aid her recovery. Consequently, Jane was packed off to Worthing to try to find somewhere to rent. Charles had received a letter that morning from his mother, which expressed her strong objections to the whole idea of staying in Worthing, on the grounds of expense. Before Jane left Charles told her that he was not going to show the letter to Florence as it would only upset her. Charles had arranged to drive into London with Florence, and at 10am the landau emerged from the Bedford Hill Road gates and after a few minutes passed Dr Gully's Orwell Lodge. It had become habit for Florence not to look in the direction of the house for fear of casting her eyes on Dr Gully, which would, undoubtedly, have brought an outburst from her husband. As they passed the house Charles asked her 'Did you see anybody?' to which Florence replied 'No, I didn't look.' Charles then began to abuse Dr Gully in his normal manner and Florence asked him how he would like it if she kept bringing up the matter of his former mistress. Charles said 'It's no good, we shall never get over it. We had better separate.' It appears that this must have been a statement made in anger, as Charles then asked Florence to forgive him and kiss him. Florence later claimed that she was too hurt, not angry, to kiss him, to which Charles then said 'If you don't kiss me, you will see what I will do when I get home.' Florence was sure that at the very least Charles was threatening to strike her and she kissed him. They drove on to the bank in Stratford Place, then the Bond Street jewellers, Bensons, where Florence paid a bill, and then into Jermyn Street, where Florence dropped Charles off at the Turkish baths. She proceeded to the Haymarket Stores where she bought Charles some tobacco as a peace-offering and a bottle of hair lotion.

Charles, after having had lunch with Mr Orr, walked along Piccadilly where he met Mr McCalmont, who accompanied him on his stroll to Victoria station. He asked McCalmont to join him for dinner at the Priory but unfortunately for Charles, the man had already organised another dinner engagement and had to decline the invitation, saying that he would come the following day.

Charles returned home at around 4pm and seemed both cheerful and affectionate towards Florence. She told him to pop upstairs to his bedroom as she had left him something there. By all accounts purchasing tobacco for her husband was something of a novelty as under normal circumstances Florence would not tolerate smoking in the house. It was acceptable for him to smoke in his own room but nowhere else in the building. It seems, however, that the tobacco, although welcome, did not delay Charles's intention to go out for a horse ride. He did not reappear until 6.30pm, complaining to the coachman and groom that the horse had bolted and that he was quite shaken after a five-mile gallop. He later claimed to Florence that the horse had taken him as far as Mitcham Common. He was pale and haggard-looking and his wife suggested a hot mustard bath, sending the butler upstairs to arrange things and light a fire in her husband's room. The butler, having completed his tasks upstairs, returned to the dining room and finished laying the table, placing a decanted bottle of burgundy in the centre of the table. Charles emerged from his bedroom at around 7.20pm; the evening meal had been delayed to ensure that Jane could join them at the table. She was due to arrive back at around 7.30pm. In fact she arrived at 7.25pm and they sat down to dinner together very punctually at 7.30.

It is worth recounting exactly what happened at the table since it has a great bearing on future events. Florence, shortly before sitting down to dinner, had joined Charles in the morning room. She asked him if he felt better, to which he replied 'I am alright now'. Jane then arrived and they sat down for their meal. Beside Charles's placing was the burgundy which was his preferred drink. Florence and Jane had two decanters of their own, one with sherry and the other with Marsala. The meal was a simple one of whiting, roast lamb and a dish of eggs and anchovies. Charles, however, did not eat the first course and instead opened a letter which had been sent to him by his stepfather. Mistakenly Charles's stockbroker, Meredith Brown, had addressed a letter to Charles at Palace Green; in it were details of Charles's stock market speculations in which he had lost £20. Charles's stepfather had forwarded the letter to Charles with a covering note of his own. In the note his stepfather upbraided him about gambling and it was clear that he was extremely angry. According to Jane 'He went on and on about it. He said the governor had no business to open his letters or write as he had done. He described his stepfather's communication as a shirty letter'.

Rowe, the butler, was later to comment that Charles looked extremely pale and was obviously in a good deal of pain at the meal.

> During the dinner that night Mr Bravo seemed in great pain. He appeared greatly put out by everything. He said in the course of dinner something about a letter from 'the governor' which he had had. Mrs Cox shewed him a photograph of the house [the one that Florence had asked her to look at in Worthing] he threw the picture down as if disgusted and said 'I shall not see it I shall not be there'.

Whatever Charles meant by this, and despite his agitated state, his voracious appetite was unaffected and he still was able to bolt down his food and consume three glasses of burgundy. It is also interesting to note that Rowe said that Florence and Jane managed to get through two bottles of sherry by themselves.

The meal seems to have lasted for around an hour, because by 8.30pm they were all sat in the morning room. At 9pm Charles suggested that his wife ought to go to bed, to which she agreed, asking Jane to get her some wine and water. Jane filled a tumbler with half Marsala and half water and took it upstairs. At 9.15pm it seems that Florence had drunk this drink as she asked Mary Anne Keeber to get her some more. En route to the kitchen she encountered Charles, who was going up to bed; she later commented on how pale and unwell he had looked. Keeber noted that Charles looked angry and did not speak to her, so when she returned with the drink and saw that he was in Florence's room, she stood outside so as not to intrude on their conversation. Here the evidence of what occurred differs. Keeber said that Charles was remonstrating with his wife that she had already drunk too much wine and should not have any more. Florence, on the other hand, later said that her husband had come into her room to wish her goodnight.

By the time Keeber had put Florence's clothes away, Charles was already in his bedroom and the door was shut. Jane was in an armchair beside Florence's bed. By Keeber's account Florence was already asleep and Jane asked the servant to take the two terriers that were asleep in front of the fire out of the room. There is contradictory evidence about whether the door to Florence's room was left closed or ajar. Jane stated that the door to Florence's bedroom was closed both before and after Keeber had taken the dogs away, whereas Keeber seems to infer that at the very least she left the door ajar.

Whatever the case, Keeber had not even got halfway down the stairs when she heard Charles's door open and him shout 'Florence! Florence! Hot water! Hot water!' Both Keeber and Jane reacted, Florence did not. They both barged into his bedroom and saw him sweating profusely. His face had turned an ashen-grey. He screamed again, 'Hot water!' then leant out of the window and was sick. Jane told Keeber to go and fetch the hot water and when she returned three or four minutes later, Charles was sat on the floor beside the window, with Jane behind him, massaging his chest. No sooner had the servant entered the room than Jane barked out another order to get some mustard. When she returned Keeber mixed the mustard into some hot water in the basin and plunged Charles's feet into the mixture. Before she had a chance to rub the mustard into Charles's feet he kicked and then went rigid and collapsed. The conversation was reported by the two women as follows:

Jane: Wake, Charlie! Do wake! Mix some mustard with water in a tumbler quickly!

Keeber: How much?

Jane: Mix and make haste.

Keeber: You had better do it yourself.

Jane unsuccessfully tried to pour the mustard and water down Charles's throat, begging him to swallow it. Charles seems to have managed to drink some but most of it ended up on his chest. Jane then told Keeber to go and make some strong coffee and when she reappeared Charles only swallowed a little before being sick into the basin. Jane then told Keeber to throw away the vomit, wash the basin and bring it back immediately. Despite the seriousness of the commotion, Jane was very much in control and then told Keeber to go and get some camphor. While she was doing this Jane went to get Rowe, the butler, to tell the groom to drive to Streatham and bring Dr Harrison to the house. During all of this Florence was blissfully asleep but Keeber made the decision to wake her up. The servant explained that Florence's husband was unwell, then helped her put on her dressing gown and accompanied her into Charles's bedroom. Florence saw her grey-faced, sweating husband with a mixture of mustard, coffee and vomit all over his nightshirt, being massaged by Jane. Immediately she asked whether a doctor had been called and was horrified to hear that the groom had been sent two miles to bring a doctor. She immediately suggested that a Dr Moore, who lived nearby, should be fetched. Florence ran downstairs to find Rowe, who later said:

She was crying as she came and called out to me to fetch someone quickly. I told her Dr Harrison had been sent for. Never mind, she said, get someone! Get someone from Balham! I don't care who it is! She screamed it at me.

Rowe ran off to get Dr Moore, explaining to him that Charles had had a fit after having been shaken from a rough horse ride.

Florence, meanwhile, had returned to Charles's bedroom and the three women managed to heave his body into an armchair. Before the doctors arrived Florence and Jane somehow managed to put a clean nightshirt on Charles. Dr Moore, who had no prior knowledge of the Bravo household, arrived there at 10.30pm. Florence quickly explained to him that her husband was ill and that she did not know exactly what the matter was. She went on to add that her husband had been very shaken after his horse had bolted but that he had had a hot bath and a good dinner and had retired shortly after 9pm. Dr Moore, with Rowe's assistance, managed to get Charles into bed and then shooed everyone else out of the room while he carried out his examination of the patient. He noted that Charles was unconscious, had dilated pupils, cold skin, a weak pulse and was breathing very heavily. He immediately realised that the patient had been poisoned, but could not identify the substance involved. The doctor went outside and when asked by Florence whether her husband was seriously ill, replied 'I do not think he will recover'. With that Florence burst into tears.

At this point, or soon after, Dr Harrison arrived and Jane sped down the stairs to meet him at the door. She quickly explained what had happened since hearing Charles's screams and then said 'Dr Harrison, I am sure he has taken chloroform'. Dr Harrison then joined Dr Moore for another examination of Charles. They were both mystified and concluded only that 'a large vessel near the heart had given way'. They decided that the patient could be revived by giving him brandy and water but since Charles's jaws were locked, they had to inject the alcohol directly into his mouth by prising open his lips. Having done this the doctors decided that they needed another opinion and confided in Jane that they 'did not think Mr Bravo would live another hour'. Florence suggested that they call on the expertise of Hutchinson Royes Bell, and Dr Harrison wrote him a note to be delivered by carriage. Throughout both doctors agreed that Florence's behaviour was entirely consistent with that of a wife concerned about her husband. Dr Harrison said:

> She lay down beside her husband for a while imploring him 'do speak to me, Charlie dear', and other endearing terms. I knew she had been very unwell. She became exhausted and fell asleep. I roused her as I was afraid she might interfere with the patient's breathing. She rose at once.

Hutchinson Royes Bell was a Harley Street doctor who knew Charles and his family and it would take two hours for the coachman to make the return journey. When Royes Bell arrived with his colleague, Dr Johnson, Jane told him that Charles had confided in her when she had first gone into his bedroom 'I have taken poison. Don't tell Florence'. Royes Bell replied 'It is no good sending for a doctor if you don't tell him what's the matter'. With that he ran into the bedroom to confer with the other doctors.

Before the two London doctors had arrived, at around 1am, Charles, despite remaining unconscious, had been purged and vomited by Moore and Harrison. By the time Royes Bell stood over Charles at around 2.30am he was beginning to regain consciousness. It seems that Charles had a brief conversation with Royes Bell and asked him what he believed to be the matter with him. By about 3.30am Charles seemed a little more relaxed and could confirm to the doctors that he had rubbed laudanum in his gums for his neuralgia and that he may have swallowed some. Johnson was sure that the laudanum could not account for the patient's illness. Rowe then appeared and told the doctors that Jane needed to speak to them. The conversation apparently went something along these lines:

> *Dr Johnson:* Mrs Cox has an important statement to communicate to you.
> *Jane:* When I answered Charlie's cry for help he told me 'I have taken some of that poison. Don't tell Florence'.
> *Dr Johnson:* Did he tell you what poison he took and why and when he took it?
> *Jane:* No nothing more than that.
> *Dr Harrison:* Why did you not tell me this?
> *Jane:* I did.
> *Dr Harrison:* You did nothing of the kind! You told me he had taken chloroform.

With that Dr Johnson returned to Charles and asked him about taking poison to which the patient simply replied that he had taken laudanum for his gums. Charles could not explain why he was ill. He was then asked whether there was any poison in the house. Charles confirmed that there was chloroform, laudanum and rat poison. With that he had another fit of vomiting and severe pain.

Dr Harrison left the house at about 4am and later, at 5.30am, Dr Johnson took away some vomit to be analysed. Royes Bell remained in charge of the patient at the Priory.

The following afternoon, Wednesday 19, at about 3pm, Charles's mother arrived and immediately began restricting the household's access to her son. She had come in response to a telegram sent by Florence. Royes Bell was still trying to discover what poison, if any, Charles had taken and asked him whether he had anything on his mind. Charles simply replied that he wanted to make a will and leave everything to Florence. Later he said to Mary Anne Keeber that they would unfortunately not be going to Worthing and that his next trip would be to Streatham churchyard. Dr Johnson was expected back at around 3pm with the results of the analysis. According to Jane, at about 1pm she had her only opportunity to be alone with Charles since the doctors had arrived. She claimed that their conversation, although brief, had confirmed that Charles had taken some poison. In the event, Johnson arrived at 3.30pm and told the other doctors that it was his belief that arsenic was the cause of the poisoning but that he had been unable to find any sign of it in the sample. It was therefore decided that a fresh sample should be taken.

Charles had another painful night and by dawn on the 20th it seemed that death was fast approaching. Jane had slipped out of the house before breakfast and had gone to the door of Orwell Lodge, where she had told Dr Gully of Charles's illness. He suggested mustard plaster and small doses of arsenic. Florence, meanwhile, was desperate to contact a friend of her father's, the eminent Dr Sir William Gull, and she sent Jane to deliver a letter personally to Gull's house at 74 Brook Street. Dr Gull arrived at the house at about 6.30pm, having been apprised of the situation beforehand by Dr Johnson. Before seeing the patient Jane changed her story once more and claimed to Gull that Charles had said to her 'I have taken poison for Gully. Don't tell Florence'. Gull, in the presence of Royes Bell, told Charles that he had been poisoned and begged him to tell him what he had taken. Charles simply replied with the same story about the laudanum. Gull then asked Royes Bell and Dr Johnson, who had recently joined them, whether there were any samples of the vomit other than what had already been tested. When Gull realised there was still some vomit at the foot of the waste pipe, he ordered that it be collected and sealed in a jar.

Gull was convinced that Charles Bravo was dying of an irritant poisoning and, after he had left, Florence told the remaining doctors that she wished to try a homeopathic remedy recommended by Dr Gully. The remedies recommended by Gully were administered by Charles's own mother. At about 10pm Charles rather dramatically and practically said goodbye to everyone who was assembled in the household. By 4.30am on the following morning his breathing became extremely laboured and he died at 5.30am.

Mr Carter was the coroner for East Surrey and it was clear that Charles's death would have to be referred to him as there could be no question of any of the doctors signing a death certificate. It was Jane who got in touch with him. She told him that Charles had committed suicide and that she would be grateful to him if the family could be spared any unnecessary trauma. She further asked him whether it would be possible for the inquest to be held at the Priory. Carter was most amenable and did not even send notice of the inquest to the newspapers.

The proceedings began on 28 April, and although the coroner seemed happy with the prospect that this was an inquest into a suicide, he was to be shocked by the evidence that would be presented. Sir William Gull had sent the specimen collected in the jar to a pathologist and the result had shown that the cause of death was antimony poisoning taken in the form of tartar emetic. Consequently Charles's stepfather had taken the report to Scotland Yard and an Inspector Clarke had searched the Priory; although he had found both Florence's and Jane's bedrooms to contain a number of patent medicines, none of these had contained the substance. Although the inquest listened to a number of witnesses who could shed light on the relationship between Charles and Florence and relate that Charles had denied poisoning himself, the coroner would not listen to the testimony of Drs Moore and Johnson, nor allow Florence to be called. In the event, the jury were unsure as to how the poison had got into Charles Bravo's body and concluded 'That the deceased died from the effects of a poison – antimony – but we have not sufficient evidence under what circumstances it came into his body'.

Charles Bravo's funeral took place on Saturday 29 April at Lower Norwood Cemetery, but already many of Charles's friends and family were unhappy with the verdict. On the following day Florence and Jane went to stay at 38 Brunswick Terrace, Brighton, as had been planned. Joseph Bravo, Charles's stepfather, had remained at the Priory and was clearly, as far as Florence was concerned, going through his son's possessions.

On 5 May Florence sent a letter to Joseph:

> I am astonished to hear from my solicitor, Mr Brooks, that you have had dear Charlie's drawers sealed, as, legally, nobody but myself has the power to touch one single thing belonging to him, he having left all he possessed to me, and I must ask you to see that nothing he possessed is touched by anyone.
>
> With regard to what he died possessed of I must leave to you: he told me he had £200 a year of his own coming from investments, and of course his books, pictures and private property at Palace Green are now mine. His watch he left at your house, and by his wish I give it to Mr Royes Bell. Please see that it is delivered to him.
>
> My father will take care that I have all my dear husband left me. Poor fellow! How he would have grieved at all this unkind feeling shewn me.
>
> Hoping you and Mrs Bravo are better,
>
> Believe me,
>
> Yours sincerely,
>
> Florence Bravo
>
> P.S. Poor Charlie told me you had promised to allow him £800 a year.

She followed this ill-judged letter to her father-in-law with another the following day:

A letter received this morning from Royes Bell fully confirms my suspicions as to poor Charlie's committing suicide. Hence his motives for reducing our expenditure, as he could not tell me how hard he had been pressed by that dreadful woman [his ex-mistress and her sister, to whom it was claimed that Charles had not paid maintenance or a £500 loan]. I wish he had, poor fellow, for I should not have been hard upon him: but it is a sad reflection on his memory for me, and I intend to sift this matter. We have Sir W. Gull's evidence, and I shall not allow the living to be under imputation such is cast upon them by such a wicked verdict.

Florence had jumped to the conclusion that Joseph Bravo was taking action on his own account and that she now believed to have discovered a reason why Charles had been driven to commit suicide. In both instances she was to be proved wrong. Charles Bravo's ex-mistress had never actually caused any trouble, so why did Florence think that she would do so now?

By now the inquest process and verdict was being called into question by both the medical and legal profession, and notably *The Telegraph* newspaper. On a daily basis Florence was receiving anonymous letters at Brunswick Terrace. In order to stave off any further unpleasantness, and on the advice of her father, Florence published the offer of a reward of £500 to anyone who could prove that tartar emetic had been sold to anyone in the Priory.

The Treasury solicitor, Mr Stephenson, carried out an independent enquiry into the inquest and decided on 11 July that a second inquest had to be called. This time it was to be held in the Bedford Hotel, next to Balham station, and unlike the first inquest it was filled with curious spectators and members of the press. The Crown had engaged Sir John Holker; Florence was represented by Sir Henry James, and Mr Murphy, QC acted for Jane Cox. Even Joseph Bravo was represented at the inquest by a Mr Lewis and later Dr Gully sent Mr Parry and Mr Smith to watch the case on his behalf. Before the inquest could formally open the jury was taken to Norwood Cemetery to view the corpse, but when the jury returned to the hotel the real drama began.

The three most important statements made by witnesses were those of Florence herself, Jane and Dr Gully. Jane was convinced that Charles had committed suicide, primarily out of his jealousy of Dr Gully. She relayed the conversation that she had had privately with Charles and much of what she was to say tallied with Florence; they had obviously rehearsed their evidence while in Brighton. Jane denied knowing that Florence and Dr Gully were lovers; she had suspected it but was not sure.

When Florence was called to the witness stand, although appearing on the verge of a nervous breakdown, her answers to begin with were clear and firm. She was taken through the whole story of her first marriage, her attachment to Dr Gully and particular attention was repeatedly paid to when her relationship with Gully had begun and when it had ended. She was mercilessly cross-examined, which *The Times* described as leaving her 'a crushed and humiliated woman'.

Finally, on the 22nd day of the inquest, Wednesday 9 August, it was the turn of Dr Gully to give what little evidence he could about the circumstances of Charles Bravo's death. Gossip and rumour had been reinforced by unflattering newspaper comments about the impropriety of Dr Gully's relationship with Florence. After all, he had met her as a professional medical man and somehow they had ended as lovers. However, there was not a shred of evidence to link Gully with Charles's death. What was sufficient was that a man in his sixties had an attractive and adoring young mistress. It had been the crown's plan to infer that Dr Gully had prescribed medicines to Florence in order to bring about a miscarriage. He flatly denied the accusation and claimed that after October 1875 he had only seen her once regarding the marriage settlement. Since then he had not seen her, although he had, through Jane, sent a bottle of laurel water.

What still remained was the fact that Charles Bravo had died as a result of ingesting forty grains of antimony. Where had it come from? It appeared that there had been a considerable amount of tartar emetic in the house just three months before he died. Griffiths, the coachman, had used it for Florence's horses and it had also been used at Dr Gully's stables in Malvern. It emerged that the amount of the substance was so huge at the Priory that despite only having four horses to care for, Griffiths had enough for a hundred animals. There was also another serious implication regarding Griffiths; Charles Bravo had dismissed him in January and before he left he claimed that he had poured what remained of the substance down a drain in the stable yard.

Although we cannot be clear exactly what was going through the minds of the jury as they delivered their verdict on the 23rd day, Friday 11 August, it seems clear that some issues had been established. Firstly, Charles Bravo must have taken the poison, probably in liquid form, sometime after 7.30pm. By the testimony of the witnesses this could have only been delivered in two forms; either in the burgundy or in the water in his bottle on the bedroom wash stand. As far as the medical experts were concerned, it was their opinion that it was probably in the water, since Rowe had been in sight of the decanter of burgundy in the dining room for most of the time. The other inference was that both Florence and Jane had been upstairs for the best part of an hour as they had gone to bed at around 8.30pm and Charles Bravo had not retired until 9.30pm. Unfortunately neither the remains of the liquid in the decanter nor the bottle could be accounted for and therefore could not be analysed. Dr Harrison and Dr Moore had been given wine from a fresh bottle of burgundy.

With all of these imponderables, the jury were initially uncertain about their verdict. Three of the 16 jurors, after three and a half hours of deliberation, still could not agree with the other 13. Reluctantly the coroner decided to accept a majority verdict, which read:

> We find that Mr Charles Delaunay Turner Bravo did not commit suicide; that he did not meet his death by misadventure; that he was wilfully murdered by the administration of tartar emetic; but there is not sufficient evidence to fix the guilt on any person or persons.

This verdict left Jane, Florence and, to a lesser extent, Dr Gully suspected of having jointly or severally organised the death of Charles Bravo. The newspapers were full of conjecture;

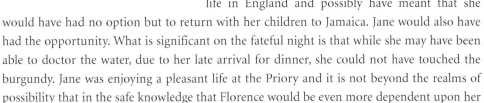

Florence Bravo after the trial.

many openly accused one or more of the three of having conspired to murder. Others, however, took a more reasonable line and suggested that the poisoning may have been no more than an accident.

What then could be the solution? Firstly we could consider Griffiths, the coachman. He had access to antimony, but was no longer employed at the Priory. If he had wished to wreak some kind of revenge on Charles Bravo for his dismissal, then in order to deliver the poison he must have had someone working for him inside the household. None of the servants readily come to mind as being potential accomplices.

Jane Cox is a much more credible suspect. She was aware that Charles Bravo wished to dispense with her services, which would have undermined her life in England and possibly have meant that she would have had no option but to return with her children to Jamaica. Jane would also have had the opportunity. What is significant on the fateful night is that while she may have been able to doctor the water, due to her late arrival for dinner, she could not have touched the burgundy. Jane was enjoying a pleasant life at the Priory and it is not beyond the realms of possibility that in the safe knowledge that Florence would be even more dependent upon her should her husband die, she may have considered murdering Charles.

As far as Florence Bravo is concerned, it seems somewhat unlikely that she had either the will or the ability to approach the murder of her husband alone. She may have wished to return to the carefree and uncontrolled life that she had enjoyed prior to meeting and marrying Charles Bravo.

As for Dr Gully, there is no evidence to suggest that he wished to renew his liaison with Florence. With the exception of the laurel water and much older homeopathic medicines which were found in the Priory, there was no way for Gully to deliver the poison into Charles Bravo's body. Gully may have mourned the loss of Florence and the circumstances under which their relationship had ended, but it seems that he had reconciled himself to a solitary and peaceful retirement.

One possible explanation is that Florence and Jane conspired to poison Charles, possibly without intending to kill him. Florence had suffered two recent miscarriages and would probably have wished to avoid falling pregnant again in the short term. Given that contraception was not widely practised, it was not unknown for women to give an emetic to their husbands to make them sick, in an attempt to dampen their husband's desire to return to their beds. If we accept that this may have been the case, then the second major point to consider is the fact that both Florence and Jane had drunk a considerable amount of alcohol that night. Possibly their initial consumption was to embolden them to put the emetic in Charles's water. Unfortunately they probably drank too much and by accident added more than they intended. Both of the women could then be considered innocent of attempted murder, but nevertheless they could have been too frightened to admit that the presence of antimony was on account of what they had done that night. This may account for Jane's contradictory statements to the various doctors.

The verdict of the jury at the inquest left the authorities with no grounds for further action. It is believed that Jane did finally end up in Jamaica with her children. Dr Gully died seven years later, his reputation sullied by his association with the Bravo case. Florence rewrote her will on 20 February 1877 and died on 21 September 1878 at Coombe Lodge, Southsea, at the age of 33, as a result of emotional collapse and alcoholism. She was buried in Buscot churchyard. She left in excess of £60,000 to her brother, William, and just £100 to each of Jane Cox's three children.

CHAPTER NINE

THE IRELAND'S EYE TRAGEDY

The Conviction of William Kirwan – Dublin, 1852

AT AROUND 10am on Monday 6 September 1852, William and Maria Kirwan boarded the boat of a local fisherman called Patrick Nangle in Howth Harbour in County Dublin. They had brought with them a hand basket and bag as it was their intention to spend a pleasant day on the picturesque little island called Ireland's Eye. The rocky isle about a mile from the harbour was an ideal picnic spot and on it was the ruined chapel of St Nessan, a Martello tower and a wonderful deserted beach. It was a hot summer's day and an ideal place for William, an artist, and his wife to visit.

William Kirwan and his wife were both in their thirties and had been married for 12 years. William Burke Kirwan, to give him his full name, was an artist, habitually seen with his sketching materials. He was described as being a stout, dark man, slightly older than his wife. Maria Louisa Kirwan was a strongly built woman, described as being very good looking, who was extremely fond of bathing and was a strong swimmer. The couple lived at 11 Upper Merrion Street, Dublin and had spent the last six weeks in Howth in summer lodgings. Monday 6 September was the penultimate day of their holiday.

Armed with sufficient food for the day, William's artist's materials and his wife's bathing costume, cap and bath sheet, they made the short journey across to the island and arranged for Patrick Nangle to collect them at 8pm that evening. They were deposited near the Martello tower in the north-west corner of the island. The sun would set at 6.36pm. Sometime later, at around noon, Nangle came out to the island again, bringing another family who were to stay on the island until 4pm.

All was not straightforward in the Kirwan household. Indeed, according to William Kirwan's landlady in Howth, Kirwan only slept in the boarding house three or four nights a week. On the other nights he would be in Dublin. While it might be assumed that William had to return to Dublin on account of his work as an artist who coloured maps of the city and was an anatomical draughtsman, it was for a completely different purpose that he made the visits. William Kirwan had a mistress called Teresa Kenny throughout his married life. Not only did Kirwan make frequent visits to Teresa and sleep at her house in Sandymount, on the outskirts of Dublin, but he was the father of her seven children. She was known locally as Mrs Kirwan and she lived in some style, even having a servant. As the prosecuting counsel would later say to the jury:

> It so happened, or was so managed, that neither Maria Kirwan nor Teresa Kenny had either of them the least notion or idea of each other's existence until a comparatively recent period. These facts, gentlemen, will appear in the evidence; nay, more, with such consummate art was this system of double deception carried on, that it was only within the last six months that either of these two women became aware of the fact that each had a rival in the prisoner's affections.

To return to Island's Eye on 6 September, what is clear is that the other group of people saw the Kirwans several times in different places on the island, apparently happy and very much alive. As Patrick Nangle approached the island at 4pm to collect the other group, one of them offered Maria a trip back to the mainland, since it appeared that she might have been ready to leave. She declined, saying that she had arranged to be collected at 8pm and was quite happy to stay on the island until then.

What happened in the next four hours can only be certainly known by William Kirwan himself. The couple were left alone until Nangle's return. Four individuals on the mainland and a fisherman who was just off the coast claimed to have heard cries from the island at some point during the afternoon or early evening. One of the witnesses was Alicia Abernethy; she lived near the harbour at Howth and in her own words she heard 'a dreadful screech as of a person in agony and pain'. She claimed that she later heard more cries but that they were fainter. She was certain about the time as she had only just asked her next-door neighbour who had replied that it was 7.05pm. At around 7pm another woman, Catherine Flood, who worked in a house on the quay, claimed to have heard 'a very wild scream'. She also stated that she had heard several other screams and that the last one was cut terrifyingly short. She claimed to have heard these screams at around 7.05 or 7.06. Despite the fact that three other people on the mainland and a fisherman heard similar cries, no one chose to investigate. John Barrett, who lived in a house near the East Pier, claimed to have heard 'screeches abreast the harbour' at around 7pm. He walked over to the pier and heard two or three more screams and was certain that they came from the direction of Ireland's Eye. Another of the witnesses, Hugh Campbell, describing the time as 'between day and dark' heard three cries from the direction of the island 'resembling the call of a person for assistance'. It was Campbell that later testified that about half an hour after he had heard the screams he saw Patrick Nangle's boat heading for Ireland's Eye. This was a significant feature as Kirwan's defence counsel would later suggest that the cries were those of Kirwan and Nangle searching for Maria.

Thomas Larkin was steering his fishing boat into Howth harbour and passed to the west of Ireland's Eye. His 38-tonne boat with nine crew passed very close to the Martello tower and he heard 'a great screech'. By now, of course, it was getting dark, but there was enough light for him to be certain that he had not seen anyone on the island. About five minutes later he heard a second scream and then one or two minutes after, a third. None of the crew had heard anything, but he was concerned that the screams sounded like someone in trouble. As he moored the boat in the harbour he looked back to the island but it was now shrouded in darkness.

At around 7.40pm Patrick Nangle, his cousin Michael and two other men left Howth harbour bound for Ireland's Eye and their rendezvous with the Kirwans. Obviously it was dark and they did not reach the island until 8pm, landing again beside the Martello tower. Nangle called out as he could see neither of his passengers waiting for him. There was now a strange conversation which began reasonably enough. Nangle heard Kirwan's voice first, saying 'Nangle, come up for the bag'. Nangle went ashore and encountered Kirwan standing on his own on a high rock, just above the place that they had landed. He took the bag and sketch book from Kirwan and headed back to the boat. His cousin Michael passed him on the way and saw Kirwan walking towards the boat.

'Where is the mistress?' asked Michael.

'I have not seen her for the last hour and a half', Kirwan replied.

'Sir, you should have had the mistress here, and not have to be looking for her at this hour of the night; what way did she go?' chided Michael.

'She went that way. I was sketching at the time she left me after the last shower. She did not like to bathe where I told her to bathe because there was a bad smell there', Kirwan explained.

He was pointing in the direction of the Long Hole, which was a narrow creek or rocky inlet on the opposite side of the island from the mainland. The Long Hole is an inlet 360ft long, narrow at the entrance and wider at the head, enclosed by steep banks and cliffs. From low to high water mark the distance is around 163ft. The area is divided into two channels by a large rock in the middle which is some 22ft high. On the landward side of the rock the tide rises about a foot at high water. The surrounding strand is of coarse gravel, interspersed with rocks, and 12ft above the low water mark a low barrier of rocks stretches across the channel, here 28ft in width. Just within this barrier, at the base of the south-eastern side of the gully, is a small rock, 3ft long and 12in high.

By now all of the men were ashore and calling for Mrs Kirwan. William shouted 'Maria, why don't you answer, the boat is waiting'. However, initially their search was in vain and they returned to the boat.

Michael, irritated, said:

This is a fine job to be here at this hour of the night. Where are we to find this woman? Let us leave the other two men in the boat and we will go round again; if Mrs Kirwan comes in the meantime, they can go on the top of the bank and hail us.

Patrick, Michael and Kirwan began their second painstaking search of the island. As they reached the Long Hole, Kirwan stumbled and fell over and it was then that Patrick Nangle saw something white lying on the rocks below. Maria's body was on a small rock, out of the water. They scrambled down and saw that she was lying on her stomach. Beneath her was her bathing sheet, which was soaking wet, as was her bathing dress, which had been pushed up under her armpits, exposing most of her body. There was no sign of her bathing cap; this would not be found for another fortnight. Her bathing boots were still on and there was gravel and seaweed all over her body, particularly in her hair. There was blood on her face and chest from a series of scratches and trickles of blood ran from her nose, eyes and ears. Patrick felt the body and it was still quite warm and flexible. Kirwan was heard to exclaim 'Oh Maria, Maria'. Patrick Nangle readjusted her bathing dress, straightened her arms and legs and tied the bathing sheet around her at the neck and knees.

Oddly, Kirwan then pointed to a nearby rock and said 'We would get them there on the rock', referring to Maria's clothes. Neither of the Nangles had seen the clothes there, despite having looked previously and seen nothing. Patrick apparently went up to the rock to collect the clothes, but again saw nothing. Kirwan then took it upon himself to find the clothes and came back with a shawl and another garment. He then asked Patrick to go up and collect the rest of the clothes and he found them despite the fact that he later said 'I had searched the very same place before and did not find them.' They wrapped the shawl around Maria's head and then Michael and Patrick left to bring the boat round to collect the body. Kirwan refused to leave his wife and apparently threw himself on the body, crying. An hour later the boat was in position at Long Hole and those in it saw Kirwan still lying with his head on the body of his wife. They wrapped the body in a sail and it was carried through the knee-deep water to the boat.

The body was taken back to Howth and laid out on the floor of Mrs Campbell's lodgings. It is interesting to note that although Mrs Campbell was short-sighted, and did not examine Maria's body closely, she did see that Kirwan's trousers were wet. In fact his boots, stockings, trousers and undergarments had to be dried in front of the kitchen fire. This was strange as neither Kirwan nor any of the other men apart from the one that carried Maria's body through the water and into the boat had got wet in the sea.

There were three other women in the house that night. One, a sick nurse with 40 years' experience called Mrs Lacy, was told by Kirwan to wash the body. The women told him that the police would not want the body tampered with until they had seen it and an inquest had been held. Kirwan said 'I don't care a damn for the police; the body must be washed.' No doubt evidence was washed away that night by Anne Lacy and Catherine M'Garr in the candlelight provided by Mary Robinson. When they unwrapped the sail from around the body they saw that there was a great deal of blood soaked into the fabric, but the body was still quite flexible. Anne Lacy later testified 'the face was covered with blood; the blood came from a cut about the eyes, and on the cheek and forehead; the ears were also loaded with blood, which was still running from the inside of them; I sponged and washed the ears, but the blood continued flowing afterwards for nearly half an hour'. The women also noted several other features about the body; there was a cut on Maria's right breast that was still bleeding, her lips were swollen, her eyes red and her neck twisted. Mrs M'Garr described the wounds around her eyes as looking as if they were torn, she said that Maria's nose was bent and her lips were covered with slime. There was blood coming out of her left breast and from her ears. Mary Robinson confirmed what Mrs M'Garr had noted.

At around 1 or 2pm on Tuesday 7 September the body was officially examined by a medical student called Mr Hamilton. He gave what he called a 'superficial examination', assuming that the woman had drowned. Unfortunately there was no other more experienced individual available to carry out the examination, but Hamilton had been studying for around six years. Later in the afternoon, under the direction of the coroner, Mr Davis, the Nangles were asked about what they had seen and done. It seems that according to the coroner, Kirwan continually interrupted them, trying to put them straight on facts that would support his version of events. Kirwan himself made only the following statement at the inquest:

> I am an artist, residing at number eleven Upper Merrion Street, Dublin. The deceased lady, Maria Kirwan was my wife; I was married to her about nine or ten years. I have been living with Mrs Kirwan in Howth for five or six weeks. I was in the habit of going over to Ireland's Eye as an artist. Mrs Kirwan used to accompany me; she was very fond of bathing, and while I would be sketching she would amuse herself roaming about or bathing. Yesterday we went over as usual. She bathed at the Martello tower on going over, but could not stay long in the water as the boatmen were to bring another party to the island. She left me in the latter part of the day, about 6 o'clock, to bathe again. She told me she would walk round the hill after bathing and meet me at the boat. I did not see her alive afterwards, and only found the body as described by the sailors.

It should be pointed out that a number of issues were not brought up at the inquest. The coroner was unaware that anyone had heard cries emanating from Ireland's Eye. Kirwan did not mention the screams, nor did he tell the inquest that his wife was an epileptic. There was no other reasonable course of action than for the jury to return a verdict of 'found drowned'. It was presumed by many that the burial of Maria Kirwan at Glasnevin cemetery would be the end of the affair.

As if the tragedy of the loss of his wife had not been enough for Kirwan, he now found that his double life was about to unravel. It soon became public knowledge that Kirwan had a mistress and seven children posing as his family. One of Kirwan's neighbours in Dublin, a Mrs Byrne, claimed to have predicted the death of Maria and went on to describe Kirwan as 'Bloody Billy'. Very soon the Dublin press were full of stories and it was clear that Kirwan's past was beginning to catch up with him. The newspapers claimed that in 1837 Kirwan had been tried before the Recorder for the burglary of a Mr Bowyer's house in Mountjoy Street, Dublin, removing property which he later disposed of. Apparently Kirwan was released, not because he was innocent but because of a legal technicality. It was further suggested that he had murdered Bowyer and had been paying his widow £40 a year to keep her mouth shut.

There was also another murder charge levelled at Kirwan from the past. It was claimed that he had killed his own brother-in-law, a Mr Crowe. 'That Kirwan murdered him, according to the statement of the parties preferring the charges, was beyond all doubt, because he accompanied him to Liverpool, and Crowe was not heard of since.'

Inevitably these stories brought the press knocking on the doors of the Nangles and the nurses that had tended the body of Maria Kirwan. The fact that there was so much blood led the press to assume that Maria had been run through with a sword. It also became common knowledge that Kirwan was a Protestant and that Maria was a Catholic, giving yet another dimension to the case. Eventually, just over 30 days after Maria had died, her body was exhumed on 6 October 1852. Two doctors, George Hatchell and Tighe, carried out another post-mortem. Unfortunately the body had been buried in a particularly boggy area of the cemetery and the coffin was actually submerged in over 2ft of water, which cannot have helped their examinations. The doctors, however, were now suspicious about the death and consequently Kirwan was arrested and charged with Maria's murder. It is significant to note that when he was arrested in his Dublin home the police found Teresa Kenny and her seven children living with him.

The trial opened on Wednesday 8 December 1852 at Green Street, Dublin. The Commission of Oyer and Terminer was presided over by the Honourable Philip C. Crampton and the Right Honourable Baron Richard W. Greene. Kirwan was defended by Isaac Butt, QC, the founder of the Home Rule party, Walter Burke, QC, William W. Brereton, QC and John A. Curran. The prosecution was led by Edmund Hayes, QC and John Pennefather. Kirwan was formally charged that he 'did wilfully, feloniously, and of his malice prepense kill and murder one Maria Louisa Kirwan on Ireland's Eye in the County of Dublin on September 6th'. Kirwan pleaded not guilty to the charge.

The prosecution began by calling Alfred Jones, who was a surveyor that had been instructed to measure and calculate all the dimensions of the area surrounding the Long Hole. He told the court that at around 3.30pm there would be about 7ft of water over the rock where Maria's body had been found. By 6.30pm the depth would be 2ft 6in, at 7pm 1ft 9in and at 7.30pm just 1ft. By 8.00pm it would be only 3 inches. This explained why, by the time the body was found, the water had receded to 2ft below the rock. He was also able to tell the court that when the Nangles arrived in their boat Mr Kirwan was standing only 792 yards from the body.

The next witness was the Kirwan's landlady in Howth, Margaret Campbell. She confirmed that they had moved into her lodgings in June and that Kirwan was often away for at least three nights a week. She also said that she had heard the couple quarrelling:

> I heard angry words from Mr Kirwan to his wife. I heard him say he would make her
> stop there; I heard him miscall her; I heard him call her a strumpet. I heard him say
> 'I'll finish you.' I do not think they had been a month with me at that time. On the

same evening I heard her say to him, 'let me alone, let me alone'. Next morning I heard her say to him she was black from the usage she had got the preceding night across her thighs.

Margaret Campbell also described Mrs Kirwan's daily routine, which included having a daily swim, commenting that it appeared to her that Maria was in good health throughout her whole stay with her. She confirmed that the Kirwans had spent the Thursday and the Friday before Maria's death on Ireland's Eye and returned to their lodgings at around 9pm. She then went on to describe what had happened when the body had been brought back the following Monday and the state of Mrs Kirwan's clothing. Even under cross-examination she repeated that she had heard the couple quarrelling but had only heard threatening language on the one occasion and was sure that Kirwan had only assaulted his wife on the one time that she had described.

Another witness who had been in the house at the time of the alleged assault against Maria by her husband was Anne Hanna, who was Mrs Kirwan's washer-woman. She claimed to have heard Kirwan shouting 'I'll end you, I'll end you.' This had been preceded by the sound of furniture being knocked over and a general scuffle.

When Patrick Nangle was called he recounted his brief and superficial relationship with the Kirwans, but his evidence regarding the body was of particular significance. He described the fact that he had had to scrub the sail that had enveloped Maria's body with a broom because it was so saturated with blood. He told the court that the body was not stiff, that the scratches on the face could not have been caused by crabs, that Maria's mouth was frothing and that there was blood flowing out of the lower part of her body. It was his opinion that the body could not have been bruised by the pebbles, although there was a good deal of bruising to the body. He admitted that he was confused about the issue of Mrs Kirwan's clothes as he claimed to have systematically searched the area and found nothing and it was not until Mr Kirwan had gone up to look for the clothes himself that their whereabouts had been discovered. He also confirmed that as far as he was aware no one else apart from the Kirwans was on Ireland's Eye between 4pm and 8pm. As for the evidence that Mr Kirwan's clothes were soaked when he arrived back at the lodging house, Patrick was certain that there had been insufficient water in Long Hole to cause this.

For the most part Michael Nangle's evidence tallied with that given by Patrick. He suggested that the Long Hole was not an ideal bathing spot; it had sharp rocks both under the water and at its mouth and head. He said that he too had looked for Mrs Kirwan's clothes and that Mr Kirwan had 'brought down something white in his hand like a sheet, and also a shawl'. He too claimed that Mr Kirwan had not had the opportunity to be soaked while he was with them. Michael had not had a close look at the body until the following day due to the darkness, and only then had he seen Maria's face.

There was still the issue of the sheet which Michael believed Kirwan had brought down from the rock. Patrick, on the other hand, had been certain that it was under Mrs Kirwan's body. If Kirwan had brought it down it would have been dry, while if it had been under the body then it would have been wet. Since it was Patrick that actually tied the sheet around Maria, perhaps his testimony was correct. If Kirwan had not brought the sheet down then what was he carrying in addition to the shawl? It was clear what clothes had been found on the rock; these were all accounted for. As we will discover, it is likely that this was Maria's chemise and it was missing.

Both Arthur Brew and Thomas Giles could add little to what the court had already been told. Brew had been part of the other group that had left Ireland's Eye at 4pm and he could only tell the court of his sightings of the Kirwans and the brief conversation with Maria. Giles, who had been on the boat with the Nangles, had seen far less than either Patrick or Michael and again he could add little to what had already been testified.

The five individuals that had heard the screams emanating from Ireland's Eye had all heard almost the same thing within a matter of minutes of one another. They were all sure of what they had heard at around 7pm that night.

The court's final business that day was to listen to the testimony of the women who had laid out and washed Maria's body. Their testimony all seemed to hang together jointly and severally and at least one of them, when asked, clearly stated that she did not believe that the scratches on Maria's face had been caused by crabs.

Joseph Sherwood, who was a police sergeant based in Howth, was the first witness to be called on Thursday 9 December. He had examined the body in Margaret Campbell's kitchen and he described the corpse's eyes as being bloodshot, the mouth as being swollen and there being a cut on the right temple. He had been present when Mrs Kirwan's bathing cap was found in Long Hole on 11 September and he described the string of the bathing cap to have had a very tight knot still in it. He had also heard the screams from Ireland's Eye on the day of Maria's death. When he had arrested Kirwan on 7 October he confirmed that he had also encountered Teresa Kenny and her children in the house in Upper Merrion Street. On the question of the chemise, Sherwood confirmed to the court that he had not seen one and that the rest of the clothes had no bloodstains on them and were clean.

The next witness, the Kirwan's servant in Dublin, could add little to the proceedings, apart from confirming that she had worked for them for twelve months and that the couple had no children of their own.

Although Teresa Kenny had been called to give evidence to the court she failed to appear. However, there were other witnesses that could shed light on Kirwan's relationship with Kenny. The first was William Bridgeford, who was the owner of Sandymount and therefore Kirwan and Kenny's landlord. He confirmed that the Kirwan's tenancy had begun in 1848 and that as far as he was concerned Mrs Kenny was, in fact Kirwan's wife and the children were his. He did concede, however, that communication with Kenny had simply been signed Teresa and not Teresa Kirwan. Kirwan and Kenny's servant at Sandymount, Catherine Byrne, also believed that Kenny was Mrs Kirwan but added that on one occasion a strange lady had appeared at the house asking questions about the couple.

The court was now to hear from the medical experts, those that had examined Maria's body soon after her death and then a month later during the post-mortem. Dr George Hatchell had been present when the body was exhumed, confirming that the coffin was steeped in water due to the boggy conditions of the land in that part of the cemetery. He said that decomposition of the body had unfortunately been accelerated by the wet conditions but that he was sure of many of the tests and examinations that he had carried out. Firstly he said that the head itself showed no signs of damage. There were scratches around the right eye and the eyes were bloodshot. The lobe of the right ear was missing and the body's lips were swollen and the tongue was marked. He was sure that neither the neck nor the back was damaged but there was a superficial scratch on the right breast. The lower part of the body was very swollen and the lungs filled with blood. He felt that this was particularly significant. He was asked by the prosecution 'from the appearances you observe on the body, are you able as a medical man, to form an opinion as to the cause of death and what is that opinion?' Hatchell replied:

> I am of the opinion that death was caused by asphyxia or a sudden stopping of respiration. I should say that in all probability the simple stoppage of respiration must have been combined with pressure of some kind, or constriction, which caused the sudden stoppage. I do not think that simple drowning would produce to the same extent the appearances I saw.

When Hatchell was cross-examined he reiterated the fact that the body would not display what he had discovered in a drowning incident. He believed that there had been a struggle of some description. He suggested that Maria could have had a fit, particularly if she had been swimming on a full stomach, but when it was suggested that it may have been an epileptic fit he was sure that he had not heard of someone suffering from epilepsy screaming more than once.

The final prosecution witness was Henry Davis, who had been the coroner at the original inquest into the death of Maria Kirwan. He believed that the scratches on the body had been caused by green crabs biting her after she had died.

Before we turn to the defence witnesses, it is significant to note that at no point had the prosecution suggested how Kirwan had murdered his wife. They had not suggested that he had strangled her, smothered her or held her head under the water. This would be a feature that would recur throughout the whole of the defence case.

Before any witnesses were called Isaac Butt, QC, leading for the defence, addressed remarks to the jury. Firstly he pointed out the fact that his client had been presumed to be the murderer by the prosecution on account of three circumstantial issues. Firstly, he said it was inferred that the state of the body led the prosecution to believe that Maria had been murdered. Secondly, that there were cries from the island which the jury was being asked to believe were cries for help. Thirdly, that the prosecution had claimed that not only was his client a bigamist, but that he had also beaten Maria Kirwan. He proposed to illustrate to the jury that whatever happened on Ireland's Eye could only have been witnessed by two individuals. The first witness, Maria Kirwan, was dead, and the second witness, William Kirwan, was unable to give evidence in the court. Butt then reiterated many of the issues that he had brought up in cross-examination of the prosecution's witnesses. Although Dr Hatchell had suggested that Maria Kirwan could have been strangled, where were the injuries to her neck and throat? If she had been smothered or crushed to death, surely there would be injuries to the face and body? If his client had struggled with the deceased, surely there would be some sign of injury on his body? Why was Maria's face scratched, and why was there sand and seaweed in her hair? Surely this illustrated the fact that she had floundered among the rocks and drowned? In any case, if Kirwan had followed his wife into the sea and drowned her, why was he not soaked from head to foot? It was Butt's opinion that his client loved his wife and that the reason that the bottom half of his body was wet was that he had clung to the body of Maria for some time while the boatmen had brought their vessel around to Long Hole to collect the corpse. Butt did not feel that the mysterious issue about Maria's clothing was particularly significant and suggested that the discrepancy had only occurred because Patrick Nangle had become confused after the shock of finding the body.

In the event Butt only called two witnesses. It is significant that they had both been sitting in court for the whole of the proceedings. They were both doctors and proposed to give their professional opinion of the potential causes of death. The first was Dr Rynd. While he admitted that the probable cause of death was asphyxia, he pointed out that there were no injuries to the body consistent with strangulation. It was his opinion that the fact that Maria had gone swimming with a full stomach could have brought on an epileptic fit. He also contradicted Dr Hatchell and said that an epileptic would scream more than once. He felt that it was perfectly reasonable to assume that the way in which the body had bled was consistent with his theory. When he was cross-examined he was asked whether he knew of another case when a drowning had caused such bleeding. He admitted that he had not but was sure that given the fact that Maria Kirwan had been drowned, the blood would remain fluid for some time. When asked whether the body would appear as it had done if someone had held a wet sheet over the mouth, the doctor admitted that this would be the case. He knew something of Mrs Kirwan's medical history and described her as being young and strong, adding that her own father had died from epilepsy.

Dr Adams, although admitting that epileptics rarely screamed more than once, confirmed much of what Dr Rynd had already told the court. He conceded that a wet sheet over the mouth and nose would appear to be a drowning incident. He recounted the fact that he had not encountered a drowning accident where there was bleeding from the organs as had been witnessed in this case. He also conceded that it was unlikely that epilepsy could have caused the bleeding. Adams was certain, however, that any pressure applied to the body would have been evident on the corpse. He was asked by one of the judges 'supposing death to have taken place by forcible submersion, or from accidental drowning, would you be able, from the appearances described, to state to which species of death they were attributable?' Adams replied 'My Lord, in my opinion, no man living could do so'.

Mr Edmund Hayes, QC began to sum up the prosecution, dealing with each issue in turn:

Is it reasonable to suppose that a man had been living with a concubine for ten years, and during all that time gave her his name, while he was beating his legitimate wife at Howth, could you entertain connubial affection for the woman he treated so grossly? If there was any evidence that this lady had been previously affected by epilepsy or anything of that kind, there might have been a shadow of ground upon which to found the assertion. As the prisoner has forborne to produce such testimony, it is not too much to infer that there was none to produce; we must take it as proved the deceased was a perfectly healthy woman. Let us suppose her in this water, two foot nine inches deep; let us suppose the prisoner coming into the hole with the sheet in his hand, after taking it from the place in which it was left, ready to put it over her head; let us suppose she saw his dreadful purpose; can you not then conceive and account for the dreadful shrieks that were heard, when the horrid reality burst upon her mind that on that desolate, lonely island, without a living soul but themselves upon it, he was coming into that long hole to perpetrate his dreadful offence? Would not the consequence have been the dreadful shrieks that were heard and sworn to? If he succeeded in putting her under the water, notwithstanding her vain efforts to rise, struggling with all her energy against his greater strength, can you not imagine the fearful, agonising and fainter shrieks that men and women from the mainland depose to having heard? That is not a mere imagination; it is a rational deduction from the evidence; and it is for you to say whether, upon all the facts of the case, that might not have occurred or whether the prisoner lost his wife without any fault of his own. You will ask yourselves, gentlemen, whether or not these scratches have any reference to the time when the horrible sheet was being put over the face of the deceased; whether that awful moment she might not have put up her hands to try and remove the sheet, and in endeavouring to do so, tore herself in the manner described.

So many questions remained unresolved yet it was still the defence's contention that the drowning was accidental. In summing up the case for the jury the Honourable Philip C. Crampton warned the jury that much of the evidence was circumstantial. He conceded that it did not appear that Mr and Mrs Kirwan were enjoying a happily married life. Turning to the death itself, while there were no external injuries to the body that could have caused the death, this did not mean that the prosecution's contention that death was caused by wrapping a sheet around Maria's face could not have been the cause of death. He asked the jury to consider how Kirwan had behaved on the day of the death and whether his apparent grief was real or for the benefit of the witnesses. He asked the jury also to consider whether Michael or Patrick Nangle was correct about Maria's clothes. What was clear as far as the judge was concerned was that screams were certainly heard at 7pm; could they have been heard by the prisoner? If so, the crucial question was what had caused these screams. Were they screams of panic or fear from a woman who was being murdered or were they as a result of a fit? The judge also asked the jury to consider whether a woman who was by all accounts a good swimmer would drown in less than three feet of water. How did the body end up on the rock? Did she have a fit there, was she placed there or did the sea sweep her onto the rock?

At 7pm the judges sent the jury to begin considering their verdict. Forty minutes later they returned to inform the court that it was their opinion that their deliberations would take a considerable amount of time. The court was adjourned to allow the jury more time, to be reconvened at 11pm the same night. When the jury re-emerged at this late hour they were still undecided, but asked if they could hear the evidence of Dr Adams once more. In the event the judges decided that it would be unreasonable to rouse the gentleman from his slumber and instead the judges summarised his evidence for the jury. The jury retired once more and within 15 minutes returned a guilty verdict.

The following morning Judge Crampton made the following statement to the court:

Upon this verdict it is not my province to pronounce opinion, but after what has been said I cannot help adding this observation, that I see no reason or grounds to be dissatisfied with it, and, in saying this, I speak the sentence of my learned brother, who sits beside me, as well as my own. You have raised your hand, not in daring vengeance against a man from whom you received or thought you had received provocation or insult; you raised your hand against a female, a helpless unprotected female, who by the laws of God and man was entitled to your protection, even at the hazard of your life, and to your affectionate guardianship. In the solitude of that rocky island, to which you brought her on the fateful 6th September, under the veil of approaching night, when there was no hand to stay and no human eye to see your guilt, you perpetrated this terrible this unnatural crime. No human eye could see how the act was done, none but your own conscience and the all-seeing Providence could develop this mysterious transaction.

Kirwan was asked by the judge whether he wished to make a fresh statement and to answer why a death sentence should not be passed. Crampton interrupted Kirwan, who was simply repeating the evidence that had already been presented to the court, by saying 'I am sorry to interrupt you at this painful moment, but you must be well aware that your counsel entered into all these subjects. It is impossible for me to go into the evidence.' Kirwan simply replied:

Convinced as I am that my hopes in this world are at an end, I do most solemnly declare in the presence of this Court, and before the God before whom I expect soon to stand, that I had neither act, nor part, nor knowledge of my late wife's death, and I state further that I never treated her unkindly as her own mother can testify.

The judges pronounced the sentence of death and Kirwan was sent to Kilmainham prison. However, he did not hang for the murder of his wife and indeed the story does not end here. Evidence was still trickling out about the strange life of the Kirwans and new evidence suggested many key points that had been overlooked during the trial.

The Reverend J.A. Malet produced a pamphlet called *The Kirwan Case.* The key issues touched on in this pamphlet included the fact that Mrs Crowe, Maria's mother, not only attested to the fact that William had been a good husband to her daughter, but that Maria was 'very venturesome in the water, going into the deep parts of the sea, and continuing therein for a much longer period than other ladies.' A Mrs Bentley who claimed to be a close friend of Maria stated that Mrs Kirwan was perfectly well aware of Teresa Kenny and had been informed of the situation by her husband only a month after they had married. She also stated that Maria was prone to having fits. Two other witnesses in the pamphlet claimed that Patrick Nangle had told them that it was his intention to implicate Kirwan by his testimony at the trial. The pamphlet also included a sworn statement by 10 Dublin doctors which claimed that the appearance of Maria's body was 'quite compatible with death caused by simple drowning or by seizure of a fit in the water'. They also attested to the fact that Maria's father had died after having a fit some eight years before. Both Anne Maher and Arthur Kelly, who had worked for the Kirwans, said that they had witnessed Maria having fits on at least two occasions, the last of which had been in the June before her death.

A second pamphlet, written by J. Knight Boswell, a Dublin solicitor, actually contained statements from Teresa Kenny. In it she confirmed that Maria was perfectly well aware of her relationship with William. Kenny had not been able to make an appearance at Kirwan's trial because she had cut her thumb. The most sensational content of the pamphlet was the suggestion that there was another person on Ireland's Eye that day between 4pm and 8pm, a man named John Gorman. He stated that 'Kirwan was as innocent of the murder as the child unborn', and claimed to have disappeared because 'he was afraid of being implicated himself'. The pamphlet also contained the conclusions of the forensic expert, Dr Taylor, which read:

> I assert as my opinion, from a full and unbiased examination of the medical evidence in this case, that so far as the appearances of the body are concerned, there is an entire absence of proof that the death was the result of violence at the hands of another. Persons while bathing, or exposed to the chance of drowning, are often seized with fits which may prove suddenly fatal, although they may allow for a short struggle; the fit may arise from syncope, apoplexy, or epilepsy. Either of the last conditions would, in my opinion, reconcile the medical circumstances of this remarkable case.

He concluded by stating that 'looking at the unsatisfactory nature of the medical evidence of violent death, it would certainly have justified a verdict of Not Proven.'

Another medical expert came to entirely different conclusions about the case. Professor Geoghegan summed up his views by stating the following:

> The preceding considerations, I think, suffice to indicate that the entire series of medical facts leads to the following conclusions:
>
> 1. That the death of Mrs Kirwan was not the result of apoplexy, or of epilepsy, nor yet of epileptic or of suicidal drowning.
> 2. That the combined conditions of the body (both external and internal) were incompatible with drowning, unattended by other violence.
> 3. That the appearances observed may have been produced by strangulation alone, or combined with compression of the chest, or with partial smothering.
> 4. That they are also consistent with a combination of the preceding mixed or simple process of strangulation, with drowning; the submersion not having been continuous from its commencement.

In essence, Dr Geoghegan believed that the murder had taken place in shallow water near the rock where Maria's body had been found. In this way he explained the fact that Kirwan's clothes were not completely soaked. He went on to say that 'the arrangement of the deceased's bathing-dress, and of the sheet beneath her, with the orderly position of the body, seemed clearly to show that wherever death may have occurred, the corpse was placed subsequently on the rock'.

Clearly medical opinion was divided on the issue, although circumstances had turned in Kirwan's favour, at least as far as the death sentence was concerned. There was an official report of the trial which concluded 'by order of the Executive Government the sentence was commuted to transportation for life'. Following the commutation of the death sentence Kirwan was conveyed to Spike Island in Cork harbour, where he spent the next 25 years.

Kirwan was referred to in an article published in the *Freeman's Journal* on 3 February 1879:

More than twenty-five years ago, a man named Kirwan, who lived in Upper Merrion Street, and had official employment as a draughtsman, was convicted in the Courthouse, Green Street, of the murder of his wife at Ireland's Eye, under circumstances of peculiar atrocity and horror. Sentence of death was pronounced; the gallows was prepared, the hangman retained, and the rope ready for its work; but at the last moment powerful influence of a very special character was successfully exerted, to rescue the culprit from the grasp of the executioner. Kirwan's death sentence was commuted to penal servitude for life, and after a short stay at Mountjoy Prison he was sent to Spike Island, where he spent nearly twenty-four years as a convict. Last week he was liberated, on condition that he should leave the country, and he has sailed, via Queenstown, for America. One who saw him just before his departure describes him as an aged and very respectable-looking gentleman, white-haired, bent, and feeble, and with nothing in his aspect or manner to suggest he was guilty of the awful tragedy on Ireland's Eye.

Perhaps the last piece of information we have about Kirwan comes from Dr O'Keeffe, who was the prison doctor at Spike Island. It is said that he 'accompanied Kirwan when, on his release, as the last prisoner on Spike Island, he proceeded to Liverpool, whence he sailed to America, with the intention of joining and marrying the mother of his children, whose name figured so prominently at his trial.'

It is also part of the folklore surrounding this story that at a later date Kirwan revisited Ireland's Eye. He was described as being an old, long-bearded man who was seen standing near Long Hole, contemplating what had happened there all those years before.

Kirwan was convicted on purely circumstantial evidence. Given the location of Maria's death, apart from the mysterious John Gorman, no one but Kirwan could possibly be certain what happened on that day. Today it is extremely unlikely that the case would ever have come to court, simply because there was insufficient evidence to establish Kirwan's guilt beyond reasonable doubt. If, indeed, Kirwan was innocent of the murder of Maria on Ireland's Eye then he paid an enormous price for the notoriety of maintaining two 'wives'.

CHAPTER TEN

THE SOUTHERN BELLE

The Trial and Conviction of Florence Maybrick – Liverpool, 1889

T HE FLORENCE MAYBRICK case is held by many to be one of the most unsatisfactory British trials in legal history. Not only did the outcome of the case paint Florence Maybrick as a notorious poisoner, but it also revealed much about Victorian prejudice and the shortcomings of the legal system. It is claimed that not only did this case directly bring about the creation of the Criminal Court of Appeal, but that as far as more recent revelations are concerned, if indeed she did murder her husband, Florence may have directly saved the lives of many other people. This was not because Florence Maybrick's case helped introduce the concept of appeals, but because her victim, if indeed he was, may have been Jack the Ripper.

In 1992 a diary, said to have been written by James Maybrick, Florence's deceased husband, was unearthed and gave stunning new insights into the Ripper murders that had taken place over a hundred years before. As if the controversy regarding the authenticity of the diary was not enough, at around the same time an antique watch was purchased in Liverpool. It had scratches on the inside cover and when read under a microscope, a signature was clear that read 'J. Maybrick'. More amazing were the words 'I am Jack', around which were written the initials of all the victims of the Ripper. Although leading Ripper experts believe that both the diary and the watch are elaborate hoaxes, there is a good deal of circumstantial evidence to link James Maybrick with the East End murders. Not only does an 1888 drawing of Jack the Ripper created by the police based on eyewitness reports look like Maybrick, but he also knew Whitechapel extremely well.

Those who believe that Maybrick was the Ripper also point to references in the diary which may well relate to Florence and her lover, Brierley. Although Maybrick himself had several mistresses, it is possible that he sought to revenge the infidelities of his wife by murdering prostitutes. As we saw in Chapter Two, it is probable that the Ripper began his work in August 1888. Maybrick was a compulsive arsenic and strychnine taker, and referred to the substances as his 'medicines'. The diary explains that he believed that taking the poisons would keep him strong enough to continue his 'campaign'. However, the unfortunate Florence Maybrick would find herself accused of poisoning her husband. According to the diary the murder of Mary Jane Kelly in early November 1888 was the last killing because of the effects of his self-poisoning and the very real fear that the police were closing in on him. It is chilling to read the diary entries which relate two

James Maybrick.

further murders; one before the Whitechapel killings and one just after Christmas 1888. The writer claims that both of these occurred in Manchester.

By March 1889 James Maybrick's poison addiction had reached such an extent that he could no longer hide the ill-effects. He died on 11 May 1889, but the last Ripper entry in the diary was dated 3 May and read:

> Soon, I trust, I shall be laid beside my dear mother and father. I shall seek their forgiveness when we are reunited. God I pray will allow me at least that privilege, although I know only too well I do not deserve it. My thoughts will remain intact, for a reminder to all how love does destroy. I place this now in a place where it shall be found. I pray whoever should read this will find it in their heart to forgive me. Remind all, whoever you may be, that I was once a gentle man. May the good Lord have mercy on my soul, and forgive me for all I have done.

> I give my name that all know of me, so history do tell, what love can do to a gentle man born. Yours truly

> Jack the Ripper

Florence Maybrick was born in Mobile, Alabama in 1862 and was the second child of William Chandler, a cotton merchant, and his wife Caroline. Her natural father died a year after she was born and her mother then married a Confederate officer who died soon after from tuberculosis. Florence's mother then took her to Paris for the remainder of the

The Maybricks.

American Civil War, returning to New York to stay with her cousin. It was back in Paris on a visit that Florence's mother met and married Baron Adolph von Roques, a Prussian cavalry officer. Florence and her mother boarded the SS *Baltic* bound for Paris, probably leaving New York on 12 March 1881. On board the ship Florence met and fell in love with James Maybrick, who was 24 years older than her; they married at St James's, Piccadilly in London, on 27 July 1881. At first they lived in Norfolk, Virginia, and it seemed that the Liverpool cotton broker that she had chosen for a husband was a successful businessman, but in reality his business was not doing well. They had two children, James Chandler, born in 1882 in America and Gladys Evelyn, born in England in 1886.

Although Florence did not know it, James Maybrick was not quite as he appeared. Not only did he have a mistress in England, with whom he had fathered several children, but he was also a habitual drug user. At some time during his trips to America he had contracted malaria and as a result of the treatment he had become addicted to arsenic and strychnine, the principal ingredients of a remedy for malaria known as Fowler's Medicine. It seems that in around 1883 he confided in one of his business associates that he was addicted to drugs:

> You would be horrified, I dare say, if you knew what this is – it is arsenic. We all take some poison more or less; for instance, I am now taking arsenic enough to kill you. I take this arsenic once in a while because I find it strengthens me.

By 1887 the couple had moved to the Liverpool suburb of Aigburth and into a fashionable 20-roomed home with five servants, called Battlecrease House. It was shortly after this that

Florence discovered that while they had been struggling financially, her husband had been sending £100 a year to his mistress and children in Whitechapel. From then on it is believed that Florence and James never shared a bed again. Florence was determined to continue her lifestyle and began borrowing against her jewellery and her expected inheritances from America. She wrote a letter to her mother in 1887 outlining her difficulties:

> I am utterly worn out, and in such a state of overstrained nervousness I am hardly fit for anything. Whenever the doorbell rings I feel ready to faint for fear it is someone coming to have an account paid, and when Jim comes home at night it is with fear and trembling that I look into his face to see whether anyone has been to the office about my bills. My life is a continual state of fear of something or somebody. Is life worth living? I would gladly give up the house tomorrow and move somewhere else but Jim says it would ruin him outright.

Money problems were not the whole story. Their son James caught scarlet fever and nearly died, Florence's brother Holbrook died of consumption in Paris, and it was around this time that Florence began to notice the fact that her husband was a drug addict.

James Maybrick began to experience severe health problems. According to one chemist in Exchange Street East, Maybrick would call for arsenic as many as five times a day. Coupled with the money problems and other pressures it seems that he also began beating his wife. Between June and September 1888 he visited the family doctor, Dr Hopper, at least 20 times. The doctor was not able to detect any particular reasons for his patient's ill-health.

Drawing of Battlecrease House.

In autumn 1888 Florence initiated an affair with a young cotton broker called Alfred Brierley. The affair continued for a considerable time before James Maybrick discovered the truth, presumably as a result of gossip as the affair seemed to be common knowledge in the neighbourhood. It seems that James discovered the affair in around December 1888, when he

Battlecrease House.

destroyed his will, which had left everything to Florence. Although Maybrick himself had a mistress for a number of years, it was the fact that everyone knew that his wife had a lover that really bothered him.

The fact that her husband knew of the affair does not seem to have daunted Florence, as in March 1889 she booked into a hotel with Brierley as Mr and Mrs Thomas Maybrick. Later that month, at the Grand National, Maybrick saw his

Alfred Brierley.

wife with Brierley and had a public row with her. When they returned home Florence threatened to leave James but he grabbed her, ripped her dress and gave her a black eye. It was only because of the intervention of the servants that the assault was not more serious. There then seems to have been some form of reconciliation; James agreed to pay off his wife's debts, while Florence promised not to see Brierley again. In the event neither James nor Florence kept their promises.

Around the 27 or 28 April 1889 James began to complain of coldness in his limbs, headaches and abdominal and gastro-intestinal problems. A little before, in mid-April, Florence had purchased some fly papers which she soaked in the sink. It was her intention to create an arsenic-based concoction to deal with several spots that had appeared on her face. She wanted to get rid of these blemishes before she attended a ball at the end of April. She did not do this secretly, but it did not prevent the household servants from gossiping about the coincidence of Florence buying arsenic-based fly papers and James's increasing illness. The nurse of the household, Alice Yapp, told one of the Maybrick's friends, a Mrs Briggs, that she suspected Florence of poisoning her husband. Mrs Briggs acted promptly and telegraphed James's brothers, Michael and Edwin, with the message 'Come at once; strange things going on here.' On the same day Florence gave Alice Yapp a letter addressed to Brierley for her to post. According to the nurse she walked to the post box with Gladys Maybrick, clutching the letter, which she unfortunately dropped in a puddle. Alice did not return the letter to Florence, but opened and read it. The letter from Florence was in answer to one which had been written by Brierley two days before, which read:

My dear Florie,

I suppose now you have gone I am safe in writing to you. I don't quite understand what you mean in your last about explaining my line of action. You know I could not write, and was willing to meet you, although it would have been very dangerous. Most certainly your telegram yesterday was a staggerer, and it looks as if the result was certain, but as yet I cannot find an advertisement in any London paper.

I should like to see you, but at the present dare not move, and we had better perhaps not meet until late in the autumn. I am going to try to get away in about a fortnight. I think I shall take a round trip to the Mediterranean which will take six or seven weeks, unless you wish me to stay in England. Supposing the rooms are found, I think both you and I would be better away, as the man's memory would be doubted after three months. I will write and tell you when I go. I cannot trust myself at present to write about my feelings on this unhappy business, but I do hope that some time hence I shall be able to show you that I do not quite deserve the strictures contained in your last two letters. I went to the D and D and, of course, heard some tales, but myself knew nothing about. And now, dear 'goodbye', hoping we shall meet in the autumn. I will write to you about sending letters just before I go.

AB

The letter which Alice Yapp read was destined to be one of the most damning pieces of evidence, and Florence should never have entrusted it to anyone. It read:

Dearest,

Your letter under cover to John K came to hand just after I had written to you on Monday. I did not expect to hear from you so soon, and had delayed in giving him the necessary instructions. Since my return I have been nursing M day and night. He is sick unto death. The doctors held a consultation yesterday, and now all depends upon how long his strength will hold out. Both my brothers-in-law are here, and we are terribly anxious. I cannot answer your letter fully today, my darling, but relieve your mind of all fear of discovery now and in the future. M has been delirious since Sunday, and I know now that he is perfectly ignorant of everything, even the name of the street, and also he has not been making any enquiries whatever. The tale he told me was a pure fabrication, and only intended to frighten the truth out of me. In fact he believes my statement, although he will not admit it. You need not therefore go abroad on that account, dearest; but, in any case, please don't leave England until I have seen you once again. You must feel that those two letters of mine were written under circumstances which must even excuse their injustice in your eyes. Do you suppose that I could act as I am doing if I really felt and meant what I inferred then? If you wish to write to me about anything do so now, as all the letters pass through my hands at present. Excuse this scrawl, my own darling, but I dare not leave the room for a moment, and I do not know when I shall be able to write to you again. In haste, yours ever.

Florie

In the event, Florence's letter was never read by Brierley as when Alice Yapp saw the contents she made it her business to show it to James's brothers.

It was not until the following morning, 9 May, that Florence confronted Alice Yapp with intercepting her mail and disclosing its contents to the Maybricks. She said 'Do you know that I am blamed for this?' to which Alice Yapp replied 'For what?' 'For Maybrick's illness' retorted Florence. The doctors on hand prescribed meat juice and took away samples of urine and faeces from James for examination. It is important to note that the results proved negative for traces of arsenic. Later that day, at some point in the evening, Florence gave James some meat juice to which James asked her to add some of his powders. The exact course of events on the 9th is derived from Nurse Gore's later testimony. She claimed that Edwin Maybrick had purchased a bottle of Valentine's Meat Juice on the suggestion of the doctors. Around midnight Nurse Gore was sat beside James Maybrick's bed when Florence came into the room and took a bottle of the meat juice into the adjoining room where she was sleeping. Florence closed the door behind her but only stayed in her own room for a few minutes, returning to James's room with a request that the nurse should go and get some ice for her husband's head. Nurse Gore declined to leave the patient and saw Florence return the bottle to the nightstand.

At some point on Friday 10 May, at the insistence of Nurse Gore, the doctors took away that bottle of meat juice. Examinations showed that half a grain of arsenic had been added to the contents. Some time in the morning Michael Maybrick saw Florence pouring the contents of one bottle of medicine into a larger one. He said to her 'Florie, how dare you tamper with the medicine?' to which Florence replied that the small bottle had a lot of sediment at the bottom and she was simply pouring it into the larger bottle so that it could be shaken more effectively. This bottle, too, was later analysed but no arsenic was found.

Some time later Nurse Callery overheard a conversation between James and Florence. He said to her 'You have given me the wrong medicine again' to which Florence replied 'What are you talking about? You never had the wrong medicine'. Later, at around 6pm, the nurse again heard a conversation between the couple. James said 'Oh, bunny, bunny, how could you do it? I did not think it of you.' Florence replied 'You silly old darling, don't trouble your head about things'.

With the assistance of Alice Yapp and some of the other servants Edwin and Michael Maybrick decided to prove conclusively that Florence was guilty of poisoning their brother. Systematically, the team of amateur sleuths searched the house and turned up an envelope which read 'Arsenic – poison for cats', five bottles, a jar of Valentine's Meat Juice, a glass, a rag and a handkerchief. It was later to be proved that all of these items contained arsenic and given the fact that two grains were sufficient to kill a normal human being; these various items had over one hundred grains of the poison in them.

These latest discoveries convinced the Maybricks that Florence was indeed poisoning their brother and to this end they made her a virtual prisoner in her own house. However, it was too late, on Saturday 11 May 1889 the doctors became certain that the patient would not live to see nightfall; they were correct. Florence was not at hand when the death occurred; she had collapsed and fainted and did not regain consciousness until some time after her husband's death.

It was inevitable, given the circumstances, that a post-mortem would be required to establish the cause of death of James Maybrick. It was the coroner's conclusion that death had been caused 'due to inflammation of the stomach and bowels set up by some irritant poison'. Meanwhile, Florence was still bedridden when the police arrived to arrest her for the murder of her husband.

Florence, as you will recall, had no money, but her mother stepped in to hire Sir Charles

Russell to defend her daughter. Some time around this period Florence also wrote to Brierley:

> I am writing to you to give me every assistance in your power in my present fearful trouble. I am in custody, without any of my family with me, and without money. I have cabled my solicitor in New York to come here at once. In the meantime, send some money for present needs. The truth is known about my visit to London [referring to the weekend that Brierley and Florence spent together under the name of Mr and Mrs Thomas Maybrick]. Your last letter is in the hands of the police. Appearances may be against me, but before God I swear I am innocent.

This letter did not reach Brierley as it, too, was handed over to the police.

The official coroner's inquest had begun on 14 May, but was adjourned until 28 May. Meanwhile, Florence was imprisoned at Walton on the 18th to be presented at the inquest after the formal identification of the body. At the inquest Florence was represented by the barrister, William Pickford. The conclusion of the inquest recommended that Florence Maybrick should stand trial at the forthcoming Liverpool Assizes in July.

Commenting on the outcome of the forthcoming trial, Florence's defence counsel confidently stated 'She'll be acquitted'.

Florence's trial opened on 31 July 1889, and was presided over by Justice James Fitzjames Stephen. What is interesting to note about this particular person is that within two years of Florence's trial he was committed to a mental asylum in Ipswich. Legal experts claim that early signs of the problems with his mental state were self-evident during the trial. The prosecution was led by John Addison, QC, supported by W. McConnell and Thomas Swift. Sir Charles Russell's aid was William Pickford. The trial opened with the charge that 'Florence Elisabeth Maybrick, age twenty-six, is indicted for having, on the 11th of May, feloniously, wilfully, and of her malice aforethought killed and murdered one James Maybrick.' The case was destined to continue for five days before Justice Stephen spent two days summing up the main points of the trial.

What must be considered shocking is that throughout the whole trial no positive conclusions were ever drawn about James Maybrick's addiction to arsenic and strychnine. The implications of this omission could only damn the accused, as the jury could not infer any other reason for the existence of arsenic in the house, or in the food that James Maybrick was given, other than that it had been put there by Florence in order to kill him. Over the course of the next few days Florence would hear doctors, household servants and both of James's brothers give evidence against her.

Much of the evidence directed against Florence revolved around three main issues. The first was the letter that Florence had written to Brierley shortly before her husband's death. The prosecution rounded on the sentences 'he is sick unto death. The doctors held a consultation yesterday and now all depends upon how long his strength can hold out'. Was this an indication that Florence was committing murder by poisoning her husband? As far as the doctors who were on hand during the last days of James Maybrick's life were concerned, one of them testified 'On 7 May I formed a hopeful prognosis and hoped he would soon recover. On the 8th I found him better.' He went on to deny that neither he nor his colleagues had ever suggested that the patient was 'sick unto death'. It was also denied that James Maybrick was delirious; as far as the prosecution was concerned, this meant that Florence's statement in the letter was either wishful thinking or a confession of poisoning her husband. The second main area of attack against Florence was the fly papers. The prosecution maintained that this is how Florence had obtained the arsenic. Witnesses recounted that she had bought a dozen fly papers on 24 April, and on 29 April she had bought two dozen from a different chemist. Several of the household servants testified that they had seen her soaking the fly papers in a basin full of water. It was, therefore, clear to the prosecution that Florence's purchases directly coincided with the beginning of James Maybrick's illness. They pointed to the fact that up until 27 April James Maybrick was extremely ill. On that day he had begun to make a recovery which, the prosecution contended, had prompted the prisoner to purchase twice the amount of fly papers than before to finish off the job. What was not reasonably established was a link between the arsenic that had supposedly been extracted from the fly papers and the third plank of the prosecution's case. Examination of the Valentine's Meat Juice did not produce any evidence that the arsenic in the fluid had been derived from fly papers. It would have been very likely that at least some fibres from the paper itself would have been discovered.

The prosecution maintained that Florence had sufficient opportunity in the first bout of her husband's illness to doctor his medicines as she pleased without any witnesses being able to be sure that the patient was being poisoned. When professional nurses had been called in the testimony of Nurse Gore gave the court the impression that Florence had tampered with one of the bottles. Indeed, as Mr Addison pointed out, this was 'one of the serious features of the case'. Why then, apart from the occasion when Florence had taken one of the Valentine's bottles into her own room, to return it a few minutes later, had she then been seen tampering with other medicines in full view of one of her husband's brothers? On the other hand, what significance could be drawn from James Maybrick's own accusation that she had been giving him the wrong medicines?

Michael Maybrick was called as the first prosecution witness. It became clear from his testimony that from the day of his arrival from London on 8 May, he had been dissatisfied with the treatment that his brother had been getting, and that he later became certain that Florence Maybrick was poisoning her husband. In cross-examination Sir Charles Russell sought to prove that Michael Maybrick had told the household servants and the nurses attending his brother to watch out for any slight indication that could incriminate his sister-in-law. In effect, Russell was suggesting that the witnesses that would be heard later had been unduly influenced by Michael Maybrick and that what they had seen was simply a self-fulfilling prophecy placed in their minds by the brother of the deceased.

The next prosecution witness was James Maybrick's regular doctor. Although Hopper had not been at hand during the last fateful days of his patient's life, he could recount a good deal of James Maybrick's medical history to the court. He confirmed that James had become his patient in 1882 and often visited him with stomach and liver problems. He confirmed that James dosed himself with arsenic and that from his recollections he believed that the patient had been doing this for some time. He also confirmed that he had had a conversation with Florence Maybrick about her husband's use of arsenic as early as June 1888. He told the court that Florence had said 'Mr Maybrick was in the habit of taking some very strong medicine which had a bad influence on him, for he always seemed worse after each dose.' This was the beginning of the opportunity for Russell to introduce the fact that there was another explanation for the presence of arsenic in the body when the post-mortem was carried out. Dr Hopper thought that his patient was a hypochondriac and that he had been trying new remedies recommended to him by friends and that he had confided in him that he had often doubled the doses that had been prescribed. It was Dr Hopper's opinion that when James had complained of numbness in his hands, feet and legs, that this was a result of the arsenic's affects on his nerves. There was an interesting insight into James Maybrick's character in as much as Dr Hopper confirmed seeing copies of prescriptions given to his patient by Dr Seguard of New York. The prescriptions included strychnine, which was believed at the time to be a 'sexual nerve tonic'. Arsenic was also present in the prescriptions as an aphrodisiac. We may read as much into this as we choose; it certainly adds fuel to the suggestion that James Maybrick wished to maintain a voracious sexual appetite. At the very least, he may have been sleeping with both Florence and his mistress in Whitechapel. If we are to believe the later revelations surrounding his character in relation to the Ripper diary, then it could be reasonable to suggest that as an outlet for his oversexed state, he was driven to the very edge of sexual fulfilment by murdering prostitutes. Russell also tried to establish the fact that once James Maybrick was bedridden he would not have had access to the large amounts of arsenic that he had been used to taking on a daily basis. The purpose of this line of enquiry was to establish that rather like any drug addiction, it would seriously affect of the health of the patient. Given that in the doctor's own view Maybrick had been taking arsenic and strychnine for at least six or seven years, and possibly more if his addiction had begun in America, then the drastic effect of withdrawal could possibly have caused his death. Therefore, it was not so much the presence of arsenic that had killed James Maybrick, it was, on the contrary, its absence.

Matilda Briggs was the next witness in the box and she was able to confirm that she had contacted the Maybrick brothers after a conversation with Nurse Yapp. She also confirmed that she had been party to the search expedition which had revealed the various items that were believed to have been used by Florence in order to poison her husband. She, too, confirmed that James Maybrick was known to dose himself with medicines, and it was clearly Russell's intention to suggest that the discovery of the items in the house had nothing directly to do with his client, but was evidence of the deceased's long-term addiction.

The next major witness was Edwin Maybrick, who began by denying that his brother took arsenic and confirmed that he had, at various times, seen his brother prior to 8 May and was concerned about his health. He had arrived at the household on the Wednesday and decided to stay and assist as best he could. In cross-examination he told the court that Florence had stayed up most nights to look after her husband, and from that day he not only suspected Florence of poisoning his brother, but expressly forbade any intervention by Florence in the care or administration of food or medicine to James. He seemed fairly certain that from then on Florence was not in a position to give his brother anything. He had tried to ensure that at all times James either had a nurse or a servant in the room with him. He also confirmed that James Maybrick had a number of medicine bottles in his office but he did not believe that these contained arsenic.

Thomas Symington Wokes, the chemist from Aigburth, was then asked about Florence's purchase of fly papers and the fact that she had an account with him. The court also heard from Christopher Hanson, a chemist from Cressington, who confirmed that Florence had purchased two dozen fly papers and some lotion from him on 29 April. He also added that he had personally analysed the fly papers that he sold and that they contained between one and two and a half grains of arsenic. He confirmed that arsenic was used to soften the skin and could easily have been used with the cosmetic lotion that Florence had purchased on the same day. It was clearly the intention of Florence's defence to establish the fact that not only was arsenic routinely used in cosmetics, but that he himself did not sell such lotions. It was therefore the inference that in order to prepare a skin lotion for herself, Florence would have had to have mixed the arsenic from the fly papers with the cosmetic cream prepared by Mr Hanson.

On the following day the star prosecution witness was Alice Yapp. She began by making the following statement:

I was a nurse in the family of the Maybricks, and when Mr. Maybrick died I had been with them one year and eight months. During that time there had been nothing the matter with my master. There was an inner room near the bedroom in which Mr. Maybrick slept sometimes, but I am not certain. I remember the day of the Grand National, the 29th April, and before that I was aware that my mistress had gone to London. Before going she said she was visiting London to see her mother, and I promised to write to her. On the day of the Grand National Mrs. Maybrick came home at ten minutes to seven, and my master returned a few minutes after. Mrs. Maybrick entered the nursery and so did Mr. Maybrick; but neither spoke.

Mr. Maybrick carried the youngest child down to the nursery. I heard Mr. Maybrick say to Mrs. Maybrick, 'This scandal will be all over the town to-morrow.' They then went down into the hall, and I heard Mr. Maybrick say, 'Florie, I never thought you could come to this.' That was all I heard. They then went into the vestibule, and I heard Mr. Maybrick say, 'If you once cross this threshold you shall never enter these doors again.' I did not know that a cab had been ordered at that time. I went down to Mrs. Maybrick, and asked her to come to her bedroom. She did not answer, and I put my arm around her waist, and took her upstairs. I made the bed for her that night, and she slept in the dressing-room. The next day, on the Saturday,

Mrs. Maybrick went out, and Dr. Hopper came in the afternoon.

About a fortnight or three weeks after the Grand National the housemaid told me something in the nursery which caused me to go into Mrs. Maybrick's bedroom. I went there, and I saw the wash-basin covered with a towel, which I took off. There was another towel on a plate. I lifted the plate and saw a basin containing some fly-papers. I cannot say how many. I knew that they were fly-papers, because I saw 'fly-papers' written upon them. There was also a small quantity of liquid in the basin. I put the things back as I found them.

Yapp's involvement in the accusations which directly led to Russell's client being accused of murder were at the very centre of the case, and the prosecution knew it. Russell had a very clear means of attack; the way in which the nurse had intercepted and read the letter from Florence to Brierley was morally reprehensible, no matter what the prosecution claimed it inferred. It was also Yapp's testimony which linked the fly papers, the arsenic and the death of James Maybrick. It was to this matter that Russell first referred when he began his cross-examination:

Sir Charles Russell: About this question of the fly-papers. Have you ever acted as lady's maid?

Nurse Yapp: No; only as nurse.

Sir Charles Russell: Was it in the morning that the girl Bessie Brierley told you as to having seen these fly-papers?

Nurse Yapp: No; it was soon after dinner.

Sir Charles Russell: But did she tell you that she had seen them in the morning when she was doing up the room?

Nurse Yapp: Yes.

Sir Charles Russell: And you, out of curiosity, went into the room after the dinner was over?

Nurse Yapp: It was about two hours after when I went into the room.

Sir Charles Russell: Out of curiosity?

Nurse Yapp: Yes.

Sir Charles Russell: You had no business in the room?

Nurse Yapp: No.

Sir Charles Russell: And having been told by Bessie Brierley that she had seen them in the morning, you found them still there as she had described them?

Nurse Yapp: Yes.

Sir Charles Russell: Where were they?

Nurse Yapp: On the washstand.

Sir Charles Russell: In the principal bedroom?

Nurse Yapp: Yes.

Sir Charles Russell: That is to say, in the bedroom which is directly approached from the landing?

Nurse Yapp: Yes.

Sir Charles Russell: Whereabouts was this washstand placed?

Nurse Yapp: By the door leading to the inner room.

Sir Charles Russell: And in a position in which you could see it on entering the door of the bedroom?

Nurse Yapp: Yes.

Sir Charles Russell: These were reported to you by Bessie Brierley as having been there early in the morning, and you have no reason to suppose that they did not continue there the whole of the day till you saw them?

Nurse Yapp: No.

Sir Charles Russell: That would be about three o'clock?

Nurse Yapp: Yes.

Sir Charles Russell: You did not think it right to ask your mistress anything about them?

Nurse Yapp: No.

So, as far as Russell could establish, the question of soaking the fly papers was as much in question as the purchase of them. Before he turned to the subject which Yapp must have been dreading, he further established a suggestion for the jury that there could be an altogether different explanation for the illness of James Maybrick. The day before James Maybrick fell ill he had been out riding with friends and had eaten out, returning home still wet. Surely there was a possibility that at least to begin with James Maybrick's illness was influenza or a chill. It was inevitable that Russell now turned to the letter:

Sir Charles Russell: Now, with regard to this letter, you had heard the name of your mistress coupled with the name of Brierley before you got the letter?

Nurse Yapp: Never.

Sir Charles Russell: Why did you open the letter?

Nurse Yapp: Because Mrs. Maybrick wished that it should go by that post.

Sir Charles Russell: Why did you open that letter?

No reply.

Justice Stephen: Did anything happen to the letter?

Nurse Yapp: Yes, it fell in the dirt.

Sir Charles Russell: Why did you open the letter?

Justice Stephen: She has just said so now.

Sir Charles Russell: Well, I did not catch it. Anyhow, I want to have it out again. Why did you open that letter?

Nurse Yapp: I opened the letter to put it in a clean envelope.

Sir Charles Russell: Why didn't you put it in a clean envelope without opening it?

No reply.

Sir Charles Russell: Was it a wet day?

Nurse Yapp: It was showery.

Sir Charles Russell: Are you sure of that?

Nurse Yapp: Yes.

Sir Charles Russell: Will you undertake to say that? I ask you to consider. Was it a wet day?

No reply.

Sir Charles Russell: Aye or no?

No reply.

Sir Charles Russell: Was it wet or dry?

No reply.

Sir Charles Russell: Had the day before been a dry day?

Nurse Yapp: It was showery.

Sir Charles Russell: Will you swear that on Wednesday it was showery?

Nurse Yapp: I cannot say positively.

Sir Charles Russell: Was the child in a perambulator?

Nurse Yapp: No.

Sir Charles Russell: Was the child able to walk?

Nurse Yapp: Yes.

Sir Charles Russell: What do you say you did with the letter?

Nurse Yapp: I gave it to Mr. Edwin Maybrick.

Sir Charles Russell: No, no. I mean when you got it from Mrs. Maybrick?

Nurse Yapp: I gave it to the child to post.

Sir Charles Russell: Did you ever do that before?

Nurse Yapp: Always, and Mrs. Maybrick always gave letters to the baby to carry to the post.

Sir Charles Russell: I was asking what you did with it?

Nurse Yapp: I gave it to the baby.

Sir Charles Russell: Always did?

Nurse Yapp: Yes.

Sir Charles Russell: Did this incident ever happen, or anything like it, before?

Nurse Yapp: No.

Sir Charles Russell: Let me see the letter. Have you got the envelope? Where did the child drop it?

Nurse Yapp: Right by the post office, in crossing the road.

Sir Charles Russell: Which side?

Nurse Yapp: Near the post office.

Sir Charles Russell: Then you had securely passed the road and were stepping on to the kerbstone?

Nurse Yapp: Yes.

Sir Charles Russell: Did any one see it but yourself?

Nurse Yapp: I don't know.

Sir Charles Russell: Then you picked it up?

Nurse Yapp: Yes.

Sir Charles Russell: And saw this mark upon it, did you?

Nurse Yapp: Yes.

Sir Charles Russell: Just take it in your hand. Is the direction clear enough?

Nurse Yapp: It was very much dirtier at the time.

Sir Charles Russell: It hasn't obscured the direction, which is plain enough?

Nurse Yapp: No.

Sir Charles Russell: You didn't rub the mud off. What did you do?

Nurse Yapp: I went into the post office and asked for a clean envelope to re-address it. I opened it as I was going into the post office.

Sir Charles Russell: Did it never occur to you that you could get a clean envelope, if you were particular about cleanliness, and put it unopened into that?

Nurse Yapp: Oh, I never thought of that.

Sir Charles Russell: Then, between the picking of it up on the post office side of the pathway and your going into the shop you formed the design of opening it, and did, in fact, open it as you were going in?

Nurse Yapp: Yes.

Sir Charles Russell: If, as you suggest, this fell in the mud and was wet, there is no running of the ink on the direction?

Nurse Yapp: No.

Sir Charles Russell: Can you suggest how there can be any damp or wet in connection with it without causing some running of the ink?

Nurse Yapp: I cannot.

Sir Charles Russell: On your oath, girl, did you not manufacturer that stain as a excuse for opening your mistress's letter?

Nurse Yapp: I did not.

Sir Charles Russell: Have you any explanation to offer about the running of the ink?

Nurse Yapp: I have not.

Although Yapp's motivation in opening the letter had been seriously questioned, what still remained was the prosecution's assertion that the two key sentences inferred Russell's client's guilt. As Russell would later say, 'That letter – take it, read it, scan it as you will – is this the letter of a guilty woman who is planning the murder of her husband?'

Yapp's testimony was followed by three other servants in the house, including the cook, all of whom added little to what the court already knew. Although the prosecution continually contended that James Maybrick had died from arsenic poisoning, it was the introduction of the prosecution's medical witnesses that gave Russell the opportunity to question even this.

The first medical witness called by the prosecution stated that the cause of death was 'arsenical poisoning'. When Russell rose to cross-examine the witness, the court could not have expected that they were about to see a real climax in the proceedings.

Sir Charles Russell: You have never assisted at a post-mortem examination of any person supposed to have died from arsenical poisoning?

Dr Humphreys: No.

Sir Charles Russell: Up to the time that the communication was made to you which, to use your own language, suggested that their might be some foundation of supposing foul play; did it in any way occur to you that there were symptoms present of arsenical poisoning? When was it that that idea was first suggested to you?

Dr Humphreys: I think on Thursday, or on the Wednesday night, when Mr Michael Maybrick came to me.

Sir Charles Russell: From a communication made to you by Mr Michael Maybrick?

Dr Humphreys: Yes, that there was something unsatisfactory.

At that the court adjourned, leaving the jury to consider whether it was the doctors that had suspected poisoning or whether the supposition had purely come from the mind of James's brother.

When the court reconvened the following morning Dr Humphreys still found himself uncomfortably in the witness box. Firstly he conceded that he had carried out a test on a sample of James Maybrick's faeces and had not discovered any arsenic in the sample. Russell asked him to confirm that the test was negative which Humphreys did, although he added that the results of the test may have been inconclusive:

Because the quantity I used was so small, and the time I boiled it so short that there might not have been time for any deposit to take place. Further I am not skilled in the details of testing and my test might have been inefficient.

Russell now had the opportunity to drive a coach and horses through the medical opinions.

Sir Charles Russell: That is candid doctor. Then you mean to say that although you tried this experiment, you were not able to conduct it successfully?

Dr Humphreys: I do not pretend to have any skill in these matters.

Sir Charles Russell: It is not a difficult test?

Dr Humphreys: No.

Sir Charles Russell: And if there is arsenic it is supposed to make a deposit?

Dr Humphreys: Yes if it is boiled long enough.

Sir Charles Russell: How long did you boil it?

Dr Humphreys: About two minutes.

Sir Charles Russell: What quantity did you take?

Dr Humphreys: About an ounce.

Sir Charles Russell: Was this quantity sufficient?

Dr Humphreys: Quite sufficient.

Sir Charles Russell: So I should have thought. Did you not at that time think your experiment was properly conducted?

Dr Humphreys: I really couldn't tell.

Sir Charles Russell: Dr Humphreys, you were making the experiment with some object?

Dr Humphreys: Yes.

Sir Charles Russell: Were you satisfied at the time that it was properly conducted?

Dr Humphreys: At the time I had no books to refer to.

Sir Charles Russell: When you came to refresh your memory from books were you satisfied that there was nothing you omitted?

Dr Humphreys: Yes, I don't know whether the instruments were absolutely pure.

Sir Charles Russell: But see, Dr Humphreys, if they were not pure, would you not get a greater amount of deposit?

Dr Humphreys: It depends on what the impurity was.

Sir Charles Russell: What impurity do you suggest may have existed?

Dr Humphreys: Arsenic.

Sir Charles Russell: If there was arsenic, would it not make it more certain you would get a deposit?

Dr Humphreys: Yes.

Sir Charles Russell: Did you find any?

Dr Humphreys: I found none.

Sir Charles Russell: Had it not been for the suggestion of arsenic by Michael Maybrick, were you prepared to give a death certificate if James had died on Wednesday?

Dr Humphreys: Yes.

Sir Charles Russell: With what cause of death?

Dr Humphreys: Gastro-enteritis.

At this admission the judge stepped in to underline exactly what the doctor had just told the court. He asked: 'If nothing about poison had been suggested to you, you would have certified that he died of gastro-enteritis?'

Dr Humphreys: Yes, my Lord.

Sir Charles Russell: Can you mention any post-mortem symptom which is distinctive of arsenical poisoning and not also distinctive of gastro-enteritis?

Dr Humphreys: No, I can't give you any.

Despite the prosecution calling two further well-respected medical witnesses, they both had to concede that it was perfectly possible that the cause of death had been gastro-enteritis. Dr Stevenson, a Home Office toxicologist, in particular, faced a severe cross-examining from Russell:

Sir Charles Russell: Will you indicate any one symptom which you say is distinctly an arsenical poisoning symptom and which is not to be found in cases of gastro-enteritis?

Dr Stevenson: I would form no opinion from one single symptom.

Sir Charles Russell: What do you mean by that answer? That you cannot point to any distinct symptom of arsenical poisoning differentiating it from gastro-enteritis?

Dr Stevenson: There is no distinctive diagnostic symptom of arsenical poisoning. The diagnostic thing is finding the arsenic.

In cross-examining this witness Russell had, in a nutshell, given the court the whole basis of his assumption that James Maybrick did not die as a result of poisoning by Florence, but as a result of a long-term addiction to arsenic delivered in non-fatal doses by the deceased himself. He had thus painted James Maybrick as a chronic arsenic-eater and suggested that his death was from natural causes derived from his addiction. This effectively ended the prosecution's case and it was now the turn of Russell to wheel in his own medical experts who would confirm in court that it was their opinion that James Maybrick had not died from arsenical poisoning but that the probable cause of death was gastro-enteritis.

Having succeeded in this, Russell then turned to casting light upon the background, character and widespread knowledge of James Maybrick's arsenic addiction. Among these witnesses was Sir James Poole, the former mayor of Liverpool, who had once, so he claimed, lectured James Maybrick on his drug addiction. 'The more you take, the more you will require; you will go on till they carry you off'.

Despite the medical opinion and the testimony, which was incidentally not disputed by the prosecution, there were still two very important aspects which Russell had not yet undermined. In modern times, Florence Maybrick would almost certainly have been called into the witness box by Russell, but the Criminal Evidence Act had not yet been passed, and she could not testify on her own behalf. She was, however, allowed to make a statement to the court, which could not be cross-examined, nor guided in any way by Russell. Russell told the judge and jury 'My Lord, I wish to tell you what has taken place. I asked Mrs Maybrick if it was her wish to make a statement. She said yes. I asked her if it was written. She said no.'

Florence Maybrick stood and addressed the court for just five minutes. She began by saying 'My Lord, I wish to make a statement, as well as I can, to you – a few facts in connection with this dreadfully crushing charge.' She went on to explain that she had purchased the fly papers purely for the purpose of creating a cosmetic lotion in order to deal with the spots that had appeared on her face. She was desperate to improve her complexion before attending a ball. It was when she turned to the subject of the Valentine's Meat Juice that she made what may in retrospect have been a very serious admission. She began by saying that her husband had been very depressed about his illness and that he had asked her to put some 'harmless' powders in his food.

> I was overwrought, terribly anxious, miserably unhappy, and his evident distress
> entirely unnerved me. I consented. My Lord, I had not one true or honest friend in
> that house; I had no one to consult and no one to advise me.

Whether this was an admission of her guilt and that she had knowingly given her husband arsenic could only be left to the interpretation of the jury. In any event, it was now the end of the fresh evidence and revelations and all that was left was for the opposing counsels to sum up the case in an attempt to direct the jury to their points of view.

Russell asked the jury to consider the two key questions as he saw them. Had James Maybrick died of arsenical poisoning? He believed that if the jury thought this was the case they needed to ask themselves whether his client had administered the fatal dose or doses. He then reviewed the medical evidence, pointing at the fact that the doctors had not been able to identify a single symptom that differentiated arsenical poisoning from gastro-enteritis. He pointed at the fact that James Maybrick was a long-term arsenic addict and that the post-mortem had revealed only a small amount of arsenic in his body. He was sure that the jury would see this as being consistent with an addict that had not enjoyed access to arsenic during the last days of his life. He summed up by saying:

> It would only be natural, that the thought should arise in your minds; if not arsenical poisoning, we should like to have some suggestion what it was. Now I am not called upon to advance any theory. Counsel representing the prisoner is entitled to stand upon a defence and to say 'You have not proved the case which you alleged.' But passing that by, is there no reasonable hypothesis? Is it improbable that a man who had been dosing himself, admittedly taking poisonous medicines – is it remarkable that this man's constitution had suffered so that he should always be complaining of derangement of the stomach? Is it or is it not reasonable to say that a man who had been pursuing such a course would have his constitution liable to attack from causes which in a healthy man would be of no effect? There is no safe resting-place on which you can justify to yourselves a finding that this was a death of arsenical poisoning. I must ask you even at the outset whether it is possible for you to find the prisoner guilty. If a woman had the nerve and fibre to plan such a murder, cold and deliberate, would she not have also had the instinct of self preservation? If, as it is clear, there was in that house a quantity of poison capable of being fatally applied; if there was one packet of arsenic with which admittedly fly papers had nothing to do; if there was a bottle in which grains of arsenic were found with which admittedly fly papers had nothing to do; I ask why, with these means at her command, should she have resorted to the clumsy, the stupid contrivance of trying to steep fly papers in water? You are in number large enough to prevent the individual views and prejudices and prepossessions of one from affecting all, but in numbers small enough to preserve to each one of you the undivided sense of individual responsibility. The verdict is to be the verdict of each one of you and the verdict of all of you. I make no appeal for mercy; let that be clearly understood. You are administering a law which is merciful; you are administering a law which forbids you to pronounce a verdict of guilty unless all reasonable hypotheses of innocence have been excluded. I end as I began by asking you, in these perplexities, in the doubts, in the difficulties which surround this case, can you with safe conscience say this woman is guilty? If your duty compels you to do it you will do it, you must do it; but you will not you must not, unless the whole burden and facts and weight of the case drive you irresistibly to that conclusion.

Addison stood up to reply for the prosecution, quickly making assertions that the deceased was a careful and healthy man and by no means a chronic arsenic addict. Ignoring testimony which had been given by Dr Hopper, Addison maintained that James Maybrick found himself ill for the first time in April 1889. He also took the opportunity to criticise Florence's statement from the dock, claiming it was 'Carefully thought out and ably delivered'. Addison spoke of the arsenic and asked the jury to consider whether it was possible that James Maybrick, who knew about drugs, would not recognise the symptoms associated with arsenic poisoning. He then turned to Florence's letter to Brierley and said

> I protest against the notion of any tenderness for a husband in a woman who wrote that letter. If she be guilty, we have brought to light a very terrible deed of darkness, and proved a murder founded upon profligacy and adultery, and carried out with a hypocrisy and cunning which have been rarely equalled in the annals of crime.

So ended the fifth day of the trial. But the court would have to endure two more days of painful, ill-considered confusion as Justice Stephen, still suffering from the after-effects of a stroke four years before, and the oncoming affects of mental illness, attempted to guide the jury through the evidence. Much of what he said in his summing up was confused, attributing statements made by doctors to the wrong witnesses and quoting from a letter which had not been produced as evidence. Other statements were both misleading and prejudicial to Florence's case: 'If you can show a sufficient quantity of arsenic to cause death, why then you need go no further.' Or, 'On that day began the symptoms of what may be called the fatal dose.' And finally, 'You are apt to assume a connection between the thing which is a proof in the result at which you are to arrive – because it is put before you – and in that way you may be led to do a greater or lesser degree of injustice according to the state of the case.'

The jury were sent to begin their deliberations at 3.20pm on the seventh day of the trial. It took them just 35 minutes to discuss the full implications of the case and the evidence against the prisoner. When Thomas Wainwright, the foreman of the jury, stood up to address the court it was widely thought that since the jury had been absent for such a short period that the only verdict could be an acquittal. In the event, those present were incorrect and Wainwright told the court that it was the opinion of the jury that the prisoner was guilty of wilful murder.

Solemnly Justice Stephen donned his black cap and pronounced:

> The court doth order you to be taken from hence to the place from whence you came, and thence to a place of execution, and that you be hanged by the neck until you are dead, and that your body be afterward buried within the precincts of the prison in which you shall be confined after your conviction. And may the Lord have mercy upon your soul.

The press and public were incensed and tens of thousands of people signed a petition demanding Florence's reprieve. The judge was called to see the Home Secretary Henry Matthews and the Lord Chancellor to discuss how the trial had been managed and whether the conviction was sound. Florence was due to hang at the end of August and from her cell in Walton jail, she could hear the carpenters erecting the scaffold. Suddenly, bowing to pressure and misgivings about the conduct of the trial, Henry Matthews reprieved Florence Maybrick and sentenced her to life in prison. He said:

> Although the evidence leads clearly to the conclusion that the prisoner administered, and attempted to administer, arsenic to her husband with intent to murder, yet it does

not wholly exclude a reasonable doubt whether his death was in fact caused by the administration of arsenic.

Florence was destined to spend 15 years in prison until she was released in 1904. Throughout her long incarceration Sir Charles Russell had sought to have the sentence quashed until his dying day in 1900. Tragically, Florence Maybrick's children were taken into the care of Michael Maybrick, who refused to allow them to see their mother. Presumably they had been sufficiently indoctrinated by the time they were old enough to decide for themselves; they chose not to see her and she never saw them again.

When Florence was freed in 1904 she initially spent six months at a convent in Truro before returning with her mother to America. Some time later she wrote a book called *My Lost Fifteen Years* and toured the American lecture circuit. After this brief brush with fame and notoriety she adopted her maiden name, Chandler, and became a recluse living in South Kent, Connecticut. It is believed that she may have returned to Liverpool in 1927 to watch the Grand National for the last time. Her hermit-like existence continued until 23 October 1941 when, at the age of 79, she was found dead in her shack, surrounded by the cats that had kept her company in the last years of her life.

Florence Chandler's shack.

Conspiracy theories come to the fore when we consider the case of Florence Maybrick. It is believed by many that her husband, James, was indeed one of the leading suspects in the Jack the Ripper Whitechapel murders. Was she set up by the authorities in order to cover the illegal execution of someone who they believed to be a serial killer? Certainly Florence and James's marriage was not exactly founded on happiness or openness towards one another; it was a turbulent relationship. But was her association with Brierley really sufficient reason for her to murder James? Could it be possible that she foolishly continued to poison James despite the fact that the whole household suspected her of slipping arsenic into his food and drinks? It seems unlikely that a woman in her position, friendless and in a foreign land, would be prepared to take such risks. Is it feasible that the traces of poison found in James Maybrick's body were nothing more than the remnants of his obsessive long-term addiction and not administered by his confused wife?

CHAPTER ELEVEN

MR CECIL HAS SHOT HIMSELF

The Trial of Alfred John Monson – Edinburgh, 1893

THE ARDLAMONT estate on the Kyles of Bute in the Firth of Clyde was the scene of what for some was a brutal and premeditated murder, and for others a tragic accident. The house lies at the foot of a peninsula overlooking Loch Fyne, a remote and beautiful place, and, in the eyes of many, the ideal spot to plan and execute a murder. From the outset, the press, the public and the police were convinced that the death was no more than an unfortunate accident, but as events unfolded, the truth behind the case became more entwined and tragic than anyone could possible imagine.

The principal players came from radically different backgrounds. The victim, Windsor Dudley Cecil Hambrough, was the son and heir of Major Dudley Hambrough. The accused, Alfred John Monson, although outwardly appearing to have impeccable credentials

Ardlamont House.

of background and breeding, lived by his wits and was not averse to resorting to criminality in order to survive and prosper.

The case was first brought to the attention of the public in a short piece in the *Glasgow Herald* on 10 August 1893:

> Greenock, 1.30 – News has been received from Greenock today of a sad gun accident which took place at Ardlamont on Loch Fyne yesterday. The report is that yesterday afternoon a young man, 21 years of age, named Hambrough, who lately came from America, was out shooting on his estate only recently acquired when, as he was going over a dyke, his gun accidentally went off and he was fatally wounded.

The newspaper can be forgiven for getting most of the facts wrong. In fact, Cecil Hambrough, as the young man was known, was the guest of Alfred Monson, who had rented the house and grounds for the shooting season. But before we begin to look at the death of the young man, it is wise to consider how the two came to be together on that fateful day in August.

Although Cecil Hambrough was the heir to the estates owned by his father, the Major, the family was virtually penniless as a result of immense overspending. The income from the

Lieutenant Hambrough

family's estates brought in something over £4,000 per year, far too little for the expensive tastes of Major Hambrough. In 1885 he had mortgaged his life assurance with the Eagle Insurance Company to the tune of £37,000 and had managed to get through that vast sum in just five years. Most of the estates were, by this time, mortgaged and finding funds was becoming increasingly difficult. The family gradually sank lower and lower in terms of their living accommodation, always just a step away from the Major's creditors. Despite his financial difficulties, the Major was insistent that his offspring should still receive the benefits due to their rank and he wanted Cecil to join the army and his two daughters to be educated in Germany.

Major Hambrough, in his search for more potential financial assistance, had made the acquaintance of one Beresford Loftus Tottenham, or 'Tots' to his intimates. Tots was about 30 years old, ex-10th Hussars, a former mercenary in the Ottoman suppression of the Cretan Rebellion in 1889 and, latterly, the owner of Kempton and Co., a finance house. Tots offered to help the Major's son join the army. Clearly, the boy had to be tutored well and introduced to the right people to ensure that he would have a glittering military career. Accordingly, Tots introduced the Major to Alfred John Monson, a blond, clean-cut man with an aristocratic bearing. Monson would tutor Cecil for the sum of £300 per year and ensure that the boy was guided well along his chosen path.

As for Monson's credentials, it appears that his bearing and appearance were sufficient to convince the Major that he was the right man for job. Certainly, Monson had the right background; his uncle was none other than Sir Edmund John Monson, the British Ambassador in Vienna. Monson had received his education at Rugby and Oxford and had been a government official in South Africa. It was there, in Cape Town, that he had married the daughter of a Yorkshire colliery owner, Agnes Maud, but South African life does not appear to have had a great allure for him, as he had returned to live in England. At the time of the appointment, Monson told the Major that he was just about to move out of his house near Harrogate to take up residence at Riseley Hall in Yorkshire.

Unfortunately, there was much about Monson that the Major would never learn until it was too late. Beneath the ordered and wealthy lifestyle lay secrets and ways of operating that would spell doom for the Hambrough family. When Monson had returned from South Africa he took up residence in Cheney Court. This large mansion was insured by Monson against fire and the place soon burned down. From the proceeds of the insurance pay-out, he moved on to Gaddesley Farm, where he became involved in an agricultural fraud case. He was acquitted of wrong-doing, but moved on to Woodlands in Harrogate. It was here that the young Mr Cecil moved to join his new tutor. On the face of it, the arrangement was perfect for Monson's protégé: his mentor lived like a lord, had extensive grounds and staff and was at the very centre of polite society's social circle. Money seemed to be no object.

The truth was very different; Monson had run up ruinous debts all around the area. His bank account was disastrously overdrawn and he owed money the length and breadth of Yorkshire. He was declared bankrupt with liabilities of £56,000 and assets of just £600. He moved on again, taking Cecil Hambrough with him to Riseley Hall. Although this was the eleventh place that Monson had lived in since his return to England, his taste for the high life was undiminished and things became pretty much as they had been at Woodlands. Not only did Monson take on a whole new batch of employees, from a butler to a governess for the children, but he also engaged a tutor for Cecil Hambrough, paying him half of the sum that the Major had agree to pay him for such duties.

Monson and the Major met in London on several occasions to discuss Cecil's progress and prospects, and it seems clear that through Tot, Monson became fully aware of the precarious financial position of his protégé's father. It also seems that Monson would sometimes give the Major small sums of money to help him out, which seems a very strange thing to do. Monson's ambition knew no bounds and he was already planning to acquire the Major's life assurance policy from the Eagle Insurance Company and thus gain control over the Hambrough estates. Given the fact that Monson was an undischarged bankrupt, it would seem unlikely that he could gain access to funds legally, but young Cecil Hambrough would help him. Monson knew that he had to continue to control the life and fortune of the Major's son; this was the key to the Hambrough estates.

Financially, Monson was aided and abetted by Tots and another London-based man by the name of Adolphus Frederick James Jerningham. They would, when the time came, bankroll Monson in the purchase of the insurance policy and share the proceeds with him. For now, however, despite the Major's poor health, the fact remained that Cecil had to be provided for and kept under the influence of Monson. Debts were again beginning to build up at Riseley Hall, but Monson had already begun to make more plans to move on again. This time, the move would take Cecil as far away from the influence of his father as was humanly possible.

Monson had entered into negotiations with Lamonts of Cowal for the purchase of the Ardlamont estate in Scotland. The asking price was a staggering £85,000, a snip for Monson, whose connections would surely be on hand for the necessary financial backing. He told the owners that he wished to sample the estate before committing himself to buy it from them. They agreed to rent it to him for the shooting season at the not inconsiderable price of £450. Tots and Jerningham came up with the rent as Monson was penniless again. At around this time, Tots began sending Cecil £10 per week for expenses, such was the confidence of the three in the eventual pay-out once they had acquired the Hambrough estates.

In April 1893, Major Hambrough was told by Monson that he had enrolled Cecil in the Yorkshire Militia. The Major was livid as he had expressly told Monson that he wished his son to join the Hampshire Militia. The Major had several old friends whose sons were in the Hampshire Militia, and they would have been on hand to help his son. The upshot of the matter was that the Major demanded that Monson send his son home and sever all ties with the family. By now, however, it appears that Cecil was completely under Monson's control, as he refused his father's demands and told the Major that he was staying with Monson. On a practical level, Cecil's decision needs to be put into the context of the lifestyle that he was enjoying against the reality of life back with his family.

Although the immediate opportunity to acquire the Hambrough estates seemed to have passed after the argument between Monson and the Major, Monson was determined to retire to the Ardlamont estate and take Cecil with him. Again, Tots forwarded the necessary funds, and Monson, his wife, Cecil and the rest of the Monson family moved to Scotland. Monson's wife pawned her jewellery and the family silver, leaving the family linen at the laundry as they could not afford to pay the bill. The £450 due to the Lamonts was not due until 1 August, but by the beginning of July, the Monson clan was installed in Ardlamont and with it a new line of credit.

Monson had but 2s 6d in his pocket when he arrived at the estate, all that remained from the money Tots had given him and the efforts of his wife to raise capital. Nevertheless, he soon assembled a new staff and ordered food and wine from local merchants and hotels. He also acquired the steam yacht *Alert,* which lay in berth at Tighnabruaich (The House on the Hill).

Matters were about to take a very serious turn for the worse. On around 9 July 1893, the

Scottish Provident Institution, based in Edinburgh, received a request for an insurance policy from Agnes Maud Monson. She wanted to insure Cecil Hambrough's life for £50,000. The insurance company requested information about the interest that Mrs Monson had in Cecil's life. The reply that the company received did not divulge this, but proposed to reduce the insurance value to £10,000. Again, the insurance company requested information about Mrs Monson's reasons for insuring Cecil. They were never to receive an explanation.

Meanwhile, Monson had his wife write to the London and Globe Company in Liverpool, again proposing a life insurance policy of £50,000. The London and Globe's response was no different from the Scottish Provident; they too wanted to know why Mrs Monson wanted to insure the life of Cecil Hambrough. Nothing ventured, nothing gained, Monson sent a second request for a life insurance policy of £26,000 to the London and Globe, this time, however, he attached a letter, dated 31 July 1893, from Cecil Hambrough himself:

> I am requested by Mrs Agnes Monson to write and inform you that she has an interest
> in my life to the extent of £26,000. I have given her an undertaking under which I
> agree to pay her this sum after my attaining twenty-one, if I should live till then.

Why would Cecil Hambrough have written this letter? How could Monson have persuaded him that this was a reasonable request? What was the basis of the so-called £26,000 interest in Cecil's life? Given the fact that Cecil Hambrough was already 20 years old, what significance was there in the words 'if I should live till then'? Unfortunately, the true meaning, as far as Monson's plans were concerned, was all too clear: his young ward would be dead within days.

In the event, the London and Globe refused the insurance policy and Monson turned to yet another insurance company in order to achieve his aims. On 2 August 1893 Monson telephoned the Glasgow branch of the Mutual Assurance Company of New York. Having been refused on two occasions, Monson had quickly created a new story to convince the insurance manager. He claimed to be the legal guardian of Cecil Hambrough and said that the young man, not yet 21, was about to inherit £200,000. Cecil Hambrough, he claimed, had set his heart on purchasing the Ardlamont estate but unfortunately, due to competition to buy the property, he would have to complete his purchase by 8 August, and before he received his inheritance. Therefore, Monson claimed, his wife, Agnes, was lending Cecil £20,000 in order to secure the property. It was therefore right, proper and prudent for Mrs Monson to insure Cecil until such time that he had received his inheritance and could pay back the advance. By all accounts the manager of the Glasgow branch was convinced by the story. However, the problem remained that Monson had to raise the capital to pay the premium. He wrote to Tots and told him that he was buying the Ardlamont estate for Cecil for £48,000 and needed his friend to forward him the deposit of £250. In confidence Monson told Tots that Cecil believed the purchase price to be £50,000 and that he and Monson could share the £2,000 difference. Tots was happy with the prospect of making a quick £1,000 so he forwarded the £250 by cheque, which Mrs Monson then paid into her account at the Royal Bank of Scotland's branch in Tighnabruaich, in which she had already deposited £15. Mrs Monson could then pay the £194 3s 4d to the Mutual Assurance Company of New York on 8 August. This was to cover the premiums for two policies, each of £10,000. Cecil Hambrough had already signed the proposal forms on 2 August and had a medical examination the same day.

We need to ask the question yet again, why did Cecil Hambrough go along with this subterfuge? Obviously he was convinced that Monson was prepared to purchase the Ardlamont estate on his behalf but what reason did Cecil have to think that he would ever be in a position to pay Monson back? He must have been aware of his father's poor financial situation and the fact that much of the Hambrough estates was already heavily mortgaged. What also is significant is the fact that earlier in 1893 Mrs Monson had sued Cecil Hambrough for £1,000. It was claimed that neither Cecil nor the Major had paid for his board, lodging and education. The Hambroughs did not contest the case in court and as a result the court found in her favour. Monson was able to sell the £1,000 judgement to Tots for £200; this was presumably part of the bigger plan to acquire the Hambrough estate. It can only be assumed that Monson was manipulating both Cecil and his wife. Certainly the former was completely taken in by his mentor's lifestyle and ability to make decisions on his behalf.

It was arranged that three of Cecil's friends from the Yorkshire Militia would join him at the Ardlamont estate on 12 August; presumably they would pay for their board and lodging as well as any shooting that could be arranged by Monson.

While Monson was in Glasgow arranging the insurance on Cecil's life, he met up with a very strange character who was a turf accountant's clerk. Edward Davis, or Edward Sweeney, was known among his friends as 'Long Ted'. He had travelled up from London to meet Monson and was introduced to Cecil as Edward Scott. They arrived at Ardlamont having travelled on a steamer from Greenock. During the voyage Monson had not acknowledged Long Ted and was engaged in a conversation with Mr Donald, a shipbuilder from Paisley, where he concluded the deal to buy the *Alert* for £1,200.

The staff and inhabitants of Ardlamont believed that Scott was a marine engineer and that Monson had brought him to the house to check over the *Alert* and confirm whether the purchase price was reasonable. On the morning of 9 August Monson and Scott went swimming in Ardlamont Bay and after lunch they approached the Ardlamont carpenter, Mr McNicol, to enquire whether they could borrow his boat for a couple of days. McNicol readily agreed and Scott and Monson rowed the boat from Ardlamont ferry into Ardlamont Bay. Monson already had the use of another boat from Mr McKellar, who hired boats at Tighnabruaich, and Cecil had used it on a number of occasions to go fishing. Monson had told McNicol that he did not think that McKellar's boat was very safe, which is strange given the fact that Monson and Scott took Monson's children out in that boat later in the afternoon.

What then was the significance of the second boat? Clearly there was one; McNicol's boat had a plug hole with a cork in it and McKellar's did not. After having taken the children onto the lake Scott began working on the cork with a knife. After they had eaten early that evening, Monson suggested to Cecil that they go out onto the lake to fish, to which the young man readily agreed. Scott installed himself beside the water and watched the two men row out onto the lake. However, it was not McNicol's boat that they had used, it was McKellar's. The two men had not progressed very far across the water when suddenly the boat inexplicably sank. Monson knew that unlike himself Cecil Hambrough could not swim. This is his version of the events:

> Hambrough took off his coat and rowed, while I busied myself preparing the nets. While occupied with the nets, suddenly there was a bump, and the boat tilted and I fell over the side. At the same time the boat capsized, and for a minute or two I was entangled in the nets. Immediately on getting clear I called out for Hambrough, and then I saw him sitting on the rock laughing. Hambrough, I knew, could not swim, so I told him to wait while I swam ashore and fetched another boat which was there.

Whether this was a genuine attempt to murder Cecil is unknown. By all accounts the three men returned from the lake to Ardlamont House and drank whisky until 1am the following morning. At some point during this drinking session Monson suggested that they should go out shooting soon after sunrise. Neither of the two men that had found themselves in the water had suffered any serious injuries, and they joined Scott to go shooting in the woods at 6.30am. Three men entered the forest, but only two would come out.

Monson's version of events was recounted to the factor, Mr Steven, who also concluded at the time that the death must have been an accident. Only Monson and Hambrough were carrying guns and Scott had accompanied them to carry any game that they were lucky enough to hit. They entered the wood near the school house, with Hambrough on the right and Monson on the left. In order to avoid a shooting accident, Scott had prudently followed them into the wood some distance behind. Very soon both Monson and Scott lost sight of Cecil, then they heard a shot. Monson shouted out 'Have you got anything?' but there was no reply, so the two men searched the wood for Cecil and found him lying near a dyke. The police were immediately called and the Deputy Fiscal of Argyll, Tom Macnaughton, helped lay out the body himself. Macnaughton knew a newspaper reporter called Neil Munro, whom he bumped into by chance at Inveraray and confided in him that he had just been to Ardlamont to investigate the tragic death of Cecil Hambrough. He told Munro 'I've very grave doubts about the character of that accident'; but he refused to expand on the matter. Munro was a reporter on the *Evening News* in Glasgow and immediately after his conversation with Macnaughton, he went to see a contact at the County Court. He asked him to let him know if there were any developments regarding the Ardlamont case. Several days went by and then a telegram from Inveraray arrived at the offices of the *Evening News* addressed to Munro, which simply said 'Go to Ardlamont'. Munro lost no time and within the space of a few hours was making enquiries at the house itself, where he was told the same story that the police had heard from Mr Steven. He headed back to Auchenlochan Pier just in time to see the *Lord of the Isles* steamer arrive from Inveraray en route to Glasgow. With considerable satisfaction that he was on the trail of a good story, he saw several court officials, as well as the Chief Constable of Argyll, getting off the boat just as he was embarking. The next day he filed a story which he entitled 'The Ardlamont Mystery' and it was, perhaps, this story that began to make the authorities realise that there was something more to the death of Cecil Hambrough than had previously appeared.

By now Ardlamont was swarming with police, delving into every issue regarding the death. They even investigated the story surrounding the capsizing of McKellar's boat. McNicol told them that his boat did not have a plug hole but clearly there was one now and what is more, there was no cork. Local fishermen told the police that they were unaware of any rocks lying under the surface which McKellar's boat could have struck, which again made them all the more suspicious, yet no action was taken. It soon became clear to the Procurator Fiscal of Argyll that the death was suspicious, particularly when they discovered that just two days before Mr Cecil had died, his life had been insured by Mrs Monson for £20,000.

On 30 August the police arrived at Ardlamont House with a warrant to search the house for papers related to Cecil Hambrough. The Sheriff, constantly accompanied by Mrs Monson in the absence of her husband, systematically searched the house until coming to Mrs Monson's own room. There he found a bundle of letters in a private drawer. Mrs Monson was ready and burst into floods of tears, claiming that the letters were private and personal. She selected two of the letters in particular which the Sheriff willingly gave back to her and he took the rest with him.

Alfred Monson, meanwhile, was driving along the road between Ardlamont and Tighnabruaich when he saw another carriage approaching him. A man stepped out and signalled for Monson to stop. The man was none other than the Chief Constable of Argyll and he told the stunned Monson 'Alfred John Monson I have to arrest you on the charge of murdering Cecil Hambrough'. The police, now convinced that Monson and Scott had murdered Cecil Hambrough in the woods that morning, were also sure that they had attempted to murder him in Ardlamont Bay. Consequently Monson and, *in absentia*, Scott, were both charged with murder and attempted murder. Unfortunately for the police one of the birds had already flown; Scott, or Long Ted, had disappeared. The last time he had been seen was on Tighnabruaich Pier waiting for the steamer back to Glasgow on the very day that Cecil Hambrough had met his maker. Long Ted would not make an appearance again until long after the trial and its outcome had been decided in an Edinburgh court. The police desperately wanted to find Long Ted and by now they knew of his aliases. To this end they circulated a 'wanted' poster to all of the police stations around the British Isles. Their description was accurate and well-detailed and also offered the sum of £200 for information leading to his arrest. The description read:

Age about 30; height about 5 ft, 10 inches, thin build, broad shoulders; complexion pale, inclined to be sallow; eyes full, steel grey, high cheek bones, long thin face, sharp chin, dark wavy hair, brown moustache (may be shaved off), carries his shoulders well back, head slightly forward, suffers from asthma, has a habit of putting his right hand to his side when coughing, indelicate health; dresses well, and generally wears a low, hard felt hat.

It was signed by the Chief Constable, James Fraser.

In due course the Argyll police traced the Sweeney family in London and they were told that Long Ted had emigrated to Australia. Meanwhile Monson was on remand awaiting his trial and on 12 December 1893 he was called before the High Court in Edinburgh on the charges of attempted murder and murder of Windsor Dudley Cecil Hambrough at Ardlamont, Argyllshire on 10 August 1893.

As far as Monson was concerned Scott's non-appearance in court meant that there was no one present that could contradict anything that Monson claimed to have happened in the woods that morning. Without doubt had Scott appeared, then the probable outcome of the case would have been entirely different. It would have been most unlikely that the two 'conspirators' statements accorded with one another. Once again Tots came forward to support Monson financially, paying for food and wine to be brought to his prison cell daily.

From the outset the case attracted considerable attention from both Scottish and English newspapers and during the 10-day trial more than 2,000,000 words were written about the case on both sides of the border.

The court soon learned of the character of Alfred Monson; the fact that he was an undischarged bankrupt, that he had not paid the Lamonts their £450 rent for the shooting season, and the fact that he had not paid Mr Donald the £1,200 for the *Alert*. It also became obvious that Monson had paid for very little, and even the cartridge that had taken Cecil Hambrough's life had been purchased on credit. The police were of the opinion that Cecil Hambrough had died from gunshot wounds from a 12-bore cartridge. Indeed, they had found the wadding of such a cartridge near where his body had lain. This was particularly significant since Hambrough usually shot with a 20-bore gun. How could Cecil Hambrough have killed himself with a 12-bore cartridge fired from a 20-bore gun? The police could not confirm which of the two guns had been fired as it would appear that Monson and Scott, soon after finding the body of Cecil Hambrough, had returned to the house, removed the cartridges from the guns and cleaned them both. It was only then that they had told anyone about the accident in the woods.

Three medical experts appeared for the prosecution. Dr Joseph Bell (who had taught Arthur Conan Doyle, who had then based Sherlock Holmes on the doctor), Henry Littlejohn and Patrick Heron Watson were of the opinion that Cecil Hambrough had been killed by a shot which had been fired nine feet behind him. They even produced in court three trees as evidence of the line of the shot. The rowan, beech and lime were each grooved with a pellet fired from the same cartridge. It is an interesting side issue that when the police made the decision to cut down the trees to present them as evidence, they set an officer the task of guarding the trees all night. The policeman pitched a tent beside the three trees and at about 2am one morning he heard the distinct sound of someone moving around in the woodland. The police officer sprang out of the tent to see the dark shape of a man clung to the rowan tree. As the officer shouted and rushed towards the figure, he disappeared into the undergrowth.

Dr Littlejohn produced a skull to show the court where the cartridge had entered Cecil Hambrough's head, apparently proving conclusively that the shot had come from behind.

The 15-man jury were then told about the financial web that had been woven around

Monson and his friends. They were also advised about the money problems faced by the Hambrough family. The prosecution also called the Solicitor General, Alexander Asher, who described to the jury Monson and Scott's attempt to drown Cecil Hambrough the night before he was shot. The truth is that Asher's evidence was purely circumstantial and that the truth behind the use of the two boats could never be adequately explained by either the prosecution or the defence.

Monson was defended by Comrie Thomson, who began by addressing the jury directly:

Gentlemen, I remember more than five-and-thirty years ago sitting in one of these benches and hearing an advocate, who afterwards became a great judge, standing where I now stand, pleading for a woman who was sitting in that dock charged with the crime of murder. He opened his address to the jury in words which have since become historical, but I repeat them to you now because of their great truth and wonderful simplicity. Gentlemen, the charge against the prisoner is murder, and the punishment of murder is death; and that simple statement is sufficient to suggest to you the awful nature of the occasion which brings you and me face to face. Gentlemen, we are all liable to make mistakes, I pray you make no mistake in this terribly serious matter. The result of your verdict is final, irreparable. What would any of you think if some day, it may be soon, this mystery is entirely unravelled, and it is demonstrated that that man is innocent, while your verdict has sent him to his death? He will not go unpunished if he is guilty. There is One in whose hands he is, Who is Infallible and Omniscient. I will repay, vengeance is mine, sayeth the Lord.

Thomson was, of course, referring to the Madeleine Smith case, which had seen a woman accused of a callous and premeditated murder but who had been saved from the gallows by the indecision of the jury. By likening Monson's case to Madeleine Smith's, Thomson was warning the jury that there was little to directly implicate Monson in the death of Cecil Hambrough. The question arose regarding Edward Scott or Long Ted. He had still not been discovered and without his corroborating evidence it was really impossible for anyone to be absolutely sure what had happened in the woods at Ardlamont in August. By implication at least from the prosecution's point of view, Monson had both motive and opportunity to murder Cecil Hambrough. Thomson's opinion was that the prosecution had proved little beyond besmirching the character of his client and that if the jury found him guilty they would be condemning an innocent man.

Lord MacDonald, the presiding judge, summed up without saying anything directly against Monson. He later wrote about the Ardlamont case in his memoirs:

I went through nine days of anxiety, such as I have never experienced before or since. So dominant was the anxiety that, morning after morning, I awoke long before my usual time, and lay in a dull perspiration, turning things over and over, endeavouring to weigh them and determine their weight in the balance. Never before had I gone through an experience the least like it, and I am well pleased that I have never had a similar experience since. It was all the more trying because I felt quite unable to form a determined opinion in my own mind. The way never seemed clear to me.

The jury returned in just 73 minutes with the unanimous verdict of 'not proven'. Monson was given leave to stand down from the dock, but it would not be the last time that he appeared before a judge and jury.

The Monson clan retreated to Scarborough, leaving behind them more merchants and retailers with unpaid bills. As for the house, Ardlamont was finally sold for about £70,000, given its notoriety and the unfortunate story attached to it.

Monson was next heard of in London. He was engaged by Mr Morritt, a ventriloquist and magician, to appear and present lectures at the Prince's Hall in Piccadilly. A packed auditorium on the first night was disappointed to be told that unfortunately Mr Monson had not chosen to appear after all. Soon after Madame Tussaud's Wax Museum acquired the clothes that Monson had been wearing in August 1893, along with the gun that he had been carrying. They proposed to exhibit a wax model of him in the Chamber of Horrors. Monson promptly acted by bringing a libel action against the waxworks, which prevented the model from going on show. Meanwhile, a carbon copy of the waxwork was being exhibited at Louis Tussaud's Waxworks in Birmingham. He, too, received a libel writ from Monson. Apparently, Madame Tussaud's had been approached by Tots on 3 January 1894. He had offered John Tussaud the clothes and gun and had promised that his friend Monson was willing to sit to have an accurate wax model made of him. Tots was paid £50 of the £100 fee agreed, but returned the money a couple of days later claiming that Monson had changed his mind about the deal. In actual fact the waxwork model never appeared in the Chamber of Horrors itself but was, in fact, placed between effigies of Queen Victoria and the Archbishop of Canterbury.

At some point soon after this, before the libel case was due to be heard before the Lord Chief Justice in London, Monson had cause to fall out with his old friend Tot. For some time much of Monson's property was stored in one of Tot's warehouses. Tots obviously decided that it was time to try and recoup some of the money that he had lent Monson over the years, and sold some of his friend's furniture. As a result Monson went to the police, who charged Tots with theft, for which he was subsequently jailed for three months.

So it was that when Tots was to appear as a witness for Monson in the Tussaud's libel case, he was brought from prison by a warder. Tots was in no mood to lie for his friend and told the court that they had taken a cab to Madame Tussaud's, stopping en route in Bond Street. Monson had brought with him the suit that he was wearing, but they did not have a gun. One was purchased in a shop and they then proceeded to meet John Tussaud and agree a deal. Monson stayed in the cab and when Tots returned to him they agreed that £100 was a derisory sum. This explained why they had backed out of the deal. The jury found in Monson's favour and awarded him one shilling for the loss of his suit and a farthing in damages. He was instructed by the judge that he would be expected to pay his own costs.

Monson was determined to make some money from his notoriety while it lasted and wrote a 72-page pamphlet called *The Ardlamont Mystery Solved*, to which is appended Scott's diary. Financially the pamphlet was a disaster and was simply a thinly veiled condemnation of the

Scottish police and the court system. Monson claimed that had the incident occurred in England, the case would never have come to trial.

If nothing else, the pamphlet flushed the mysterious Mr Scott out of his hiding place. In many respects this was a brave thing for Edward Sweeney to do, as since he had failed to appear in court, by Scottish law he was considered an outlaw. Sweeney asked the editor of the *Pall Mall Gazette* to interview him so that the truth about Cecil Hambrough's death could finally be told. The editor immediately contacted Scotland Yard and offered them the opportunity to arrest Mr Scott when he appeared at the *Gazette*'s offices for the interview. However, Scotland Yard had already removed Scott's name from their list of wanted persons as the case had been heard in Scotland and as far as they were concerned the matter was closed. In his interview Sweeney told the editor: 'I am a moral coward; I must confess it. I must also lack much reasoning power in the hour of danger, for I had but one idea, and that was flight.'

He went on to claim that he had left Ardlamont completely oblivious of the fact that the police would be interested in speaking to him, but once he had discovered that he was wanted for murder, he had shaved off his moustache, adopted a disguise and become Mr White. He went on to complain that he feared a return to Scotland as it was his impression that he would immediately be arrested.

Sweeney did return to Scotland of his own accord on 4 May 1894, giving his occupation as a commission agent and a home address of 66 Meadow Road, Clapham. He told the Lord's Commissioners in Edinburgh that he was perfectly prepared to stand trial for the attempted murder and murder of Cecil Hambrough. The case was called on 21 May, but to the dismay of the three law lords that had been assembled, the prosecution failed to appear. Consequently there was nothing to be said or done, apart from revoking Sweeney's outlaw status and telling him that he was no longer wanted on either of the charges.

Nearly a year later Monson too found himself in Edinburgh. It was April 1895 and the aforementioned Mr Morritt was appearing at the Operetta House. During his run a letter purporting to be from Monson appeared in one of the Edinburgh newspapers. It read:

> I challenge Mr Morritt to try his hand on me, with a view to clearing up the
> Ardlamont Mystery. I see he is to appear at the Operetta House on Monday next, and
> as I shall be in Edinburgh at the same time, I am willing to afford him an opportunity
> of publicly testing his theories.

It seems that hypnotism was among the multi-talented Morritt's tricks, and he was famed for being able to extract information from those that he called up on stage. Monson was indeed in Edinburgh on 25 April 1895 and he was seen with Morritt walking into a public house in the Lothian Road. It was clear that this publicity stunt had been well planned between the pair of them. In the evening, after Morritt had performed a series of conjuring tricks, he stepped forward to the front of the stage and replied to Monson's challenge by saying 'If Mr Monson is in the building, I shall have pleasure in accepting his challenge.' Monson immediately rose from his seat in the dress circle and it was announced that the mesmerism would occur at 9pm the following evening.

The audience assembled at the Operetta House on the Tuesday evening and watched, entranced, as Morritt directed his powers on Monson. Morritt asked the audience to pose their own questions directly to Monson. In his trance-like state Monson denied murdering Cecil Hambrough and claimed that he did not know how he was killed. The performance met with mixed response from the audience and not all were convinced of either Morritt's abilities or Monson's truthfulness.

After his last public appearance Monson tried to obtain the £20,000 from the Mutual Assurance Company of New York on behalf of his wife, but seems to have failed. He then took up the alter-ego of Alfred John Wyvill and lived in Douglas on the Isle of Man. He insured the property that he was living in for £500, and again it was soon burned to the ground. Somehow the insurance company discovered his real identity and refused to pay out. He then moved back to London, and it seems that he spent the next two years or so working for money-lenders. His speciality, it appears, was to lend money at exorbitant rates to young heirs who needed quick money for their fast lives. He was arrested and charged in 1898 for an attempted fraud on the Norwich Union Life Assurance Society. He and two other men were sentenced to five years in prison. It was while he was in prison that he attempted to divorce Agnes on the grounds of adultery. He claimed that in 1891 she had been unfaithful to him on two occasions with two different men; one he named, the other he did not know. Paradoxically one of the men that Agnes was accused of sleeping with was none other than Cecil Hambrough. The court rejected Monson's claims, provoking Agnes to write her own book about the terrible life that she had led with Alfred John Monson. It is significant that, knowing her husband's litigious nature, she did not accuse him of murdering Cecil Hambrough.

As for Edward Scott, or Sweeney, he, too, appeared in 1896 in Glasgow with the intention of telling his own story to the audience at the Gaiety Theatre in Sauchiehall Street. According to witnesses at this event, from the moment Scott appeared on the stage the audience hissed and booed at him and not a word of what he said was understood.

The last words on the case perhaps belong to the Hambrough family. With no one brought to justice or a reasonable explanation offered for the death of their son, they posted the following message in the *Glasgow Herald* on 10 August for many years after Cecil's death.

> In loving memory of our dear son, Windsor Dudley Cecil Hambrough, found shot dead in a wood at Ardlamont, Argyllshire, August 10th, 1893, in his 21st year.
> 'Vengeance is Mine, I will repay, sayeth the Lord'.

All the evidence in the case was circumstantial, and we cannot blame the jury for having returned a verdict of 'not proven'. Even if Cecil Hambrough had not died accidentally by his own hand, there was no firm evidence to suggest that the shot had been fired by Monson. The time and the place, if it was a murder, had been perfectly chosen. Within the depths of the woods no one could witness what happened shortly after 6.30am on 10 August 1893.

CHAPTER TWELVE

THE UNCONSUMMATED MARRIAGE

The Capture and Trial of Christina Gilmour - Paisley, 1843

CHRISTINA or Christian Cochran was born at South Grange, near Dunlop in Ayrshire on 25 November 1818. She was the daughter of a strict Presbyterian, Alexander Cochran, who was a wealthy landowner and the owner of several farms at South and West Grange. Christina had been educated at a Glasgow boarding school and had then worked for a short time on the farm before being sent to Paisley where she was taught dressmaking. Both her looks and family's wealth brought a number of potential future husbands knocking on the Cochrans' door. It was obvious that her parents had set their sights on her marrying someone that they considered a social superior. Christina had already formed a close friendship, which blossomed into love, with John Anderson, who was the son of a neighbouring farmer and about 10 years older than her. Christina and John had an agreement that when his circumstances permitted it, they would marry, but the childhood sweethearts, as they had been, had not accounted for the fact that Christina's father had another man in mind for his daughter. Christina had already turned down many suitors in the belief that one day she would marry John Anderson.

When John Gilmour appeared on the scene he was not only younger than Anderson, but Christina's parents obviously considered him to be an ideal match. He was the son of another wealthy neighbouring farmer and actually had his own farm in Renfrewshire. Gilmour was well educated and was keen to woo Christina. When he proposed to her initially she refused. He told her that if she did not marry him then he would kill himself. Christina was clearly impressed with this devoted declaration and agreed to be his bride.

Meanwhile, John Anderson continued to visit Christina at South Grange and she had the unfortunate task of telling the besotted man that she was to marry another. It may be that Christina had hoped that this bombshell would prompt Anderson to make his own proposal of marriage. In the event, although surprised and shocked, Anderson agreed to abide by what Christina wanted and to renounce his intention to marry her. It seems that Anderson's reaction changed Christina's outlook on life entirely. Previously she had been a cheerful and happy woman but now she became preoccupied and moody. Christina took to wandering around the countryside at night and often had to be searched for by her sisters and the rest of the family. She also began to eat to extreme, whereas normally she had picked at food and had a very meagre appetite.

The marriage ceremony was put off twice, her parents becoming increasingly concerned that the marriage would never happen, particularly given the fact that she was still corresponding with John Anderson. John Gilmour was becoming impatient and he persuaded Christina to go with him to Glasgow in order to post the banns for a third time, finally fixing the date of the marriage for 29 November 1842. The ceremony was performed by the Reverend Dickie, minister of the Dunlop parish. After the ceremony Christina and her new husband, accompanied by one of her sisters, left for John Gilmour's farm at Town of Inchinnan, near Paisley in Renfrewshire. The house stood beside Inchinnan Bridge and although Gilmour had made every attempt to make the place as inviting for his new wife as possible, it seems that even on the first night there were problems. Christina sat up in front of a fire, brooding, for the whole of her wedding night.

The days passed by with little change in Christina's manner. It was said that Christina did not even undress during the short period that the marriage lasted. Certainly it appears to be almost certain that the marriage was never consummated. Christina apparently told her new husband that she did not know why she had married him and that although he had her respect, she could not be a true wife to him. Within six weeks of the wedding, John Gilmour was dead. But before then Christina had confided in the maid, Mary Patterson, who had been a long-serving employee of the Gilmours, that she had only married John Gilmour because that was what her father had wished and that by some means she would reunite herself with the man that she truly loved, John Anderson.

Throughout their short marriage John Gilmour was convinced that Christina would gradually adjust to married life and her existence at his farm. During those six weeks Gilmour also played host to one or other of Christina's sisters. Oddly Christina and John would always eat their meals in the parlour alone. Even Christina's sisters were not allowed to intrude and were forced to eat their meals in the kitchen.

On Monday 26 December 1842, just a month after the couple had married, Christina gave Mary Patterson 2d to purchase some arsenic in Paisley during the servant's visit to see a relative. Curiously she told Mrs Patterson not to buy the poison herself but to go to a particular house and ask a boy to get it for her. Christina explained that she wanted to poison the rats which she felt were overrunning the farm. Unfortunately, by the time Mary got to Paisley she had forgotten the address that Christina had given her. She personally visited Dr Vessey's chemist shop and purchased the arsenic. The chemist asked her for whom the arsenic was being bought, to which Mary innocently replied Mrs Gilmour of Inchinnan. Consequently, when Mary gave Christina the packet labelled 'arsenic poison' it had her own name on it.

On Wednesday 28 December Christina accosted Mary in the boiler house and told her that she was too frightened to use the arsenic because she was not sure how to prepare it. Mary later testified that Christina then threw the packet of arsenic into the boiler. Later that day Mary Patterson took a short New Year's holiday, leaving the Gilmours alone without a house servant. John Gilmour was a strong and vigorous 30-year-old man, but the following day he became seriously unwell and was violently sick. The couple had arranged to visit John's family in Ayrshire on 2 January 1843 and, despite the fact that John had continued to be extremely ill over the weekend, they left that morning in a gig bound for Dunlop. Gilmour's father witnessed his son with a swollen face, complaining of internal pains and suffering from bouts of vomiting throughout the visit. On the following day, Tuesday 3 January, they drove home and arrived late in the afternoon. Gilmour again suffered from severe sickness symptoms; throughout he was carefully looked after by Christina, who, in the absence of Mary Patterson, prepared her husband's food, drinks and medicines.

It appears that Gilmour was not entirely confined to bed during this period and certainly on Wednesday 4 January he was seen near the stables by one of the farmhands. The man described Gilmour as having a swollen face and watering eyes. Gilmour apparently explained to the man that he had been suffering from a sickness. By the Thursday Gilmour's condition had considerably worsened and he was confined to his room.

By Friday 6 January, with Mary Patterson back, John Gilmour was on his deathbed. Christina explained to Mary that she was going to Renfrew, about two miles away, as 'she wanted something, to see if it would do her husband any good'. Christina must have left at the crack of dawn as she was back at the house by breakfast. We can accurately time Christina's reappearance at the farm by the testimony of John Muir, one of the farmhands. He claimed to have passed the boiler house between 8 and 9am that morning and went to have his breakfast. On his return there was a black, silk bag propped up against the wall. Inquisitiveness got the better of him and he opened it; in the bag he found a small phial of liquid and a paper packet. The paper packet was tied with thread and had a single word written on the paper, 'poison'. He unplugged the phial and smelt the liquid and was convinced that it was some kind of women's scent. In any event, he replaced the phial and paper packet and took the bag to Mary Patterson. She, too, looked at the two items and then approached Christina to ask her whether the bag was hers. Christina took the bag from her and commented that she had purchased some turpentine to rub into her husband's skin. This was an interesting explanation since when John Muir had smelled the liquid he had not recognised the smell. He would certainly have known if the liquid was turpentine. As far as Mary Patterson was concerned, the packet looked very much like the one that she had brought back from Paisley herself, but she could not be sure.

Much later in the day Christina again left the house, taking with her John Muir, who also worked at the farm. She explained to him that since her husband was refusing to see a doctor, she felt that the only thing she could do was to ask her uncle Robert Robertson in Paisley what she should do. In the event, her uncle hardly recognised Christina, particularly as he had not seen her for almost four years. She told him that she was married to John Gilmour but 'she would rather have preferred one Anderson'. Robertson offered to send his own doctor but Christina told him that she would prefer it if he made the visit to see her husband himself in order to sound John Gilmour out about seeing a doctor at all.

While Christina and Sandy were in Paisley the events of the day had been preying on John Muir's mind. He was unable to reconcile what he had seen and heard and went up to see John Gilmour in his bedroom at around 8.30pm. He could see that Gilmour was in great pain and offered to get him a doctor, but his employer told him that this would be the best course of action should he not feel better in the morning. Muir was insistent and Gilmour finally agreed that he should go and fetch Dr McLaws at Renfrew. Muir took one of the other farmhands with him. Fortunately they did not have to travel far, as they happened to bump into Dr McLaws at the Inchinnan Tollhouse. Although by this time it was nearly midnight and the doctor had had a fair bit to drink, he agreed to come back with them and see Gilmour straight away.

McLaws found Gilmour suffering from fevers, pain and thirst and concluded that the patient had some kind of inflammation. He bled Gilmour and then told Muir to rub turpentine into his body. Christina arrived to see the doctor's horse tied up near the front door and went straight up to her husband's bedroom. It appears that she told the doctor that she had already purchased some turpentine and that she had matters in hand and that his services were no longer required.

At 8am on Saturday 7 January a well-dressed woman entered the shop of the chemist, Mr Wilie, in Renfrew. She wanted to purchase some arsenic for killing rats and told the chemist that her name was Mrs Robertson and that she was purchasing the arsenic on behalf of John Ferguson, who was a local farmer. The chemist asked her what was the name of Ferguson's farm but the Mrs Robertson could not tell him. Luckily for the chemist a local man called James Smith, who knew the farmers in the area well, was outside the shop at the time and could confirm that he did not know of a man called Ferguson owning a farm in the area. Mrs Robertson then told the chemist and Smith that his farm was closer to Paisley, which seems to have satisfied the two men because Wilie gave her 2d worth of arsenic in a paper parcel and marked it 'poison arsenic'. The chemist, by law, had to enter the transaction into a book and James Smith signed the entry as his witness. Wilie's wife noted that when Mrs Robertson left the shop she was not heading in the direction of Paisley. Later at the trial Mrs Wilie was certain that Christina Gilmour was Mrs Robertson.

Between 10 and 11am that morning John Gilmour's father, Matthew, came over from Dunlop to see his son. He saw that John was extremely ill but was pleased to see Mr Robertson arrive at about 4pm and left content that the best was being done for his son. Robertson was told by John Gilmour about Dr McLaws visit and that Christina had arranged for Dr McKechnie, who was Robertson's own doctor, to make a visit if he got worse. Once again, out of earshot of her husband, Christina spoke to her uncle about her unhappy marriage and said 'it had been against her mind in taking Gilmour'.

At 9am the following morning Robertson received a message from Inchinnan asking him to bring Dr McKechnie as soon as possible. When Dr McKechnie arrived he found that John Gilmour's pulse was 112 and that he was very feverish and thirsty. He was told about the vomiting and diarrhoea but unfortunately Christina had not kept samples for the doctor to look at. He told Christina that she should ensure that she retained anything that her husband excreted or vomited for him to have a look at the following day. In the meantime, McKechnie prescribed a concoction of camomile, tartaric acid and soda powders; he believed that John's problem was a bilious one. Shortly before the doctor left Mr Robertson arrived himself and spent the night helping Christina nurse her husband. John Muir, meanwhile, was sent to Mr Wilie's shop in Renfrew to collect the prescription Dr McKechnie had given.

On Monday 9 January McKechnie returned and found that Gilmour's pulse had reduced to 94 and that although the vomiting and diarrhoea had not abated, their frequency had lessened. When asked whether she had collected samples from the patient, Christina replied 'there was so little I did not think it worthwhile keeping them'.

Matthew Gilmour returned to his son's bedside on Tuesday, finding him actually worse than the last time that he had visited. Throughout the remaining hours of John Gilmour's life either his father or his wife was at his bedside to give him the powders which had been prescribed to him.

On Wednesday 11 January Dr McKechnie's son, who assisted his father, found the patient to be in a dangerous state of health. John Gilmour was bled again, which probably con-tributed to his final death. When he finally passed away his bedroom was positively heaving with friends, family and employees; his wife, his father, his 14-year-old cousin Andrew and John Muir were all present. Although slightly differently reported, both John Muir and Andrew Gilmour claim that shortly before John's death he whispered that he 'wished to be opened' and added, more loudly, either 'Oh, that woman! If you have given me anything!' or 'Oh, if you have given me anything, tell me before I die'. Neither of their statements were corroborated by John's father, as being rather hard of hearing he missed both statements.

On the following Monday, 16 January, the body of John Gilmour was buried in Dunlop churchyard. Soon after the funeral Christina wrote a letter to John Anderson. It soon became widely believed that Christina had poisoned her husband with arsenic. This probably began as rumours, circulated by the employees of the farm. Inevitably the gossip reached the ears of Superintendent McKay who, at some point in mid-April, paid a visit to the farm in order to make some preliminary enquiries. Whether he was convinced or not by the story of poisoning is probably reflected in the fact that the Procurator Fiscal granted a warrant to exhume the body and arrest Christina Gilmour for suspected murder. The warrant was signed on 21 April 1843.

The gossip had also reached the ears of Alexander Cochran, Christina's father, who advised his daughter to make herself scarce. He claimed later that Christina was not willing to leave the area and that she had no idea that it was his intention to send her to America. It seems that Alexander asked his brother, Robert, to make all the necessary arrangements. As Christina made her circuitous journey to Liverpool it seems that she was blissfully unaware of how her disappearance might be interpreted by the authorities. As far as her family was concerned, they later claimed that Christina had no idea what they had planned for her and that they had told her that she just needed to be away from the area for a few days. On the day that Christina left Robert had arranged for a man to take her on foot to an arranged place where another stranger drove her in a carriage to a house. Waiting there was a third stranger who may have been either a man called Simpson, a gardener from Renfrewshire, or a shoemaker from Ayrshire. In any event, this man was also going to America and Robert had arranged for him to chaperone Christina safely to America.

Paradoxically it does appear that Christina had some inkling, at least by the time that she reached the boat, that she was not coming back and that efforts had been made to conceal where she was and where she was going. Her companion signed them onto the *Excel*, bound for New York, as Mr and Mrs John Spiers. Christina also wrote another letter to John Anderson, which was dated 28 April.

While Christina was making her difficult journey to Liverpool and America, the body of John Gilmour was exhumed on 22 April and a post-mortem was carried out by the Paisley doctors, Wilie and McKinlay. Their internal examination of the body revealed the tell-tale signs of arsenic poisoning but to be sure they removed several parts for further examination.

On 24 April the police arrived at South Grange with a warrant for Christina's arrest on a charge of murder. Superintendent McKay soon discovered that Christina had fled the scene via Carlisle and Liverpool. He now knew that Christina was bound for America and obtained a warrant for her extradition on 18 May. He boarded Cunard's *Acadia*. Amazingly, he made it to New York three weeks before the *Excel* sailed into the harbour. By then he had secured co-operation with the authorities there under the Treaty of Washington, which had been signed on 9 August 1842.

Unaware of the welcoming party awaiting her, Christina was astonished when she was accosted by Superintendent McKay on 21 June after he had boarded the *Excel* in a custom house boat. It was most unfortunate for Christina that her attempts to deny the fact that she was Christina Gilmour were foiled by the fact that McKay, who had known her husband, had actually met her and knew her by sight. Somehow in the confusion 'Mr Spiers', who had accompanied her on the voyage, disappeared and was never seen again. One final point on the mysterious Mr Spiers is that apparently he took his role of being Christina's 'husband' to its logical conclusion during the voyage. Apparently, Christina had cause to ask for the protection of the captain of the vessel from his unwanted advances.

The United States Commissioner, Sylvanus Rapalyea, heard the initial extradition proceedings with a New York lawyer, Mr Warner, appearing for Christina. He claimed that his client was insane and was therefore seeking asylum and, at the very least, the hearing should be postponed until medical professionals had had the opportunity to examine his client. By 12 July no fewer than eight New York doctors had examined Christina, five of whom presented evidence in great detail. Of the others, one's evidence was disallowed, and the remaining two failed to appear. Their combined opinion, after much cross-examination, was that Christina was mentally ill. Throughout their observations of her she had talked gibberish, shown signs of self-mutilation, sat rocking on the floor and asked them whether she could go home by coach. The bombshell was that although Christina displayed all of these signs of insanity, it was their opinion that she was play-acting. Mr Warner, her lawyer, now questioned the validity of the proceedings against his client. The only course of action was to appeal directly to the President of the United States, John Tyler. Accordingly, on 9 August, the Secretary of State delivered his conclusions, which were that Christina Gilmour be surrendered to George McKay as a legal officer of the government of Her Britannic Majesty. Warner was not beaten and he now requested a writ of *habeas corpus* to the Second Circuit of the Southern District of New York. He claimed that not only had proceedings been illegal on the grounds that the Treaty of Washington was not fully in place, but also that Mr Sylvanus Rapalyea had failed to prove that the murder charge against Christina was valid.

On 12 August the request was denied and by 16 August McKay and Christina were back en route to Liverpool. The police officer and the prisoner were accompanied by a woman who originally came from Paisley and, by luck, wished to return to Scotland. It took them 26 days to reach Liverpool. From there they boarded the *Achilles* steamer to Greenock and then took a train to Paisley.

On Wednesday 14 September 1843 Christina was examined before the Sheriff and committed for trial. In her declaration Christina described her journey to America and the fact that she knew before she left that her husband's body was going to be exhumed. Concerning her husband, she said that prior to the New Year, John had been suffering from headaches and chest pains which he personally believed was a heart problem. At some point the husband and wife had had a conversation in which they told one another that the other had broken their heart. She admitted buying arsenic from Mr Wilie in the name of Mrs Robertson and claimed that she intended to take her own life with the poison. As for the original packet of arsenic, which Mary Patterson had seen her burning, Christina claimed that the packet was neither opened nor used, as she was too frightened to scatter it around to kill the rats. She denied at any time giving arsenic to John Gilmour. She claimed that it was her husband that had refused to see a doctor, despite the fact that she had urged him to do so. She could not account for the fact that there was arsenic in her husband's body and said 'he got none from me, and I am not aware that he got any from anybody else'.

Paisley prison was her home until she was brought to trial before the High Court of Justiciary in Edinburgh on Friday 12 January 1844. This was four months after her examination by the Sheriff and a year and a day after the death of her husband. The presiding judge was Lord Justice-Clerk Hope, assisted by Lords Moncreiff and Wood. The prosecuting counsel was the Lord Advocate Duncan McNeill, assisted by Advocate-Deputies Charles Neaves and David Milne. Christina was defended by Thomas Maitland and Alexander McNeill. Here, in the Edinburgh court, she was formally presented with the accusation that between 26 December 1842 and 12 January 1843 at Town of Inchinnan and between 2 and 3 January 1843 at South Grange she administered arsenic to John Gilmour who fell ill and died on 11 January 1843. In addition to the murder she had sought to escape justice by travelling to America.

The keystone of the prosecution's case was that they claimed that there was enough circumstantial evidence to suggest that Christina had given her husband several doses of arsenic. From the outset they ruled out the possibility that John Gilmour had either committed suicide or accidentally taken arsenic. The truth of the matter, as we will see, is that on no occasion did anyone see Christina administer arsenic to John Gilmour. They may have seen arsenic in her possession; they may have witnessed her purchasing arsenic; they may have belatedly suspected that she had administered it, but they did not see her give it to her husband.

The two purchases of arsenic by Mary Patterson and 'Mrs Robertson' were both confirmed by the relevant chemists. Both Mary Patterson and John Muir confirmed that John Gilmour used arsenic for killing rats. Christina's uncle, Mr Robertson, described his niece as being very attentive and kind to her husband but conceded that she had told him that her marriage was not a happy one. Dr McKechnie also confirmed Christina's proper behaviour towards her husband.

The prosecution then called John Anderson. He confirmed that the letters that Christina had sent him in January and on 28 April 1843 had both been destroyed. He claimed that in one of the letters that she had confessed that she had 'bought arsenic to take herself, but she did not admit she had administered it to John Gilmour'. It also appears that Anderson gave at least the second letter to Christina's father, Alexander, via her brother, Thomas; they had both read it and there was no mention of arsenic.

The doctors that had been involved in the exhumation, post-mortem and subsequent examination of samples taken from John Gilmour's body now presented their evidence. Dr McKechnie, Dr Wilie and Dr McKinlay all believed that the fatal dose had been given to John Gilmour shortly before his death. They had found a considerable amount of arsenic in John Gilmour's stomach and bowels. In any event, they had sent samples of John Gilmour's organs to Professor Christison for independent analysis. He had found arsenic in the stomach and in the liver and it was his opinion that death had occurred as a result of several doses of arsenic, as this would account for the widespread retention of the poison in the organs.

The medical witnesses were the last called for the prosecution and on Saturday 13 January Duncan McNeill summed up the prosecution case. The 15-man jury, upon whose shoulders Christina's fate lay, was told that the medical evidence that they had heard the previous day conclusively proved her guilt. It was clear, McNeill contended, that Christina had administered arsenic to her husband on several occasions from 29 December 1842 until his death on 11 January 1843. He suggested that there was nothing in John Gilmour's history to suggest that he would have committed suicide. He contended that John Gilmour had regularly used arsenic to kill rats at the farm and was therefore perfectly well aware of any risks and would have known exactly how to avoid accidental poisoning. He told the jury that while it was unlikely that there would be any case before the Scottish courts where a poisoner was actually witnessed administering the drug, this did not mean that the accused was innocent of the deed. He stated that Christina had both opportunity and motive and, what was more, it was known that she had at least three packets of arsenic in her possession at some point between 27 December 1842 and Saturday 7 January 1843. He asked the jury to consider why Christina had acquired the arsenic under such strange circumstances. The first had been acquired via Mary Patterson, but had it really been destroyed in the boiler house fire? The third packet, which had been purchased under a false name in Renfrew on 7 January, was, by Christina's own admission to the Sheriff, unopened and in the possession of her mother, who had destroyed it. Where did the packet and phial that were found by John Muir on the morning of 6 January come from? If the first packet and the third packet were, indeed, destroyed, where was the second packet? It was the prosecution's contention that Christina had used this to kill her husband.

McNeill asked the jury to consider the following question in relation to the fact that Christina had claimed that she had married John against her will and that the poison had been acquired in order to end the marriage:

> Gentlemen, there are two ways in which arsenic might be used by her to attain that end; she might have poisoned herself, or she might have poisoned her husband. Her husband is poisoned, she is not. By a most extraordinary chance, the cup which she mixed for herself has not been quaffed by her, but by some unknown and mysterious hand was conveyed to the lips of her husband. Can you, then, doubt the purpose for which that poison was obtained or the purpose to which it was applied?

He went on to draw the jury's attention to the fact that no sooner had her husband died than she wrote to John Anderson. McNeill cleverly connected the initial purchase of arsenic on 27 December with the beginning of John's illness on 29 December and the fact that no doctor saw him until eight days later. Even then, Dr McKechnie did not see John Gilmour until the Saturday. The majority of his instructions had been ignored and the patient had died. He pointed out that although Christina was perfectly well aware of the fact that her husband's body was to be exhumed, she had fled to America and, what is more, under an assumed name. He asked the jury to ignore Christina's protestations that she had been sent on this journey as an unwilling traveller. McNeill also highlighted the fact that, unlike Anderson's evidence, both Alexander and Thomas Cochran denied that there was any reference to arsenic in the missing letters. He asked the jury to consider the fact that given Alexander and Thomas Cochran's involvement in the flight of Christina Gilmour, would they not be prepared to perjure themselves in the witness box on the matter of the arsenic?

When Mr Maitland, the leading defence counsel, rose to address the jury he began by telling them that the prosecution had not, in his view, proved conclusively that his client was guilty of poisoning her husband. He conceded that, given her flight to America, there was reasonable cause for some suspicion, but he asked the jury to consider whether it was impossible for Christina Gilmour to be innocent.

Maitland described to the jury the character of Christina before her marriage and suggested that, regardless of any provocation, it was not in her nature to have been able to carry out the crime. He conceded that his client was not entirely satisfied with her marriage but, on the evidence of her own uncle, she continued to make the best of it and at no time showed aggression or ill-feeling towards John Gilmour. Maitland pointed to the demeanour of his client during John Gilmour's illness and suggested that throughout she behaved properly and correctly, and her behaviour was witnessed by both Dr McKechnie and Mr Robertson. Surely, Maitland claimed, given the gravity of the situation, if she had been poisoning her husband, some kind of reaction would have been noticeable? Throughout her husband's illness, he went on, medical aid was sought; friends, family and employees were given access to John Gilmour. Was this consistent with the activity of a woman who was poisoning her husband?

Maitland did not attempt to contradict the testimony of the medical witnesses and conceded that it was clear that John Gilmour had died from poisoning and that it was established beyond doubt that arsenic was in his body. What, he claimed, they had not proven was the source of the arsenic, how it had been administered and over what period of time.

Maitland then turned to the far more sticky problem of the two or three packets or arsenic. He maintained that there were only ever two arsenic parcels and that both Mary Patterson and John Muir were incorrect in their assertion that the bag incident had occurred on Friday 6 January and that it had, in fact, happened on Saturday 7 January. From Mary Patterson's own testimony it had been proven that the first arsenic packet had been destroyed in the boiler house. The second had been found by Christina's mother in her daughter's pocket, unopened, and had been destroyed by her mother after Christina had admitted that she been intending to commit suicide with the poison. Maitland concluded that although his client had had two parcels of arsenic, both were reasonably accounted for and could therefore have not been used to facilitate her husband's death.

Maitland then turned to the question of Christina and John Gilmour's marriage, stating 'a broken heart may lead to suicide but not to murder'. He claimed that John Gilmour's death was suicide and that it had been established that the dead man had access to arsenic and that he had as good a reason as Christina to want to end the unhappy union. Alternatively, he suggested, given the fact that he had been prescribed white powders by Dr McKechnie, could the victim not have either been accidentally poisoned or have been given the opportunity to add the arsenic to the medicine himself? Maitland concluded by saying that the jury needed to be sure beyond any reasonable doubt that there was conclusive evidence that his client had, in a most premeditated manner, murdered her husband. Finally he said:

You may not be satisfied that this unhappy lady is guiltless of her husband's blood. Nay, you may suspect or even be inclined to believe that she is guilty. But that is not the question at issue. You are sworn to say upon your oaths whether guilt has been brought home to her by legal and conclusive evidence, and, applying this test, I feel confident you can arrive at no other verdict than that of Not Proven.

The trial was coming to an end, but not before Lord Justice-Clerk Hope spent four and a half hours summing up to the jury. He first asked the jury to consider whether they were sufficiently convinced that John Gilmour had died from arsenic poisoning. He told them that if they were then it could have been administered in one of three ways; firstly, the defendant or some other person might have administered it. Secondly, the deceased might have taken it voluntarily and thirdly, John Gilmour might have accidentally poisoned himself. He told them that the possibility of either accidental or voluntary poisoning would have to be dismissed by the jury in order to come to the conclusion that Christina Gilmour had committed murder. He cautioned the jury not to accept as being proven the fact that Christina Gilmour had married John under duress; no one, likewise, had seen unpleasantness between the husband and wife. On the question of arsenic poisoning he suggested that in his view it would be unlikely for anyone to choose this long and painful death as a means of committing suicide; this did not, however, mean that he had not done so. He also asked the jury to consider whether Christina Gilmour had had the opportunity to administer poison and that they should think about how the arsenic was obtained, what it was to be used for and whether they were convinced that it was all accounted for.

Hope began his conclusions to the jury by saying:

You see, therefore, that with all the improbabilities which the charge rears up, there are strong and weighty facts proved; and it will be for you to say what result you can arrive at, taking the whole evidence into view. It is a sad and fearful alternative that is presented to you by the prisoner's own statement in her declaration, that she bought the poison for the purpose of dissolving her marriage by committing suicide, especially considering the mysterious result that her husband dies of the same kind of poison, and that she lives. Still, that statement may be true, and the panel [defendant] be innocent, and you, who are the only judges of the facts in this case, may say that without any proved act of administration on her part, your minds revolt from the notion that she committed the crime charged against her.

The 15-man jury was then told to retire and consider the evidence which had been presented to them. They discussed the case for an hour before returning to the court. When asked, the verdict was unanimous; they had concluded that the case against Christina Gilmour was 'not proven'.

We know very little of the exact life of Christina Gilmour after she was dismissed from the court and given her freedom. She had been married for just six weeks before she became a widow. She would now spend another 62 years unattached before her death at the age of 87.

BIBLIOGRAPHY

Alexander, Marc *Royal Murder* Muller, 1978

Altick, Richard D. *Victorian Studies in Scarlet: Murders and Manners in the Age of Victoria* Norton, 1970

Borowitz, Albert *The Woman Who Murdered Black Satin: The Bermondsey Horror* Columbus, 1981

Butler, Ivan *Murderers' London*, Robert Hale, 1973

De Vries, Leonard Ilonka Van Amstel, comp. *'Orrible Murder: An Anthology of Victorian Crime and Passion, Compiled From the Illustrated Police News* MacDonald, 1971

Ford, Franklin L. *Political Murder: From Tyrannicide to Terrorism* Harvard UP, 1985

Franklin, Charles *World Famous Acquittals* Oldhams, 1970

Goodman, Jonathan, *The Fictions of Murderous Fact* Encounter, 1984

Gretton, Thomas *Murders and Moralities: English Catchpenny Prints, 1800–1860* British Museum Publishing, 1980

Harris, Melvin *The True Face of Jack The Ripper* Michael O'Mara, 1994

Harrison, Michael Clarence *Was He Jack the Ripper?* Drake, 1974

Hartman, Mary S. *Murder for Respectability: The Case of Madeline Smith*, Victorian Studies 1973

Hodge, Harry *Famous Trials I* Penguin, 1941

Hodge, Harry and James H. Hodge (ed.) *Famous Trials* Viking. 1984

Hodge, James H. (ed.) *Famous Trials III* Penguin, 1950

House, Jack *Murder Not Proven* Penguin, 1989

Jenkins, Romilly Janus Heald *The Dilessi Murders* Longman, 1961

Kaliloff, Rita Beth *Murder and the Erosion of Authority in Victorian Popular Literature* Dissertation Abstract International, 1983

Knelman, Judith *Twisting in the Wind: The Murderess and the English Press* Toronto UP, 1998

Lethbridge, J.P. *Murder in the Midlands: Notable Trials of the Nineteenth Century* Hale, 1989

Lewis, Roy Harley *Edwardian Murders* David & Charles, 1989

Marshall, Tim *Murdering to Dissent: Grave-Robbing, Frankenstein and the Anatomy Literature* Manchester UP, 1995

Massie, Allan *Ill Met by Gaslight: Five Edinburgh Murders* Harris, 1981

Sellwood, Arthur and Mary *The Victorian Railway Murders* David & Charles, 1979

Sparrow, Gerald *Vintage Victorian Murder* Arthur Barker, 1971

Taylor, Bernard and Stephen Knight *Perfect Murder: A Century of Unsolved Homicides* Grafton, 1987

Taylor, Bernard and Kate Clark *Murder at the Priory: The Mysterious Poisoning of Charles Bravo* Grafton, 1988

INDEX

ND - #0202 - 270225 - C0 - 234/156/10 - PB - 9781780915012 - Gloss Lamination